RISE
OF THE
BARTENDER

Adam-Jamie Hussein

Clink
Street

Published by Clink Street Publishing 2022

Copyright © 2022

First edition.

ISBNs:
978-1-914498-59-6 - hardback
978-1-914498-60-2 - ebook

ESSENTIAL
INGREDIENT
PREPARATION

As a general rule, I use a gram scale for measuring out ingredients when making syrups for use in cocktails. When measuring ingredients by sight or volume it tends to be less accurate than the use of a scale, which will yield consistent results – important when making any cocktail.

When scaling for high-volume service, having a scale that can measure out kilograms is desirable, however it is just as important to have one that can weigh out extremely small quantities.

Most syrups are mixed with the addition of heat however this can cause water to boil off in the process yielding a less accurate result. Hand mixing is labour-intensive but accurate, although a hand blender or Thermosmix is the most ideal solution.

SIMPLE SYRUP

The standard in a bartender's repertoire. This is a mixture of white sugar and water and has a neutral flavour, which is why it is best suited for mixed drinks. The purpose of simple syrup is to heighten flavour and reduce bitterness, without eliminating it.

100 grams filtered water
100 grams white sugar

METHOD
- Place both ingredients in a mixing bowl and mix until sugar is dissolved completely.
- Transfer to storage vessel and keep refrigerated until use. Keep for up to fourteen days.

HONEY SYRUP

Most honey sold commercially at the moment is clover honey, which can be rather dominant in flavour. While it is possible to find lighter styles of this honey, more appropriate styles of balanced drinks would be something like acacia honey.

Obtaining good quality honey is becoming increasingly difficult and costly nowadays, making it complex to justify its use.

Due to honey's natural viscosity, it is generally better to mix it with more water than other syrups – roughly 3:1 yields the best result.

340 grams acacia honey
100 grams warm filtered water

METHOD
- Place both ingredients in a mixing bowl and mix until sugar has dissolved completely.
- Transfer to storage vessel and keep refrigerated until ready for use. Keep for up to fourteen days.

GINGER SYRUP

Ginger in cocktails generally comes in the form of ginger beer for cocktails like the Dark 'N' Stormy or Moscow Mule. There are indeed delicious ginger beers available but some people enjoy using a ginger syrup with soda water to achieve a similar flavour profile.

Generally you would juice fresh ginger but if you do not have access to a juicer that is capable of this, you can purchase fresh ginger juice from speciality retailers.

200 grams washed fresh ginger, chopped
250 grams white sugar

METHOD
- Pass cut up ginger (you can keep the skin on) through the juicer and collect the juice.
- Filter the collected through a fine-strainer or sieve.
- Weight out collected contents and add 1.5 times the amount of sugar.

Add both ingredients to a mixing bowl and blend until sugar has dissolved completely. Add to storage vessel and keep refrigerated until ready for use. Keep for up to ten days.

GRENADINE SYRUP

There are plenty of good bottled grenadine syrups available to purchase on the market and they will suffice for mixed drinks. They tend to be electric red, made with high-fructose corn syrup, however they pay homage to the era of which the ingredient was popular.

If you are so inclined to make your own grenadine, he is a recipe for you.

300 grams Rubicon pomegranate juice
300 grams white sugar
2.5 grams malic acid
Two grams citric acid
Three grams orange blossom water
One gram vanilla essence

METHOD
* Add all ingredients to a blender and blend until sugar has dissolved completely.
* Add to storage vessel and keep refrigerated until ready for use. Keep for up to eighteen days.

RASPBERRY SYRUP

Raspberries are very interesting as there is several ways to go about turning them into a syrup.

Blending raspberries with sugar is the most efficient method, however this will extract bitter flavours from the berries which is not ideal in the final product.

Adding too much heat with overcook the berries and will likely yield a jam-like texture product rather than a syrup.

Adding a small amount of heat to raspberries in simple syrup will extract their flavour without turning them into 'jam'. To do this, use a sous vide or temperature-controlled water bath.

300 grams simple syrup
100 grams fresh raspberries
1.5 grams citric acid

METHOD
* Set water bath to 60 degrees Celsius.
* Add all ingredients to heatproof bag and seal the bag.

• Place bag in water bath and leave for 90 minutes.
• After 90 minutes, remove the bag and allow the mixture to cool to room temperature.
• Pass the mixture through a fine strainer and coffee filter.
• Add to storage vessel and keep refrigerated until ready for use. Keep for up to ten days.

If you don't have access to this piece of equipment, there is another method you can use:

400 grams white sugar
400 grams fresh or frozen raspberries
200 grams hot water

METHOD

• Add raspberries to mixing bowl and cover with sugar, then leave for 30 minutes.
• Add hot water afterwards and then cover – leave for additional 90 minutes.
• Stir the mixture through and then strain through a sieve.
• Add to storage vessel and keep refrigerated until ready for use. Keep for up to ten days.

CINNAMON SYRUP

Not used in many cocktails use this as a component, but it is a useful tool to add to your arsenal. There are two techniques that yield similar results, firstly you can simply steep cinnamon sticks in simple syrup for 24 hours.

Secondly you can add heat to the simple syrup and cinnamon syrup together. Either way the ingredient list is the same.

400 grams simple syrup
Eight cinnamon sticks (snapped)

METHOD ONE

• Add cinnamon sticks to simple syrup in airtight container and leave for 12 hours.
• Strain the mixture and then add to storage vessel and keep refrigerated until ready for use. Keep for up to fourteen days.

METHOD TWO

- Add simple syrup and cinnamon sticks to pan. Gently add heat and stir throughout.
- Remove from heat after 30 minutes.
- Allow to cool to room temperature, pass through a fine strainer.
- Add to storage vessel and keep refrigerated until ready for use. Keep for up to fourteen days.

LIME CORDIAL

This component can be used as a potential replacement to fresh citrus juice or in cocktails such as the Gimlet. This adds a subtle, elevated richness to the cocktail and remains shelf stable for a longer period than fresh juice.

200 white sugar
200 grams lime juice
Ten grams grated lime peel
Three grams citric acid
Two grams ascorbic acid

METHOD

- Combine the juice and acids together in a mixing vessel and blend until they are dissolved.
- Add lime peel and leave to rest in an air tight container.
- Pass through a fine strainer.
- Add to storage vessel and keep refrigerated for up to one month.

HALF AND HALF

This component is a more suitable replacement for cocktails that use cream or milk as one of the ingredients. Blending both milk and cream together yields an ingredient that adds weight and viscosity without the downsides of using either individually.

200 grams milk
200 grams double cream

METHOD

- Add both ingredients to a mixing bowl and mix thoroughly until combined.

- Pass through a large fine strainer. Add to storage vessel and keep refrigerated until ready for use. Keep for up to four days.

THE
HOW
& WHY

The first question that generally arises when I spoke about cocktails is "why classics, what is so interesting about them?" I tend to get caught up and go off on a tangent when I speak about classic cocktails, as the sheer mount of information is staggering. However it has always been about their historical significance such as where they came from, why they were designed, and who created them. This all started during a time in Melbourne, Australia whilst I had taken mantle in a classic-focused bar, 1806. The collective knowledge within that venue was something, a new experience, and in order to consistently add to and push the team I decided to make note of everything I had picked up and further research on my own time. To me knowledge is key, the more concise information you can give a guest the better able they are to make their own decision. Thus my journey began. Starting with an A4 notepad I wrote down facts and drinks I had never heard of before in order to learn as much as possible. Believe me when I say I never thought that notepad would stem into a second or a third, let alone a book. Almost three years on and this unknowing passion has turned into a manual that I hope you will enjoy and take something from.

There is such a vast wealth of information available and nowadays there is little need for you to collect such valuable and scarce texts like *The Bartenders Guide* or *The Gentleman's Companion* as these books are available online. The issue with too much of anything is that you need to decipher what is true and what is fabricated. This is what I have attempted to achieve within this text for you, to provide everything I discovered about each classic – historical background, informational wonders and matters of debate or interest. What has been provided are details I have gathered along the years and would have liked to have known myself many years ago. To achieve this I have turned to auction sites, bar owners, personal books, virtual libraries and the farthest parts of the internet regarding cocktail history – this took an incredibly long period of time, but I had a great time undertaking such research.

This book is laid out in such a way that I believe best to convey the information contained within – the recipe, where it was first published, who first created it, followed by factual information or points of contention. This is not an A–Z of classic cocktails rather they have been separated into their own historical time periods to give a better insight into what style of drink was being sipped on at that time. I began asking things such as "What would the champagne used to create the first French 75 have tasted like?" or "Was the vermouth used at the time drier or sweeter than it is now?" and even though you may not get the exact the answer, it should lead you to a new line of questioning about ingredients, drinks, techniques and tasting notes. Believe it or not things we typically associate with modern-day venues were almost unheard of at a time, such as ice or citrus juice, and thus the cocktails of the time reflected this in their make-up. Just as drinks were named after famous people or events throughout history, I have dedicated several cocktails in this manual to colleagues and friends I have been lucky enough to encounter during my career with their own personal story.

The recipes within the book are my own balanced interpretations, tried and tested through many days and nights to ensure that they are suited for a modern-day palate and do not have measures such as 'a wine glass of cognac' but more concise and accurate measurements to yield a consistent cocktail. There are certainly some recipes that many may not consider classic, however I believe that a bar professional should be well-equipped to handle a wide variety of guest's needs and thus have included some beverages that will come from left of field – all have been tried and all are delicious. What is not included are specifics about how to stir, shake and throw, or a detailed look at bar tools. Rather I am taking the impression that this is known by the reader or they have a book covering this written by someone far more qualified than myself.

As much as I tried to list as many cocktails as possible, I feel as if that would have diluted the content of the book and become an unmanageable read. The book as a spread of drinks to cover many styles and spirit bases in which I hope your favourite is among them – if this was solely for myself I would have included many more sherry cocktails. This is a non-exhaustive list of classic cocktails and is really the tip of the iceberg with new drinks being made and discovered every day, and perhaps it may be worth looking into a sole recipe manual in the future to accompany this book. As for now there are in excess of 200 recipes listed with histories and information to pique your interest.

Stretching back to a time before phones and internet the intimate relationship between bartender and guest was key, therefore most of what was communicated was word of mouth and done so after a night of imbibing concoctions. So it is likely we will never know the first person to create a cocktail, mix cognac and vermouth or use fresh citrus juice however this is the exciting concept of cocktail history and what we hope to uncover. As with most areas of interest, there is constant ongoing research bringing new information to light and replacing what was previous thought to be correct. Cocktail origins change and facts can be altered, therefore I will continue to discover and provide the most relevant and accurate information in coming editions of this book.

My ethos of hospitality is and always has been regarding education and passing on information, as through sharing of information we preserve our industry and inform more people to make it better and stronger than ever before. Reducing the barriers to entry within the industry and in particular the cocktail culture we invite new eyes and ideas to push past what may have been holding us back.

Even though some of these old texts were written only around 150 years ago, if not less, they seem like ancient history and so out of touch for bartenders today when in reality that is really not that long a time. The problem with cocktails and modern techniques is that even though new advancements are made few are documented and even less are shared, more guarded for competitive gain. You do not learn how to bartend from a book but you do learn much information that is better shared than kept, so what you are reading is my collective and gathered knowledge regarding classic cocktail history and insight into mixed drinks during their time.

INDEX

PUNCH
(1600–1800)

THE SIGNIFICANCE OF PUNCH

We never have discovered the first date liquids were mixed together, but we do know they became popular during the seventeenth century under the flag of 'punches'. These were popular when the world felt much smaller and time was less of an obstacle. During this period European sailors were exploring much of the world, both old and new, and discovering land, peoples and ingredients.

Widely considered the earliest cocktail the name punch comes from the Hindi word *panch* meaning five, this being the number of components that go into a mixed drink – spirit, water sugar, citrus and spice. An excerpt from *A Historical Dictionary of Indian Food* (1998) lays this out rather clearly;

> *"Punch in Hindi means five, and the first 'paunch',*
> *and then punch, was the name that was eventually*
> *settled on the five-component drink made up of*
> *arrack, spices, sugar, lime juice and water.*

In course of time, numerous recipes for the drink developed, including one with milk in it, described in AD 1823 in Madras."

The first known written reference to punch appears in a letter sent on 28th September 1632 by Robert Addams who was stationed in India and worked for the British East India Trading Company, and the first recorded punch recipe dates from 1638 when Johan Albert de Mandelso, a German in India, recorded workers drinking a concoction of aqua vitae, rose water, juice of citrus and sugar.

Punch also means something short and stout and was a description of a barrel and that's how it was served, so more suspect it came from that. Such is the barrel name puncheon – a 500L barrel most identifiable with the rum industry.

However most people who were drinking punch in the early days of its creation were sailors travelling the world, and illiterate, so miscommunication is a possibility.

As far as spotty records show punch began in British controlled East India Trading Company. Around this area of the world, sailors swapped to drinking the widely available spirits, such as arrack in India and even coconut flavoured arrack from neighbouring islands. Due to the high alcohol volume, someone suggested turning it back into a wine, but how could this be achieved? The acidity that had been distilled out needed to be replaced, so lemon juice would have been used; then a sweetener would be required to balance that out – sweet wines were extremely popular at the time so that covers that aspect. Most importantly, is that it would need diluted back, you the use of water to yield a drink similar to the strength of a wine was achieved.

As England continued to colonise sugar-producing nations, the Royal Navy were quick to swap their daily allowance of a gallon of beer for a half pint of Jamaican rum as it took up less room and wouldn't spoil on voyages. Spirits from such colonies were unrefined and the rum tended to be particularly intense, so the punch drink was used as a method of taming the rum.

Punch would be rationed to sailors in long voyages as the citrus would help protect them from diseases such as scurvy, which rampant in that line of work. The ships would normally be overprovisioned so they would trade it for new spirits such as arrack from the East Indies, along with new and exciting ingredients. It soon became a popular celebration to share in a punch bowl with returning sailors as they always had new ingredients to add to the bowl.

As travel expanded and extended, the desire for punch made with arrack, and rum, became fashionable within London coffee houses. These establishments loved punch as it was not taxable at the time, due to how new it was, so they could avail of higher profits. Punch would remain the drink of choice for English social elite for many years, as it was a sign of significant wealth – in the 1690s a three-quart bowl of punch would cost half a week's living wage.

Punch bowls would continue to spread throughout the world, especially into what would become the United States, notably it is said the founding fathers drank 76 bowls at the signing of the declaration of independence.

However as with most drinks, punch fell out of fashion as people didn't have time to sit in public houses all day, imbibing on lavish punches.

MILK PUNCH

The Milk Punch may have origins stemming from Medieval Ireland. One discovered punch from Irish roots contained whiskey, melted butter, hot milk, sugar, honey, nutmeg, cinnamon and cloves (the original Milk Punch). Another theory, one slightly more documented, is that the concoction was created by Aphra Behn (1640–1689) imbiber, spy and author regarding the Restoration. Working in Charles II secret service, Behn became romantically entangled with a powerful royal, and divulged many political secrets to her. George Woodcock wrote:

"Her talent for companionship evidently extended beyond conversation and music, for she is credited with having introduced into England that liquor favoured of eighteen-century topers, milk punch."

It would seem that William Oldys, a known specialist in the history of the stage, heard an actor say that:

"The first person he ever knew or heard of, who made the liquor called Milk Punch..."

... was none other than Aphra Behn. If anyone was going to have known, it would have been this particular actor having appeared in at least three of Behn's plays including *The Widow Ranter*. Bowman's character has the line;

"Punch! 'Tis my morning Draught, my Table-drink, my Treat, my Regalio, my everything."

My concern is whether or not Behn was simply a promoter of the drink or if she actually coined it, as the drink is first mentioned in an account of William Sacheverell's account of his visit to the Scottish island of Iona, 1688.

Like many cocktails of the time, the Milk Punch would run its course until its fabulous rediscovery and rebirth in the mid-eighteenth century when it would become a highly desirable drink again – preferably in bottled form as it was shelf staple.

A young Queen Victoria enjoyed this bottled version by Nathaniel Whisson & Co. that in 1838 she issued a royal warrant declaring them as 'Purveyors of Milk Punch to Her Majesty'. Imagine a monarch enjoyed your drink that much, they only wanted you to supply it.

On the other side of the ocean, Benjamin Franklin devised his own version of the Milk Punch. On a trip from Boston to Philadelphia, October 11 1763, Franklin sent a letter to James Bowdoin, disclosing a recipe for 'Milk Punch'. Within this letter Franklin dissects two types of beverage – possets and syllabubs.

Possets were generally used as a cold remedy and combine hot milk with ale, wine, or brandy, sugar and several spices. Syllabubs combine wine with milk and lemon juice (most readily available acid); the acid from the juice and wine curdled the milk.

I believe most credit should be given to Franklin's recipe as, according to Montague Summers who discovered it in 1914, it stems from

"A tattered manuscript book, the compilation of a good housewife named Mary Rockett, and dated 1711."

As you can see, there I have not provided my own personal recipe here. There is no 'individual' recipe for a Milk Punch as it is meant to be created as a communal cocktail to be shared and be highly flexible in its approach.

In its most basic form, it is warm milk that is broken with high acid citrus juice and then complemented by other flavours like fresh fruit, tea, brandy or gin. From there, the choice is yours. Go wild and enjoy the flavour exploration.

FISH HOUSE PUNCH

30ml Aged Dark Rum
30ml Cognac
10ml Crème de Peche
25ml Lemon Juice
10ml Simple Syrup
Soda Water Top

METHOD
- Shaken and strained into a highball over ice
- Garnished with a lemon wedge

Never has a beverage held such symbolic positioning amid those such as George Washington. In 1732, 104 years before Texas declared itself a Republic, Schuylkill (Skoo-Skul), home of the Fish House Punch, was its own colony, and later its own sovereign state.

At its core, it was a club: The Schuylkill Fishing Company. Those involved – including politicians, fishermen and Philadelphia locals who fished, ate, smoked and drank. Located between Schuylkill and Delaware rivers in what is now Pennsylvania.

Gary Regan's *The Joy of Mixology* (2003) suggests that George Washington once visited and stayed at the club. Following an afternoon of drinking he made a small note in his dairy followed by three blank pages, which I would say speaks for itself in regards to the potency of the mixture.

The drink was prepared as a lunchtime punch bowl that would sit on the bar and slowly be emptied by thirsty customers. Washington himself declared this punch was the only way to celebrate national holidays. Indeed, at several viewings of the troops, the corps would be presented to the president before moving away to where huge cauldrons of this punch had been prepared. It is no surprise that the president would receive three rousing cheers from the soldiers.

The secretary of an embassy of Virginia Commissioners, William Black, was greeted by members of this club in 1744 and *"was very kindly welcomed into their province, with a Bowl of fine Lemon Punch."*

Jerry Thomas relayed a simple (yet probably accurate recipe) using lemon juice, sugar, water, peach brandy, cognac and rum in his *The Bon Vivant's Guide or How to Mix Drinks* (1862) – here he credits Charles Godfrey Leland, an early member of the club. This however is unlikely to be the first recorded print of this cocktail, *The Philadelphian Telegraph* (1880) has a reprinted piece about the club from 1795 and states;

"To 1 pint of lemon or lime juice add 3 pints of mixture given below; 10 pints of water, 4 pounds of best loaf sugar.

The Mixture; ½ pint Jamaica rum, ¼ pint Cognac Brandy, ¼ pint best peach brandy. "

NOTES:
- A recipe as old as this has probably seen its fair share of iterations.
- Another recipe by Mrs. Goodfellow's cooking school in 1907 added oranges, strawberries or pineapple.
- Recreating this drink nowadays is overly difficult because peach brandy is no longer available. The best bet is to recreating your own with Crème de Peche, or infuse some yourself.

ROMAN PUNCH

30ml Aged Jamaican Rum
20ml Cognac
10ml Maraschino
10ml Curacao
15ml Orange Juice
15ml Lemon juice
10ml Port
Two Raspberries

METHOD
- Add all ingredients to a highball and churn over crushed ice
- Garnished with a lemon wedge, mint sprig & orange slice

Punches tend to be inspired by something that would be served at the White House during Rutherford Hayes' tenure, most likely to mask the alcohol from temperance-minded folks such as Mrs. Hayes. Other sources to the drink have led to a cocktail named Punch a la Romaine, which seems to be a Papal libation from the 1800s. Perhaps this may be more of a 'Papal Punch', which may be too 'in your face'.

This concoction was virtually an obligatory item at a dinner of any importance during the nineteenth century.

The first listed cocktail in text with this name comes from Jerry Thomas' *How to Mix Drinks* (1862) as reads;

> *"1 table-spoonful of sugar.*
> *1 table-spoonful raspberry syrup.*
> *1 tea-spoonful of Curacoa.*
> *1 wine-glass of Jamaica rum.*
> *½ wine-glass brandy.*
> *The juice of half a lemon.*
> *Dash of port wine."*

During the 1890s, orange juice was being introduced to the cocktail and was almost eliminating other citrus juice entirely, unbalancing the cocktail.

William Schmidt's *The Flowing Bowl* (1892) contains an updated version of the Roman Punch;

> *"The juice of an orange,*
> *The juice of half a lime or lemon in the bottom,*
> *A spoonful of sugar,*
> *A squirt of mineral water,*
>
> *Dissolve this well;*
>
> *½ pony of curacao*
> *½ pony of maraschino*
> *1 pony of brandy*
> *one dash of Jamaica rum*
>
> *Ornament the brim with orange and pineapples,*
> *and the centre with ice-cream and berries."*

This recipe omits port but makes way for ice-cream and berries, a drink fit for an emperor.

LORD RUTHVENS GOSSIP CUP

40ml Cognac
40ml Brown Ale
10ml Brown Simple syrup
5ml Ginger Juice
One Lemon Peel

METHOD
- Preheat a digestive wine glass with boiling water
- Build ingredients into metal tankard with a handle
- Steam on coffee wand
- Garnished with a lemon peel which is then discarded

The earliest form of Punch recipe comes from *Experiments in Cooking* (1654) by Lord Ruthvens and an excerpt from the book found states:

"A pint of Table Beer (or Ale if you intend it for a supplement to your 'Night-cap'), a table-spoon of Brandy, and a tea-spoonful of brown Sugar... – a little grated Nutmeg or Ginger may be added... Lemon-peel.

As Lord Ruthven says, 'This is a right Gossip's Cup that far exceeds all the Ale that ever Mother Brunch made in her life-time.'"

I would associate this cocktail to the original style of cocktail, Punch. Punch would have many interchangeable facets, and would evolve with arrivals of new and wonderful products from across the world. Spices like nutmeg, ginger, cardamom, and then spirits like Arrack would soon follow.

Punch would become the drink of choice for the next few hundred years, however with the inclusion of such 'New World' spices, it would be extremely expensive and so only be enjoyed by the social elite of the world.

RISE OF THE BARTENDER (1800–1850)

It is common place to assume that the American Revolution changed the world in many ways. This new society didn't have the time to sit about and lazily consume lavish concoctions from an ever-flowing punch bowl. The time of punch was over, and it was time to set the stage for the individualistic beverage known as the cocktail.

In 1806 Harry Croswell, editor of a conservative newspaper, was describing a bill received at a bar by a political candidate campaigning for votes, in which 25 dozen cocktails had been consumed. A reader wrote in explaining that they had never heard this term and wanted to know what it meant.

Croswell made it his duty to reply to this question and in the editorial edition of *The Balance, Columbian Repository* – May 13th 1806 – stating that:

> *"a cocktail is a stimulating liquor combined of*
> *spirits of any kind, sugar, water, and bitters*
> *– it is vulgarly called a bittered sling."*

During this time, ice began available for sale in America and the United Kingdom as it started to become extracted from frozen lakes; and several years later refrigeration would make its way into several industries. This led to the obvious correlation with the rise of the individual cocktail, and bartending as a whole.

In 1826 Robert Stein created continuous distillation, that would then fuel the fires of invention for Aeneas Coffey and his Coffey still, so that spirits of better quality could be produced more effectively.

Beyond this, bitters had just come onto the scene. Angostura bitters, created in 1824, had begun to make a statement on the world and would pave the way for Antoine Peychaud to develop his signature bitters several decades later. Bitters first played a role in apothecary and healthcare, but much like anything else packing flavour, would soon find their homes in many cocktails – even the first cocktail was dubbed a 'bittered sling' early that century.

Mixed alcohol was already seeing much use, particularly in the United States where drinks like the mint julep were being given to workers on farms in the South before work, almost like coffee stimulus. Even though they didn't know it, the golden-era of bartending was just being born.

Similarly the Gold Rush of 1949 started to bring many people, and wealth, to San Francisco. This started national trade with places such as Panama that would bring new ingredients, like pineapple, to the state in exchange for the riches being mined there. This is also where the great Professor Jerry Thomas would begin to make a name for himself, and foster the information for his *How to Mix Drinks or The Bon-Vivant's Companion.*

GEORGIA JULEP

60ml Cognac
10ml Crème de Peche
15ml Simple Syrup
Ten Mint Leaves

METHOD
• Add all ingredients to Julep tin and cover in crushed ice
• Churned crushed ice and ingredients in tin
• Cap with crushed ice and add straw
• Garnish with orange wedge and cherry

The cocktail first appears, from what I have read, in Jerry Thomas' *Bartender's Guide* (1887), and not his original copy in 1862, therefore it would be unlikely that he created this cocktail, more so he popularised it.

This may come as a surprise, but the first julep was made with grape brandy, not Bourbon. This cocktail is heavily associated with southern American states, horseracing and whiskey.

The Mint Julep was born in the late eighteenth century where the cotton industry was at its peak, but Bourbon had yet to come to the forefront of drinking culture. Brandy was the preferred tipple of choice among the plantation owners, and so they wanted to use that in new beverage.

Peach brandy was one of the most sought-after drinks at the time. It was likely used in this cocktail due to the abundance of fresh peaches that were available, as they were used for eating, cooking and animal feed. The issue here was that peaches grown for summer were difficult to preserve.

Future distilling techniques allowed for better preservation of flavour from the peaches. This also fell in line with the Julep craze at the time, and the common Georgia Julep consisted of a split base of peach and grape brandy.

Sadly, peach brandy virtually went extinct with the rise of canning food and refrigerated transportation, which is why it is extremely difficult to replicate drinks like this and the Fish House Punch.

HOT TODDY

50ml Scotch Whisky
25ml Lemon Juice
10ml Honey Syrup
10ml Ginger Syrup
15ml Hot Water

METHOD
- Preheat a digestive wine glass with boiling water
- Build ingredients into metal tankard with a handle
- Steam on coffee wand
- Garnished with star anise

The Toddy as we know it started in British Controlled India. In 1610, the Hindi word 'Toddy' meant;

"Beverage made from fermented palm sap."

The British, appropriating from conquered colonies, took the beverage as their own, and with British trade routes from India allowing access to exotic spices, public houses began using just spirit and hot water.

The history of this drink is naturally disputed as another story suggests an Irish doctor named Robert Bentley Todd, ordered his patients to drink hot brandy, cinnamon and sugar water. As with most tales the truth is most likely a combination of the two; doctors hearing about the mixture, and began using them as remedies.

The Hot Toddy was a vessel for all spirits at one point, from rum to brandy, and this can be seen in Jerry Thomas' *The Bon Vivant's Guide or how to Mix Drinks* (1862) in which he lists an apple, brandy, whiskey and gin toddy;

"133. BRANDY TODDY
1 teaspoonful of sugar.
½ wine- of water.
1 wine-glass brandy.
1 small lump of ice

Stir with a spoon.
For a hot brandy toddy, omit the ice, and use boiling water."

Thomas would also include each spirit in the form of a 'sling' cocktail, which was the same drink only with the inclusion of grated nutmeg on top.

These cocktails endured a long life until the 1870s when the French vineyards were destroyed due to the phylloxera plague, after this scotch became the go-to spirit and remains that way to this day.

NOTES:

• In an article called *'How to Take Cold'* in the *Burlington Free Press*, 1837, the Hot Toddy is heralded as a cure-all.
• In 1781, poet Allan Ramsay published a poem called 'The Morning Interview' that mentions Todian Spring. This spring, also called Tod's Well, was the main water supply to Edinburgh. So it may have also been named after this. Ramsay's poem refers to Todian Spring water being used for a tea party.

MINT JULEP

60ml Bourbon
15ml Simple Syrup
Ten Mint Leaves

METHOD

• Brush the inside of the julep tin with a mint sprig.
• Add mint leaves to julep tin, then add sugar and whiskey.
• Fill with crushed ice and muddle gently until mint is pulled sufficiently through the vessel.

- Top and cap with more crushed ice.
- Add three large, fresh mint bouquet and place straw beside them.

The world 'julep' comes from the Persian word *gulab* a sweetened rosewater. In classic Arabic, the word is *julab*, only to cross into Latin *julapium.* The Mint Julep was originally prescribed, and appears in literature as early 1784, as a medicinal remedy.

Originally, a julep was any sweet and syrupy drink, often used as a vehicle for medicine, according to *William Buchan's Domestic Medicine* (1789). Rumour has it that farmers yearned for it as a medicine, and it was used akin to coffee before they took to the fields as stated by British medical researcher John Ferdinand Smith during a tour of the United States in 1784:

> *"He drinks a julep made of rum, water*
> *and sugar, but very strong."*

Of course at this stage this stage the drink would not have had ice, nor mint. Mint wasn't introduced to the cocktail until around the 1790s as David Wondrich recalls a 1793 description of the cocktail as being a breakfast beverage *"of rum and water, well sweetened, with a slip of mint in it."*

First appearing in Jerry Thomas' *The Bon Vivant's Guide or How to Mix Drinks* (1862) and is made with Cognac and rum, not the standard Mint Julep we would consider today.

The Mint Julep predates cocktails and might, in fact, pre-date American whiskey, the key ingredient. In one sense 'julep' refers to the production method as much as the drink itself. One of the first julep-style drinks to be popularised was the Georgia Julep, a mix of brandy and peach liqueur with mint and ice. However the julep we know today has to be the classic 'Mint Julep' that is consumed at the Kentucky Derby and is also responsible for inspiring the creation of the first commercially produced straws.

Following this, once ice was formerly introduced to the Mint Julep in the 1820s, a strainer would be served with the cocktail in order to protect the imbiber's teeth from coming into contact. Sensitive teeth and dental health were likely not a cause for concern during this time and so there needed to be a solution for the cocktail of choice, and the strainer was the answer. Not exactly what it is used for these days.

The bourbon cocktail made its way to Kentucky from Virginia, where at one point it was made with rum and brandy from trade-ships exploring those travel routes. It is worth noting that any recipe listed as 'whiskey' unless specified as bourbon, is likely to have been rye in a pre-Prohibition America, as it was the grain of choice for most distillers.

Post-Prohibition, corn was much more cost-effective, and therefore was used by a larger proportion of the agricultural population to build business, and sadly rye whiskey never really recovered from this decision.

The Mint Julep appeared in a book *One Hundred and One Beverages* (1904) printed with a rye-base in place of brandy. This same year John Applegreen's *Barkeeper's Guide* (1904) referenced the first 'Whiskey Mint Julep'.

Prohibition made it more difficult to get cocktail books and alcohol of any kind, although after repeal Irvin S. Cobb's *Own Recipe Book* (1934) suggested there were only two juleps worth mentioning;

"The Original Kentucky Mint Julep and the Georgia Mint Julep."

Both of these called for Four Roses Bourbon or Paul Jones Whiskey (a pre-Prohibition blend of Kentucky whiskey).

This was made the official drink of the Kentucky Derby in 1938 as it was served in the room of the Churchill Down, home of the derby that year.

As many as 120,000 mint juleps are consumed during the Kentucky Derby.

NOTES:
- Known by Jerry Thomas as a *"peculiarly American beverage."* It was later introduced to England by Captain Maryatt.
- Was originally made with corn whiskey due to availability and ease to produce.

MOJITO

60ml White Rum
25ml Fresh Lime Juice
15ml Simple Syrup
Ten Mint Leaves
Soda Water top

METHOD

• Add all ingredients except soda to a shaker tin
• Whip shake with a small amount of crushed ice
• Dump contents into chilled highball and cap with crushed ice
• Garnish with straw and large mint bouquet.

The origin of the name is hazy and there are a few sources of where it could have stemmed from.
• Some say it comes from the word *mojar* which is a Spanish verb suggesting wetness.
• There was a Cuban lime-based seasoning called 'Mojo'.
• And the African word 'mojo' which means to cast a little spell.

Quite a lot of these islands were inhabited by African slaves brought over by the Spanish to work in their 'New World' and farm riches for them, so the African influence holds most promise, however it is likely a combination of the three coupled with miscommunicated word of mouth.

One theory is that the Mojito was a spinoff that came from the Mint Julep, that crossed over during American slave trading. These slaves would work sugarcane fields and it is likely they would try and curb the sharp and harsh flavours of unrefined rums the island was producing.

Another theory is (more romanticised I would say) Sir Francis Drake, a privateer in service to Queen Elizabeth I, was sent to plunder Spanish-held cities in the Americas and take their riches. In 1586, after successfully raiding the city of Cartagena De Indias, he headed to Havana, Cuba to do exactly the same thing. King Philp II of Spain warned his governor of Drake's approach so they could be better prepared to withstand the attack. Havana was well-prepared, but everyone was amazed when after several days of waiting, Captain Drake sailed away from the richest port in the West Indies after only exchanging a few bullets. Drake left Havana without its gold, but his visit did spark a larger event.

His crew were suffering from scurvy, dysentery and other illness, as most sailors of that time were, so one Richard Drake went ashore to source ingredients for a well-known medicine that was being consumed in South America. The medicine consisted of aguardiente (a crude cane spirit that was the forerunner for rum), mint leaves, sugarcane and lime juice. We know that lime juice was effective in combating the disease, but the other ingredients would make it much more palatable. A cocktail made of the same ingredients was already being consumed on the islands, named after Drake himself, the 'El Draque'.

Whichever the story, the birthplace of the cocktail was Havana.

The 'El Draque' would remain unchanged until the Bacardi Company was formed in 1862, at which time rum would be swapped in to become the base spirit. Bacardi would take the drink under a new name, the Mojito, and use it to showcase their rums to the world. It is fair to say the Mojito would not be nearly as popular without Bacardi using it as their posterchild.

The Mojito would first appear in *Sloppy Joe's Cocktail Manual* (1932), it is listed under "*Bacardi Drinks*" as:

"1 Teaspoonful of sugar.
One half of a lemon.
1 Part of Rum.
Seltzer water.
Leaves of Mint.
Serve in a High Ball glass with Cracked ice."

This again shows how closely associated the cocktail was with the Bacardi company.

The Bodeguita del Medio Bar, Havana is by myth credited with making the first Mojito and this is apparently where Ernest Hemingway went to drank his.

There is a framed note by him saying;

"My mojito in La Bodeguita and my Daiquiri in El Floridita."

However none of his books mention either the bar or the Mojito.

OBITUARY COCKTAIL

50ml Gin
12.5ml Sweet Vermouth
5ml Absinthe

METHOD
* Stirred and strained into a coupe
* Garnished with a lemon peel

I felt I had to include this cocktail, based on name alone. The 'Obituary' cocktail is essentially a gin Martini, heightened with Absinthe (or pastis). With this in mind there is only one place this cocktail could have been created, New Orleans.

Believed to have been created at Lafitte's Blacksmith shop (one of America's oldest bars) in the French Quarter, this drink still has an odd cult-like following. There is talk of an open, yet secret society of French Quarter residents who take their name from this cocktail. The full name is 'The Grand and Secret Order of the Obituary Cocktail', interesting if nothing else.

But how can something be open yet a rumour, or grand yet secret? This is the whole concept, the embodiment of New Orleans night life and culture, a playful humour if you will. This is the perfect New Orleans secret, a good cocktail, with a mysterious ambiance to boot.

OLD FASHIONED

60ml Choice Whiskey
10ml Simple Syrup
Three dashes Angostura Bitters
One dash Orange Bitters

METHOD
* Stirred and strained into a large rocks glass with block ice
* Garnished with lemon peel and orange peel

If you say the word 'cocktail' to someone, chances are this is one of the first drinks that comes to their mind. The drink has become

such an icon in the drinking world that even those whom tend not to dabble know of its presence.

There are plenty of other authors who cover this cocktail in much more depth than myself, notably David Wondrich in *Imbibe!* (2007) so I would implore you to pick up a copy of that if you would like delve deeper.

One of the first recipes is credited to the May 13th, 1806, editor's issue of the *Balance and Columbian Repository* in New York. It became synonymous with a drink style being described as *"a potent concoction of spirits, bitters, water and sugar."*

One of the many tales about the inception of this cocktail is that it was coined at the Pendennis Club, Kentucky, 1880, although further research seems to have debunked this claim to fame, with the club itself being founded in 1881, several years after mentions of the cocktail had been in books and newspapers. Alongside the fact that the bartender who is famed for making it, Martin Cuneo, didn't actually start there until 1913.

James. E. Pepper, a bartender and Bourbon aristocrat was said to have invented the drink in Louisville, before he brought the recipe to The Waldorf-Astoria Hotel. This cocktail was made of local Kentucky whiskey, and muddled fruit (lemon, cherries and orange). This is even mentioned in the Waldorf-Astoria cocktail book of 1931, however author Jacques Straub of the time worked at the Pendennis Club for almost twenty years, and the 'Old Fashioned cocktail' listed in his books look nothing like the one described.

However the Waldorf-Astoria Hotel didn't open its doors until 1893, further debunking the claim that James Pepper brought the Old Fashioned there from Kentucky, as the cocktail was already known and being served across America.

Other mentions of the Old-Fashioned in legitimate texts are:

Lafcadio Hearn, *La Cuisine Creole,* 1885

> *"Two dashes of Boker's, Angostura or Peychaud's bitters –*
> *either will make a fine cocktail. One lump of sugar, one piece of*

lemon peel, tablespoonful of water, one wineglassful of liquor,
with plenty of ice. Stir well and strain into a cocktail glass.

Spoon cocktail
One lump of sugar, two dashes Angostura bitters,
one piece of lemon peel, one lump of ice. Serve
plain in a small bar glass with spoon."

Neither of these drinks are called an Old Fashioned, however they read familiarly similar to what we can suggest one to be. Originally the Old Fashioned was called a 'Whiskey Cocktail', and this followed for gin, brandy and the like, appearing in Jerry Thomas' *The Bon Vivant's Guide or How to Mix Drinks* (1862) listed as:

"3 or 4 dashes of gum syrup
2 do. Bitters (Boker's)
1 wine-glass of whiskey, and a piece of lemon peel.
... shake and strain in a fancy red wine-glass."

The 'Spoon Cocktail' was in reference to when the bartender would prepare the glass for the guest, but then hand them over the bottle of spirit for them to pour their own drink. This privilege is mentioned in a piece published by the *New York Times* (1936) by someone who disapproved of the modernising of drinking culture, dubbed an 'Older Timer':

"Stuck in a miniature barspoon and passed the glass
to the client with a bottle of good bourbon from which
said client was privileged to pour his own drink."

The name 'Old Fashioned' begins to circulate, not from some clever turn-of-phrase, but from the ever-increasing number of Europeans making their way to the new world that was America. Due to this cultural taste difference, bartenders began 'improving' cocktails with ingredients that the new arrivals may be more accustom with, absinthe and curacao namely, which led to an unwelcomed change amongst American drinkers. They demanded a 'Whiskey Cocktail' as they knew it, the 'Old Fashioned' way, and thus the name stuck.

By 1930 the recipe had twisted out of recognition with muddled cherries, dashes of absinthe or curacao, and even the addition of a pineapple garnish. The following are some of the known written recipes of the Old Fashioned, and how it developed.

The first written record of the Old Fashioned, under that guise, was in *Modern American Drinks* (1895). George J. Kappeler called it an 'Old Fashioned Whiskey Cocktail'.

What we do know about this drink is that it is effectively a bittered sling on the rocks:

> *"Dissolve a small lump of sugar with a little water in a whiskey-glass; add two dashes Angostura bitters, a small piece ice, a piece lemon-peel, one jigger whiskey. Mix with small bar-spoon and serve, leaving spoon in the glass."*

Paul E. Lowe's *Drinks As They Are Mixed* (1904):

> *"Sugar, 1 lump.*
> *Seltzer, one dash, and crush sugar with muddler.*
> *Ice, one square piece.*
> *Orange bitter, one dash.*
> *Angostura bitters, one dash.*
> *Lemon Peel, 1 piece.*
> *Whiskey, 1 jigger.*
>
> *Stir gently and serve with spoon."*

Hugo Ensslin in his *Recipes for Mixed Drinks* (1917) puts out a recipe that contains a variety of fruit, which was commonplace after Prohibition, but not so much prior. His recipe reads as:

> *"OLD FASHIONED COCKTAIL (GIN)*
> *Use Old Fashioned Cocktail Glass*
>
> *½ piece Domino Sugar*
> *two dashes Angostura Bitters*
> *1 drink El Bart Gin*
> *1 slice Orange Peel*
> *1 slice Lemon Peel*
> *1 slice Pineapple*

OLD FASHIONED COCKTAIL (WHISKEY)
*Made same as above, using Whiskey instead
of Gin and two dashes Curacao."*

Finally, *The Savoy Cocktail Book* (1930) calls for both a lemon peel and a slice of orange, whilst the *Old Waldorf Bar Days* (1931) the following year still yearns for the use of a spoon.

NOTES:
- The Savoy calls for the use of rye or Canadian Club Whiskey, due to being cost effective, and one of the few accessible whiskies due to Prohibition.
- Simply adding a dash of absinthe to this cocktail will make it a 'Hendrick'.
- Also, if you add scotch in place of bourbon with a dash of absinthe you yield yourself a 'Choker'.

SHERRY COBBLER

60ml Manzanilla Sherry
20ml Dry Curacao
15ml Pineapple Juice
10ml Lemon Juice
10ml Lime Juice
10ml Simple Syrup
5ml Pedro Ximenez Sherry Float

METHOD
- Add all ingredients to shaker
- Add crushed ice to highball glass and pack to create a solid block
- Whip shake ingredients with small amount of crushed ice
- Strain into ice filled glass
- Cap with crushed ice and float P.X sherry
- Garnished with mint sprig, orange wedge & straw

'A mix of any spirit, sugar, crushed ice and fruit.'

This cocktail fast became America's most loved drink after the fall of the 'Mint Julep'. During the nineteenth century the Sherry Cobbler swept America and it claims responsibility for launching the use of commercial ice into public consciousness, and also the use of straws.

Although there are many mentions of 'cobblers' in print prior to 1838 they generally refer to madeira and not sherry. In 1975, the diary of one Katherine Jane Ellice was uncovered, explaining her travels to New York in 1838. The dairy references Sherry Cobblers twice – once on Friday, August 24, 1838 and the second on Friday, August 31st, 1838 – both entries recall a Sherry Cobbler being made and that it was refreshing on a hot day. David Wondrich has been cited by many sources on this being the first time Sherry Cobbler was named specifically.

The *Mississippi Free Trader* from April 7th, 1841 notes that *"a piece of lemon peel out of a sherry cobbler which had fallen out,"* which would reference that lemon was the initial garnish was this cocktail, and additional fruit came later.

Interestingly, Charles Dickens novel *The Life and Adventures of Martin Chuzzlewit* (1842) actually mentions on of his characters creating the beverage and first printed mention of the use of a straw in the cocktail. The book goes on to praise and name the cobbler:

> *"[It] is called a cobbler. Sherry cobbler when you name it long; cobbler when you name it short."*

This use of straws, and popularity of the cobbler, spread after this and not just in America. The *Commercial Advertiser* (1843) from New York noted that 'upper class' drank Sherry Cobblers

> *"sucked through a straw in the most delicate manner imaginable. some of the emigrants from Great Britain are mightily taken with our sherry cobblers."*

There is information linking a man named Otis Field, an ex-cobbler, to being the creator of the cocktail, however the evidence is insufficient but presents a reasonable case. There are several newspaper references, but the most satisfying comes from *New York Atlas*, May 24th, 1846;

> *"Blessed be the man who invented sherry cobblers and who do you think that man is? Why, Otis Field, to be sure, and it aint anybody else.' Reader, if you call at Bassford's rooms, entrance 149 Fulton or 1 3/4 Ann sts.,*

and drink a cobbler, made by Otis, and don't say it is the
very best you ever tasted, you need not pay for it; let it
be charged to us; we are willing to risk that much."

The Sherry cobbler first sees print in a cocktail book when Jerry Thomas lists it in his *The Bon Vivant's Guide or How To Mix Drinks* (1862) and shows the sheer popularity of the cobbler style cocktail. He lists seven cobbler drinks, the first of which being the Sherry Cobbler served with a straw.

The year, in 1863, it is recorded that the price of ice had risen and the cocktail now cost no *"less than $2.50, ice being so expensive a luxury."* The term cobbler is thought to have come from the cobblestone appearance of the ice that made up the cocktail. Ice had only recently been introduced to many parts of America, and it was being shipped from Norway to fulfil many of the bar needs due to the increasing demand.

In 1888 Harry Johnson wrote of the Sherry Cobbler noting:

"This drink is without doubt the most popular beverage
in the country, with ladies as well as gentleman."

Alas, as with many cocktails, the drink fell out of favour due to its low-ABV nature during Prohibition. Less people were drinking for flavour and more so for the alcoholic component, which the cobbler lacked.

SAZERAC

30ml Rye Whiskey
30ml Cognac
7.5ml Simple Syrup
Three dashes Peychaud's Bitters
One dash Angostura Bitters
Absinthe Rinse

METHOD
- Stirred and strained into a chilled, absinthe-rinsed sours glass with no ice
- Garnished with lemon zest then discarded.

This drink became the Official Cocktail of New Orleans in 2008.

According to David Embury in his *Fine Art of Mixing Drinks* (1948) Sazerac is *"essentially it is merely an Old Fashioned made with Peychaud bitters instead of Angostura and flavoured with a dash of absinthe."* However, is that all it is, or is there more to the story?

The attraction of classic cocktails for me is the history – the how and when – the mystery behind the liquid. Some cocktails have so little history or information that it is neigh impossible to connect a story whilst others, such as the Sazerac, are surrounded by such a plethora of information that making sense of it all is like a hunting predator – a slow and calculated process.

This cocktail has so many tales that there is bound to be falsities within each as that is the nature of generation stories, so I will recall each and break down the facts that coincide with each.

Firstly, the famed Stanley Clisby Arthur has much to say regarding the Sazerac cocktail. At one point, much that we knew of the Sazerac stemmed from his book *Famous New Orleans Drink and How to Mix 'em* (1937). Considering this was a New Orleans beverage and Clisby worked there his word was taken at face value, however there are some points to take note off in this story

We begin with a young Antoine Peychaud (inventor of Peychaud's bitters on less) arriving in New Orleans in 1795 after fleeing from Haiti due to a slave rebellion. When he landed he had little to his name, aside from a secret family recipe for medicinal bitters, and an education in French apothecary. He would open shop in 1834 and from there the bitters became rather famous as medicinal tonic were fashionable at the time. Peychaud would serve the ever-popular cognac with his bitters in a large eggcup (that you wouldn't mistake for a modern-day jigger) and that would often be mispronounced by Americans. The word 'coqutier' was often spoken as 'cockt-tay' which then led to 'cocktail'.

- As Dave Wondrich would say, *"Never let the truth stand in the way of a good story."* Sorry Clisby, but it doesn't check out.

Next, one Sewell Taylor decided to move into the spirits distribution rather than bar ownership and in the 1850s his bar – Merchant's Exchange Coffee House – was taken on by John B. Schiller.

Schiller (the local agent for the Sazerac de Forge et Fils cognac brand) had opened a dispensary to sell his products in the mid 1850s. He dubbed it the 'Sazerac Coffee House' and his 'Brandy Cocktail', coupled with Peychaud's bitters was one of New Orleans most popular serves.

In 1870, Thomas Handy, the venue's accountant, took control of the bar after Aaron Bird had renamed it the Sazerac Coffee House as respect to the popularity of the cocktail being served. Cognac became hard to obtain due to the phylloxera plague that destroyed many European vineyards in the 1870s, so he replaced it with Maryland rye whiskey to keep up with demand and appease local American tastes.

Lastly, the absinthe, where did it come from?

Clisby in his book recites;

"The absinthe innovation has been credited to Leon Lamothe who in 1858 was bartender for Charles Cavaroc and Co.,... More likely it was about 1870, when Lamothe was employed at Pina's restaurant in Burgundy Street that he experimented with absinthe and made the Sazerac what it is today."

FACT CHECK

According to David Wondrich, there are articles found in the Times-Picayune (1843) that show of hotel bars serving "brandy, absinthe, bitters and ice" long before Leon Lamothe was credited with that addition to the cocktail.

There are several other characters who play a part in this story, yet their influence on the cocktail is not as great. As mentioned previously Sewell. T. Taylor owned the Merchant Exchange Coffee House, sold this business to Aaron Bird so he could start importing spirits instead. Bird then renamed the venue 'Sazerac House' where he would sell the Sazerac cocktail using the Sazerac de Forge et Fils cognac that Taylor was importing, paired with the local Peychaud's bitters. Later, Thomas Handy (the accountant) would take over the business.

FACT CHECK

To make things complicated, there were several venues called 'Exchange' in the area. The 'Merchant Exchange Coffee House' that Taylor sold in 1850 was not the first venue to sell Sazerac de Forge et Fils, but it did popularise it due to the extensive range of rare vintages available.

Taylor died in 1861 and then Aaron Bird took over the business. He died in 1864 at which time the business and stock was sold at auction. According to David Wondrich, there was no mention of them renaming it to Sazerac House and selling the famous cocktail. The business imported spirits, it wasn't a bar. So neither really had a huge part to play in the cocktail's creation but Taylor did certainly popularise the cognac brand, which is sometimes just as important.

Next we have Thomas H. Handy and his role. He worked for Sewell Taylor's spirits business before going to fight in the American Civil War until 1865. Upon his he worked alongside John Schiller, another wholesaler as well as owner of Sazerac Coffee House which was across the street from Sewell Taylor's business. Handy would take over Schiller's company in 1871 and rename it 'Thomas H. Handy and Co.' listing himself as one of the few importers of Sazerac de Forge et Fils cognac, fine champagne and bitters (although not Peychaud's bitters). Come 1873, Handy bought the rights to Peychaud's bitters when Antoine fell on financial difficulty, becoming an employee to Handy Co. and sealing the bitters as a vital component to the Sazerac cocktail in future.

After years of competition with another local business owner – Vincent Micas – Handy died in 1893 and his prime investor William McQuoid, along with two bartenders, Billy Wilkinson and Vincent Miret, continued to run the business. But with all the stories out of the way there is still no mention of the Sazerac cocktail that is credible. David Wondrich clears this up in his article *'Is the Sazerac a New Orleans Cocktail?'*

A lot of miscommunication would have occurred regarding the interchangeability of the Sazerac and a Brandy Cocktail. The Brandy Cocktail was found all over New Orleans (highly popular since around 1825) and would have been made with brandy, sugar, whatever bitters you had on hand, and sometimes absinthe. If this cocktail was called a Sazerac before Handy switched the base spirits, it was likely a brandy cocktail made with Sazerac de Forge et Fils.

We know that Handy made the switch from cognac to rye whiskey in the 1870s due to the phylloxera plague and changing consumer tastes. There was massively increased American influence overtaking the French culture of New Orleans and the most popular cocktail was the *Improved Whiskey Cocktail* as listed in Jerry Thomas' *The Bartender's Guide* (1887):

"IMPROVED BRANDY COCKTAIL
two dashes Boker's (or Angostura) Bitters.
three dashes gum syrup.
two dashes Maraschino.
one dash Absinthe.

1 small piece of the yellow rind of a lemon,
twisted to express the oil.
1 small wine-glass of brandy.

IMPROVED WHISKEY COCKTAIL
Prepared in the same manner as the Improved Brandy Cocktail,
by substituting Bourbon or rye whiskey for the brandy."

Time-Democrat newspaper (1895) is the first time any cocktail is praised coming from Sazerac House where it mentions bartender Vincent Miret, Billy Wilkinson and that their whiskey cocktails were *"the best in New Orleans"*. Handy and Co. began bottling their cocktails for nationwide sale and their offerings were extensive including Martinis and Manhattans, but it was the improved whiskey cocktail consumers desired – which would go on to be labelled the 'Sazerac Cocktail'. So the theory arises that there was never a spirit base transition and the two cocktail were always different drinks – Sazerac du Forge et Fils went into the famous 'Brandy Cocktail', and the Sazerac was a simply spin on the 'Improved Whiskey Cocktail' – meaning the bartenders simply made something better and claimed it as the city's own.

The bottled cocktail service was a success and the recipe continued to develop under Christopher O'Reilly who worked for the Handy company from 1904 until Prohibition. His recipe included both Peychaud's and Angostura bitters, but no absinthe which is interesting, and is likely due to absinthe being banned between 1912 up to Prohibition.

Appearances
* In 1898, at the 16th biennial conference of the Alpha Tau Omega fraternity held in New Orleans, the Sazerac would make its first appearance by name.
* The first time it appears in a cocktail book is in William Boothby's *The World's Drinks and How to Mix Them* (1908). He likely got the recipe from someone he knew who worked for the Handy Company who was spilling company secrets;

"A small barspoonful of gum syrup, three drops of Selnar bitters and a jigger of Sazerac brandy; stir well, strain into a cocktail-glass which has been rinsed out with a dash of absinthe."

NOTES:

• The lemon twist is essential but as Stanley Arthur Clisby said in *Famous New Orleans Drinks and How to Mix 'Em* (1937)

"Do not commit sacrilege of dropping the peel into the drink."

TOM AND JERRY

45ml Jamaican Aged Rum
15ml Cognac
15ml Simple Syrup (cinnamon infused if you wish)
One Whole Egg
Hot water

METHOD

• Preheat brandy balloon with boiling water
• Build all ingredients into a tin and dry shake
• Pour the mixture into a metal tin with a handle
• Steam on coffee wand
• Throw the mixture between two tins
• Pour into empty preheated glass
• Garnished with grated nutmeg

This cocktail creeps up first in Jerry Thomas' *Bon Vivant's Guide* (1862) with a batch recipe and a how to:

"5lbs. sugar.
12 eggs.
½ small glass of Jamaica rum.
1 ½ teaspoonful of ground cinnamon
½ teaspoonful of ground cloves
½ teaspoonful of ground allspice.

Beat the whites of the eggs to a stiff froth, and the yolks
until they are as thin as water, then mix together and
add the spice and rum, thicken with sugar until the
mixture attains the consistence of a light batter.
To deal out Tom and Jerry to customers:
Take a small bar glass, and one table-spoonful of the above
mixture, add one wine-glass of brandy, and fill the glass
with boiling water, and grate a little nutmeg on top.

*This drink is sometimes called Copenhagen,
and sometimes Jerry Thomas."*

Following this recipe and style, the batter would be served from a large bowl into individual guest vessels and then lengthened with either hot water or milk. To this degree it was essentially a hot eggnog, which sounds delicious.

In numerous accounts, Jerry Thomas is credited for the drink in 1847, long before he printed it, and named after two white mice he kept as pets named Tom and Jerry. However reports of the drink being made in the Americas have been documented from 1820 in the *Salem Gazette* (1827) by David Wondrich, and this was before Thomas was alive.

Another tale credits the cocktail to an English playwright Pierce Egan, who named the drink after a play called *Tom and Jerry, or Life in London* in 1821, however there is no evidence to corroborate this. It is possible the drink bears some influence from his characters, but he is certainly not the creator.

Another theory that makes for a good tale is that this drink inspired by the cartoon of the same name. During Prohibition there was a cat and mouse game between bootleggers of alcohol and government 'G-men'. The bootleggers would send informants to tip off speakeasys before the G-men arrived so they could shut up shop, therefore there was nothing to see. Perhaps this was the concept for the cartoon, perhaps not.

Thomas may not have created the cocktail, but he is certainly the reason it was so popular, and there is no denying that. Sadly we still do not know who created it.

This cocktail appears in *The Savoy Cocktail Book* (1930) with an accompanying note:

*"1 Egg.
½ glass Jamaica Rum.
1 tablespoonful Powdered Sugar.
½ Glass Brandy.*

Fill with boiling water, grating nutmeg on top.

**The Tom and Jerry was invented by Professor Jerry
Thomas – rise please – over seventy years ago, in the days
when New York was the scene of the soundest drinking
on earth. The Tom and Jerry and the Blue Blazer were
the greatest cold weather beverages of that era."*

I have included my personal recipe that is for a single serve cocktail. The sugar syrup can be turned into a spiced syrup with vanilla, cinnamon and allspice if you want to be more authentic, however I find it a rare occasion where you would wish to batch this cocktail traditionally.

NOTES
- The drink originally contained hot milk.
- According to Pierce Egan's play, to go Tom and Jerrying was to go out on the town.

WHISKEY SOUR

50ml Bourbon
20ml Lemon Juice
20ml Simple Syrup
20ml Egg White

METHOD
- Wet and dry shaken and strained into a rocks glass over ice or served up in a coupe
- Three drops of Angostura bitters carefully on top once cocktail is finished

The most prolific family of cocktails, sours are cocktails that have a strong citrus presence. They shouldn't necessarily make the guest pull a 'sour face', but the citrus must be present in the balance. Traditional sours are spirit, citrus, sugar and often contain egg white/emulsifying agents.

A basic recipe for a sour was known much longer before it was printed. Travel seemed to take forever and up until the twentieth century, refrigeration was lacking along with the concept of contamination.

Land travel wasn't nearly as bad as sea ventures as food wood spoil over a multi-month trip, and water wasn't always considered to be safe.

Professional sailors suffered from scurvy, primarily, until one Vice Admiral Edward Vernon of England would begin to give his sailors rations of limes, lemons and safe liquids on his ships. In order to prevent full intoxication the safe liquid, usually rum once it was discovered, was watered down with citrus juice and water was added to mask the flavour. Hence, the early version of the sour was born.

When this concept was brought ashore, the concoction began to get refined as it became more popularised. The English would substitute gin and brandy, whilst Americans would use easier to obtain whiskey, and this refined recipe would later be codified in text by Jerry Thomas.

The recipe for a 'Sour' cocktail was first listed in Jerry Thomas' *How to Mix Drinks or The Bon-Vivants Companion* (1862) as:

"140. BRANDY FIX
*1 table-spoonful of sugar. ½ a wine-glass of water .
¼ of a lemon. 1 wine-glass of brandy.*

Stir with a spoon, and dress the top with fruit in season.

142. BRANDY SOUR
*The brandy sour is made with the same ingredients as
the brandy fix, omitting all fruits expect a small piece of
lemon, the juice of which must be pressed in the glass."*

Next it appears in the *Waukesha Plain Dealer* newspaper, therefore highlighting its increased popularity with the masses, in 1870 in which the cocktail is actually demonised.

*"'Then may God have mercy on your soul.'
'Amen,' says the Methodist, as he order another whisky sour."*

The next appearance, and the addition of egg white, is listed in Robert Vermeire's *Cocktails and How to Mix Them* (1922) in which he writes:

"A few drops of egg white improve all Sours."

However the addition of egg white occurred before this printing. There was a cocktail called a 'Boston Sour' that required egg white in the drink, whilst a 'Whiskey Sour' at the time usually had a red wine float, or what we now know as 'New York Sour'.

The New York Sour would eventually go on to be an acclaimed cocktail in its own right once it matured and spread.

NOTES

- National Whiskey Sour Day is August 25th in the United States of America.
- The New York Sour was also known as a Continental Sour for a period of time when the base was exclusively rye whiskey.
- Cognac in place of bourbon is known as a Brunswick Sour.
- Garnishes range from bitters on top of the finished cocktail, to fruit wedges.

BIRTH OF
COMMERCIAL
ICE
(1850–1920)

It comes as no surprise that the explosive popularity of cocktails comes hand in hand with the addition and usage of ice, an item nowadays taken as standard practice.

With drinks such as the Mojito or Mint Julep it is evident that ice was available for the most part of the nineteenth century, however in days prior to refrigeration or cooling techniques it was a highly expensive commodity, and therefore used sparling in saloons and hotels.

However, moving into the latter half of the nineteenth century there was more ice than ever being transported from lakes to cities. This increased practise, married to the creation of the ice machine and affordable refrigeration meant that ice was more widely accessible and available than ever.

It was Jerry Thomas, born in 1830, who would capitalise on these factors and spread the cocktail wildfire across the world via New York, London and New Orleans. His first stint where he would gain recognition would be El Dorado, San Francisco. Unlike regular saloons this venue came equipped with antiques, art pieces, and luxury furniture. Sadly Thomas would die before his book would be available in print, but he left a lasting legacy that many still call on today.

As time went on gold rushes, oil booms and the implementation of railroads continued to occur so other cities wanted to cash in on the wealth being found, soon places like New York would open grand hotels birthing cocktails such as the Manhattan and popularising others such as the Old Fashioned. Word travelled fast, even then, and so the flair and libations started to attract holiday makers from all over the world and places such as the Old Waldorf Hotel and Hoffman House started to become destination hotspots.

Thomas wasn't the only person to see this gap in a newly revitalised market. Across the ocean European bartenders such as Harry Johnson began to realise that gone were the times of simple saloons and that grand hotels and resorts were required in order to compete with the new American bars. These venues would require signature drinks and added flair to avail of the wealth, and Johnson himself would take over the lease on a successful establishment, make it his own and produce several, more digestible books than Thomas highlighting such accomplishments.

Europe would go one to build on what America had started and propel the cocktail scene to new heights. There was little that could be done to prevent this forward traction, even World War One had little stopping power and would actually spawn cocktails such as the French 75 and Sidecar as products of their environment. With the whispers of Prohibition looming stateside, many American bartenders would abandon ship to take mantle in one of the booming European venues, notably, Harry Craddock going to the Paris before venturing to the Savoy Hotel.

ALASKA

50ml Gin
12.5ml Yellow Chartreuse
Two dashes Orange Bitters
Stirred and strained into a coupe
Garnished with lemon peel

The drink made its debut in *Straub's Manual of Mixed Drinks* (1913) as:

> *"One dash Orange Bitters.*
> *⅓ Jigger Yellow Chartreuse.*
> *⅔ Jigger Tom Gin."*

Harry Craddock then included it in *The Savoy Cocktail Book* (1930) although he removed the orange bitters and altered the ratio from 2:1 to 3:1 and swapped to a London dry gin from the original Old Tom.

A slight riff on the drink appears in Embury's *Fine Art of Mixing Drinks* (1948) as the 'Nome Cocktail' and has the addition of dry sherry, with another cocktail appearing on the modern drink's scene coming from the famed Sam Ross at Attaboy:

> *"ANCHORAGE*
> *45ml Gin*
> *15ml Fino Sherry*
> *12.5ml Yellow Chartreuse*
> *One dash orange bitters*
> *Stirred*
> *Lemon peel."*

ALBEMARLE FIZZ

50ml Gin
20ml Lemon juice
20ml Simple Syrup
Two Raspberries
Soda Water Top

METHOD
• Shaken and then strained into a highball over ice
• Top with soda water and lemon peel discarded

A classic gin fizz with the addition of raspberries or raspberry syrup and both yield a similar result, the deciding factor here is picking a single method for consistency.

This cocktail first appears in in Hugo Ensslin's *Recipes for Mixed Drinks* (1916) and later again in Harry Craddock's *The Savoy Cocktail Book* (1930).

This cocktail is essentially a raspberry 'Tom Collins' but there is a small debatable as to whether this cocktail should include egg white or not, closely relating it to the *'Clover Club'* cocktail. The choice is yours.

A small addition to this cocktail occurs when you add a dash of Maraschino liqueur to it, it becomes a 'Bayard Fizz'.

ALEXANDER

40ml Gin
15ml Crème de Cacao Blanche
15ml Crème de Cacao Dark
30ml Half and Half

METHOD
• Shaken and strained into a coupe
• Garnished with grated nutmeg

The original drink is made gin, chocolate liqueur, cream. However, the drink has spawned several variations that work on this 1:1:1 build. The recipe was first printed in Hugo Ensslin's *Recipes for Mixed Drinks* (1916).

The cocktail was said to have been created at Rectors, New York by one Troy Alexander. It was made to celebrate the birth of a fictional character called Phoebe Snow who was being used to promote the use of clean-burning coal on the Delaware and Western Railroads. Her character was depicted in an all-white outfit and thus the cocktail needed to follow suit.

A few years later, in 1922, Princess Mary married Viscount Lascelles in London. This is when many people believe the base spirits were swapped as brandy was the drink of choice for most English Nobility – thus spawning the Brandy Alexander. However this story is highly contested and several other theories pop up in regard to this cocktail's namesake such as the Russian Tsar, Alexander II believing this cocktail was named after him and an opera critic named Alexander Dragon thinking the same.

BRANDY ALEXANDER

Interestingly, Popkin also mentions an article in the 1915 edition of the *Philadelphia Inquirer*, which claims the Alexander was invented in honour of Philadelphia pitcher Grover Cleveland just before the 1915 World Series against Boston, however, this is an unlikelier story – no spec is given, so I have no idea what this drink was like, or if it is even relevant to the modern variant.

The switch from gin to brandy – this change as seen in print happens for the first time in the book *Harry of Ciro's ABC of Mixing Cocktails* (1923):

"ALEXANDER COCKTAIL: ⅓ Crème de cacao, ⅓ Brandy, ⅓ fresh cream."

In Harry Craddock's *The Savoy Cocktail Book* (1930) he covers all bases, calling the gin version '*No1*' and the brandy version '*No2*'.

ALEXANDER COCKTAIL (NO.1)
⅓ Dry Gin, ⅓ crème de cacao, ⅓ fresh cream

ALEXANDER COCKTAIL (NO.)
⅓ brandy, ⅓ crème de cacao, ⅓ fresh cream

There is also a drink called a Panama Cocktail which is an exact duplicate of his Alexander no.2

In W.J. Tarling's *Café Royal Cocktail Book* (1937), it appears with a more modern 2:1:1 ratio and is seen as:

"ALEXANDER: ½ Brandy, ¼ crème de cacao, ¼ cream."

And from this, it seems the spirit base changed before the name.

AMERICANO

40ml Campari
40ml Sweet Vermouth
Soda Water top

METHOD
* Built in a highball over ice and then given a short stir
* Garnished with an orange wedge

Born in Milano-Torino (Campari from Milan and red vermouth from Torino) in the nineteenth century, this cocktail was named after the influx of American tourists coming to Italy to escape the horrors of Prohibition.

Like many cocktails, its origin is unknown but there are a number of stories. The oldest tradition is that the Americano was invented in 1860, at Gaspare Campari's bar in Milan. Another story dates back to the 1930s where the cocktail is said to have been named in honour of the Italian boxer Primo Carnera who was an active fighter in the United States, and dubbed 'the Americano'.

The Americano has become a modern-day staple and has become increasingly popular with the focus on 'No and Low ABV' drinks. An earlier claim to fame for the cocktail was the drink's mention in the Ian Fleming novel series, James Bond, as it is the first drink the famed spy orders in *Casino Royale*.

NOTES
* Add a dash of absinthe to get a Young American cocktail.

AFFINITY

50ml Scotch
15ml Dolin Dry
15ml Sweet Vermouth
Two dashes Angostura Bitters

METHOD
* Stirred and strained into a coupe
* Garnished with discarded lemon peel and a cherry

In essence, this cocktail is a Scotch-laced 'Perfect Manhattan' and is first found in *The New York Sun* in 1907 which states:

> *"There's another new cocktail on Broadway. They call it*
> *the Affinity. After drinking one, surviving experimenters*
> *declare, the horizon takes on a roseate hue: the second*
> *brings Wall Street to the front and centre proffering to*
> *you a quantity of glistering lamb shearings: when you've*
> *put way the third the green grass grows up all around,*
> *birds sing in the fig trees and your affinity appears.*
>
> *One medium teaspoonful of powdered sugar, one*
> *dash orange bitters, one jigger of Scotch whisky,*
> *and a half jigger of Italian vermouth."*

In that same year there was a popular hit song released by composer John W. Bratton named 'Molly McGinnity, You're My Affinity'. Seeing as the timelines match up, this is very possibly a theory as to where the cocktail drew its rather odd name.

The cocktail was first put into print when Hugo Ensslin released his *Recipes for Mixed Drinks* (1917) when he listed it as:

> *"⅓ French Vermouth*
> *⅓ Italian Vermouth*
> *⅓ Scotch Whiskey*
> *two dashes Aromatic Bitters."*

It is uncommon for the cocktail to follow this equal parts format in modern bartending, but this is the style in which it started.

BAMBOO COCKTAIL

40ml Fino Sherry
40ml Dry Vermouth
Two dashes Orange Bitters

METHOD
* Stirred and strained into a Nick and Nora
* Garnished with a lemon peel

Aside from the 'Adonis' cocktail this is likely the best-known of all sherry-laced beverages. Much like its sweet vermouth counterpart, this cocktail also lacks a full spirit base allowing it to become one of the most beloved 'low-ABV' drinks of the modern era.

Like many classic cocktails before it, and many to come after, there are conflicting stories about where it came from and who created it.

It's best to begin with the first time it appeared in a cocktail book, that being Thomas Stuart's *Stuart's Fancy Drinks and How to Mix Them* (1904) as:

"BAMBOO COCKTAIL
⅔ sherry, ⅓ Italian vermouth, one dash orange bitters."

It is interesting that Stuart decides to use sweet vermouth in his recipe making it identical to the 'Adonis'. It isn't until its appearance in William Boothby's *The World's Drinks and How to Mix Them* (1908) where a differentiation occurs when he writes:

"BAMBOO COCKTAIL
*Half a jiggerful of French vermouth, half a
jiggerful of sherry, two dashes of Orange bitters
and two dashes of Angostura bitters.*"

There is a note attached to this recipe that credits one Louis Eppinger, Yokohama, Japan of creating and naming the cocktail. Eppinger was a famed German bartender who began his career in San Francisco before going to Japan to take up mantle at the Grand Hotel as bar manager.

Another story regarding the origins of the Bamboo comes from the *Western Kansas World* newspaper printed September 11th, 1886, in which it credits and Englishman for the cocktail's creation. The paper reads:

*"A new drink has been introduced by some Englishman and
is becoming popular in New York... It consists of three parts
sherry to one part vermouth and is called 'bamboo'."*

If this story were true, it is highly contradictory of Boothby's claim of Eppinger creating the drink. If Eppinger did coin the cocktail, he would have done so in San Francisco before moving to Japan, and whether this was the case or not he is certainly attributed to promoting the cocktail.

NOTES
• Manzanilla sherry also works well here.

BACARDI COCKTAIL

60ml Bacardi Carta Blanca
25ml Lime Juice
15ml Grenadine

METHOD
• Shaken and strained into a coupe

The first written to this cocktail come from the November edition *Oakland Tribune* (1913) in which a they speak of a cocktail from New York in which you *"take half a whisky glass of Porto Rican rum, add the juice of half a lime and dash into it a squirt of grenadine."* It was named 'Rum and Grenadine', so a daiquiri turned pink without specifying Bacardi by name.

This changes in *Drinks* (1914) by Jacques Straub when he lists the 'Bacardi Cocktail' with Bacardi branded rum for his recipe.

When Hugo Ensslin published *Recipes for Mixed Drinks* (1916) he lists two cocktails – one named 'Bacardi Cocktail' and another 'Cuban Cocktail'. These cocktails are identical aside from the way in which the author describes the volume of the Bacardi used: *"drink Bacardi Rum"* and *"1 jigger Bacardi Rum"*, meaning their volumes must have differed. Neither of the cocktails had grenadine in their recipe.

Lastly, Tom Bullock's *The Ideal Bartender* (1917) lists two 'Bacardi Cocktail' recipes – one *'Country Club Style'* and one not. The prime difference is that the country club version contains lime juice, and the regular version does not.

The cocktail grew in popularity post-Prohibition as consumers took a likely to the taste of rums and grenadine, so Bacardi took legal action to the Supreme Court in 1936 to ensure only their rum could be used as the cocktail has their name.

NOTES
- J.A. Gohusko's *Jack's Manual* (1910) lists a 'Bagardie Cocktail' which is rather different to the recipes seen before as it is cited as "*50% Bagardie rum, 25% Italian Vermouth, 25% French Vermouth.*"

BLACK VELVET

Equal Parts Guinness and Champagne

METHOD
- Built in flute and gently stirred

The ever-debated mix of Guinness and champagne, the Black Velvet was coined in London at Brook's Club, 1861. The cocktail was said to be a commemoration of the death of Prince Albert.

The Prince died as a result of typhoid on December 14th, 1861, at the age of 42. A fitting mixture if you ask me – champagne which is used as a celebratory beverage, and the stark contrast of the black stout.

After this, Queen Victoria was famously known, and remembered, for wearing black until her death in January 1901.

David Embury makes a statement regarding the cocktail in his *The Fine Art of Mixing Drinks* (1948):

> *"Actually, it is excellent. The champagne cut the heavy, syrup consistency of the stout, and the stout takes out the sharp, tart edge off the champagne. Each is the perfect complement of the other."*

BLUE BLAZER

40ml Rye Whiskey
20ml Single Malt Whiskey
10ml Simple Syrup (2:1)
One dash Orange Bitters
One dash Angostura Bitters
15ml Hot Water

METHOD

- Preheat a digestive wine glass with boiling water
- Build ingredients into metal tankards with handles
- Cover the tin with the ingredients and allow to heat up
- Set ablaze and throw
- Garnished with lemon peel then discarded

This is one of the most famous cocktails of all time, not because it is the most balanced, but because it epitomises bartending showmanship like no other. Jerry Thomas is credited with creating this cocktail during his tenure at the El Dorado, San Francisco during the Gold Rush of the 1850s. Thomas was a man that wasn't afraid to draw attention to himself, as is described by British travel writer during his stay in San Francisco in 1863:

> *"He is a gentleman who is all ablaze with diamonds. There is a very large pin, formed of a cluster of diamonds, in the front of his magnificent shirt, he has diamond studs at his wrists, and gorgeous diamond rings on his fingers..."*

I would only make sense for a man of such personality to want a cocktail serve matching this. Thomas listed the cocktail with a story in his *Bartender's Guide* (1862):

> *"1 wine-glass Scotch whiskey.*
> *1 wine-glass boiling water.*
>
> *Put the liquid and the boiling water in one mug, ignite the liquid with fire, and while blazing mix both ingredients by pouring them four or five times from one mug to the other...*
>
> *The 'blue blazer' does not have a very euphonious or classic name but it tastes better to the palate than it sounds to the ear... The novice mixing this beverage should be careful to not scald himself. To become proficient in throwing the liquid from one mug to the other, it will be necessary to practice for some time with cold water."*

Even then the cocktail came with a warning, and I cannot stress this enough. This cocktail can be rather dangerous so be sure to practise throwing with cold water.

The drink quickly became a sight to behold, and a popular cocktail through the cold winter months. A popular tale is that a gentleman came into the bar and asked for *"some hellfire that'll shake me right down to my gizzard.* "Instead of informing the guest that humans don't have gizzards, Thomas told him to come back later that day and he would have something for him. Later that night upon the gentleman's return, Thomas set ablaze whiskey and boiling water.

Thomas said that the drink would only be made if the temperature outside was below ten degrees Celsius, however if someone came to the bar at noon and asked, I'm sure he would have obliged their request.

Now the previous tale is likely to be untrue, and Thomas himself never claims to have credited the cocktail (seeing as it is a simple spin on a 'Hot Toddy'), however he is certainly the ultimate spokesperson for the blazer.

There was a running joke in an Australian bar that I worked in many years ago in which we would all jest *"Did you even work in 1806 if you don't have a picture of you throwing a Blue Blazer?"*

And so this cocktail is for all the Bar 1806 family, past and present.

NOTES
- When preparing this cocktail preheat you glass with boiling water, build your cocktail, then empty your glass.
- Build cocktail and cover the tin that has the ingredients in it with another tin or mug. It is actually the alcohol vapour that catches fire first, the more you have the easily it will light.

BIJOU

40ml Gin
20ml Green Chartreuse
20ml Sweet Vermouth
Two dashes Orange Bitters

METHOD
- Stirred and strained into a coupe
- Garnished with lemon peel discarded and a cherry

> * this drink is also called an *'Amber Dream'*
> in the Savoy cocktail book *
> At the Ritz Paris, Frank Meier's spec was gin,
> curacao, dry vermouth and orange bitters.

Bijou in French means 'jewel' which depicts the breakdown of the components used in its making:

Gin – (Diamond)
Sweet Vermouth – (Ruby)
Green Chartreuse – (Emerald)

The Bijou first appeared in C. F. Lawlor's *The Mixologist* (1895) as:

"1/3 Grand Marnier.
1/3 Vermouth.
1/3 Plymouth Gin."

This recipe isn't what we would expect today if we order the cocktail and the invention of the drink is commonly attributed to bartender Harry Johnson, who included the recipe in his *The Bartender's Manual* (1900) in which he specifies Italian vermouth in place of Grand Marnier.

The drink was popular enough that it found its way into Frank Newman's French language book, *American Bar*, a few years later in 1904 — albeit with a few alterations: Newman's recipe calls for four dashes each of Green Chartreuse, orange bitters, and curaçao, two drops of grenadine, and a liqueur glass each of sweet vermouth and sloe gin.

The 'Bijou' was popular for several decades, however unlike the 'Manhattan' and the 'Martini', it disappeared after Prohibition. It was rediscovered by the 'King of Cocktails' Dale DeGroff in the 1980s, when he stumbled upon the recipe in Johnson's book. While the original cocktail had equal parts of the three ingredients, DeGroff tripled the ratio of gin to vermouth and chartreuse to soften the profile. Eventually, his recipe became the standard.

BOBBY BURNS NO.1

50ml Scotch Whiskey
20ml Sweet Vermouth
7.5ml Benedictine

METHOD
* Stirred and strained into a coupe
* Garnished with lemon peel

How did the cocktail did its name? – The 'Bobby Burns' was thought to have been created to commemorate the famous Scottish poet Robert Burns (1759–1796) however, Crockett mentions under his 1931 spec that it was probably named after the Robert Burns brand of cigar, rather than the poet. It falls in a family of alliterative cocktails along with the 'William Wallace' and 'Rob Roy'.

This cocktail first sees some sort of print in Jacques Straub's *Drinks* (1914) as the:

"BOBBIE BURNS COCKTAIL (FOR TWO).
1 barspoonful orange juice.
1 barspoonful maraschino.
Crush 1 lump of sugar.
½ jigger Scotch.
½ jigger Italian vermouth."

Now this cocktail doesn't contain Benedictine as we would know the drink to today, however like many classics it does evolve over the years.

The first time the modern, Manhattan-style cocktail appears is in Hugo Ensslin's *Recipes for Mixed Drinks* (1917) as "*½ Italian Vermouth, ½ Scotch Whiskey, two dashes Benedictine.*"

Two conflicting recipes exist around similar times: Harry Craddock's *The Savoy Cocktail Book* (1930) recipe, and *Old Waldorf Bar Days* (1931) by Albert Crockett. Craddock's recipe is the same as Ensslin's 13 years prior, whilst Crockett lists:

> *"Dash of Orange Bitters*
> *One dash of Absinthe*
> *One-quarter Italian Vermouth*
> *Three-quarters Scotch Whiskey."*

Coupled with this recipe, Crockett writes that the cocktail may have been named after the famed poet, or else it was named after a "*cigar salesman, who bought in the Bar.*" The cigar story would make for a much less interesting tale.

NOTES
- *Bobby Burns No.2* swaps Benedictine for Maraschino.
- *Bobby Burns No.3* replaces Benedictine for Drambuie.

BRANDY CRUSTA

40ml Cognac
10ml Grand Marnier
5ml Maraschino
15ml Lemon Juice
7.5ml Simple Syrup
One dash Angostura Bitters

METHOD

- Shaken and strained into a sugar-coated sours glass with a lemon Crusta shell
- Rim the glass with a lemon wedge and dip in caster sugar.

Assumed to have been created by Italian bartender and caterer, Joseph Santini, in New Orleans venue, Jewel of the South or City Exchange bar around 1850. Like many drinks of the era, it can be made with a variety of base spirits, however cognac became the flag-bearer of the family.

This cocktail remained a local star until Jerry Thomas visited New Orleans sometime in the 1850s and became bedazzled by the concoction and the serve. Thomas would go on to list this cocktail in his *The Bon Vivant's Guide or How to Mix Drinks* (1862) in contrast to his already established 'Fancy Brandy Cocktail'. Thomas rarely had cocktails that used lemon juice, and particularly not drinks that were so spirit-forward in nature.

This cocktail has seen a resurgence in popular due to Chris Hannah of Arnaud's French 75 Bar, New Orleans.

A typical fault in this cocktail is not getting the proportions right and mistaking this drink for a 'sour'. The use of citrus in this cocktail is meant to coincide with the like of bitters, using it as a flavouring agent to modify the cocktail.

NOTES
- The drink's base became its undoing as the phylloxera plague destroyed European vineyards making cognac unattainable in America.
- The peculiar spirit/citrus ratio has caused plenty of confusion as to where the Crusta fits into the cocktail family tree.
- Maraschino was added in the latter part of the nineteenth century appearing first in Harry Johnson's *New and Improved Bartender's Manual* (1882).
- This cocktail is said to have popularised citrus as a cocktail ingredient.

BRONX

40ml Gin
12.5ml Dry Vermouth
12.5ml Sweet Vermouth
25ml Orange Juice
One dash Orange Bitters

METHOD
- Shaken and strained into a coupe
- Garnished with an orange peel

DUPLEX
(PRECURSOR TO THE BRONX, MADE FAMOUS AT THE WALDORF-ASTORIA)

40ml Sweet Vermouth
40ml Dry Vermouth
Two dashes Orange bitters

METHOD
- Stirred and strained to a coupe
- Garnished with a lemon peel

This cocktail made its first appearance in William Boothby's *The Worlds Drinks and How to Mix Them* (1908) listed as:

> *"One-third Plymouth gin, one-third French Vermouth and one-third Italian vermouth, flavoured with two dashes or orange bitters and a barspoonful of orange juice."*

It also makes several appearances in other books at the time, but without the vital orange juice component.

The first-ever mention of the Bronx was in the newspaper *The Virginia Enterprise* in 1901. The excerpt credits three bartenders who made up a committee commissioned to create a cocktail to celebrate a visit from Carrie Nation to Virginia. Mrs. Nation was an avid supporter of the temperance movement, so this could be interpreted in many ways:

> *"Frank Curtis of The Gilsey house, inventor of 'Long Branch punch': J.E. O'Connor of the Waldorf-Astoria, inventor of the Bronx cocktail and William Gilbery of the Manhattan Hotel, inventor of the 'Clover Club Mystery'."*

Until this article, no one had even heard of John 'Curley' O'Connor, who started at the Waldorf-Astoria in 1893 and stayed there some 35 years. This led to the assumption of the following story being the accepted version.

The accepted story is that it was created in 1906 by Johnny Solon (a teetotaller), a bartender at New York's Waldorf-Astoria Hotel, and named after the newly opened Bronx Zoo.

Solon (the *Guys and Dolls* actor) and the bartender were challenged to whip up a cocktail on the fly, they came up with a riff on the (Duplex – perfect Martini with orange bitters). They so named it after the Bronx Zoo which he had visited the day before.

If this story is true, Solon must have created the drink between 1899 (when he started at the Waldorf-Astoria) and 1901 (when the article was published). In saying this, the Bronx Zoo opened in November 1899.

In the 1935 Waldorf-Astoria cocktail book, A. S. Crockett published he says:

> *"Solon's own story of the creation – of the Bronx: We had a cocktail in those days called the Duplex, which had a fair demand. One day I was making one when Traverson, head waiter of the Empire room – the main dining room in the original Waldorf. A Duplex was composed of equal parts dry and sweet vermouth, shaken up with a squeezed orange peel, or two dashes of orange bitters. Traverson said 'Why don't you make up a new cocktail?'"*

He didn't try it but handed it straight to Traverson as he was a good judge and he swallowed it whole.

> *"The demand for Bronx cocktails started that day. Pretty soon we were using a whole case of oranges a day, then several. Customers used to tell me of the strange animals they used to see after consuming lots of mixed drinks."*

By mid-century, however, the cocktail had mostly faded into obscurity as vodka supplanted gin as the clear spirit of choice.

Like all cocktails of a certain age, the Bronx's origins are somewhat contested. Some evidence suggests it was the creation of Philadelphia bartender Joseph S. Sormani in 1905. Sormani's *New York Times* obituary even credits him as the cocktail's creator. The recipe cited, however, omits dry vermouth, which technically makes it an Orange Blossom.

One thing can be confirmed, it originated at the historic Waldorf-Astoria Hotel.

Adding to the confusion, both Henry Craddock and William Boothby further cloud the history of the Bronx in their respective cocktail manuals. Craddock presents three different versions. Boothby, meanwhile, credits one Billy Malloy from Pittsburgh with a recipe that keeps the orange bitters but reduces the orange juice down to just a spoonful.

NOTES
- This is reputedly the first cocktail to have fruit juice in it.
- Add an egg yolk and it yields you a 'Golden Bronx'.

BROOKLYN COCKTAIL

50ml Rye
10ml Dry Vermouth
7.5ml Maraschino
7.5ml Amer Picon

METHOD
- Stirred and strained into a coupe
- Garnished with a cherry

I used to have a guest who solely ordered Brooklyn's and one day he asked me about the cocktail and I was stumped, so if anything this one goes out to you.

The much lesser known of the other cocktails named after Boroughs of New York, this cocktail dates back to the early twentieth century. Falling close to a Manhattan cocktail, it includes Amer Picon and Maraschino, two very difficult to come by liqueurs post-Prohibition – this is the prime reason it lost its place among classic cocktail canon.

The first appearance in cocktail text comes from J.A. Grohusko's *Jack's Manual* (1908). Jack was head bartender at Baracca's on Wall Street, which was owned by a gentleman from Brooklyn. His originally recipe read:

> *"one dash Amer. Picon bitters*
> *one dash Maraschino*
> *50% rye whisky*
> *50% Ballor Vermouth."*

The vermouth used was a classic sweet vermouth from Torino.

Several years later Jacques Straub listed his own recipe in his book *Drinks* (1914) listing it with dry vermouth instead of sweet. It was this recipe that put this cocktail, and the borough, on the drinking map:

> *"One dash Amer Picon*
> *One dash Maraschino*
> *½ jigger French Vermouth*
> *½ Jigger good Rye Whiskey."*

Many in recent years have agreed that the original recipe with sweet vermouth actually yield a better cocktail, and it was the brands and recipes for dry vermouth at the time that made it the more suitable choice for this cocktail. I would give both versions a try and see which you prefer.

CORPSE REVIVER NO. 1

25ml Calvados
25ml Cognac
25ml Sweet Vermouth
One dash Angostura Bitters

METHOD
- Stirred and strained into a coupe
- Garnished with a cherry

The concept surrounding this family of cocktail is that they serve as a 'pick-me-up' or a 'cure what ails you' style of refreshment.

The first recipe for a drink named *'Corpse Reviver'* comes from E. Ricket and C. Thomas' *The Gentleman's Table Guide* (1871) and is as such:

> *"Half wineglass of brandy, half glass of Maraschino,*
> *and two dashes of Boker's bitters."*

This was seen as one of the Savoy's most popular drinks, and author Harry Craddock says, *"To be Taken before 11am, or whenever steam and energy are needed."*

The less-known 'Corpse Reviver No. 3' is listed in *Patrick Gavin Duffy's Official Mixer's Manual* (1956) as:

> *"Place 1 or 2 ice cubes in a highball glass and add the Juice of ¼ Lemon, 1 jigger Pernod and fill with chilled Champagne."*

Joe Gilmore from the Savoy in 1954 had another variant of this cocktail listed as an equal parts cocktail containing Cognac, Fernet Branca and Branca Menta.

CORPSE REVIVER NO. 2

30ml Gin
20ml Cointreau
20ml Lillet Blanc
20ml Lemon Juice
Absinthe Rinse

METHOD
- Shaken and strained into a coupe
- Garnished with a cherry

One of the earliest written references to this family of cocktails comes from an English magazine *Punch, or the London Charivari* in which it is name dropped along with the 'Stone Wall' and 'Sling' cocktails:

> *"After liquoring up a Sling, a Stone Wall, and a Corpse Reviver."*

The first written reference in industry text regarding the cocktail comes from *The Gentleman's Table Guide* (1871) by E. Ricket and C. Thomas where they simply list it as:

> "CORPSE REVIVER
> *Half wineglass of brandy, half glass of maraschino, and two dashes of Boker's bitters."*

So clearly this is extremely different to what we would normally expect and the cocktail would continue to evolve from this point on.

It is likely that some semblance of cocktails that fall into the family of 'Corpse Revivers' were already present in the drinking world around the 1850s, they did not exist in a publication until Harry Craddock would have that pleasure in his *The Savoy Cocktail Book* (1930). Craddock would write of the soon-to-be-famous number two variant as:

> " ¼ *Wine glass Lemon Juice.*
> ¼ *Wine glass Kina Lillet.*
> ¼ *Wine glass Cointreau.*
> ¼ *Wine glass Dry Gin.*
> *One dash Absinthe.*
>
> *Four of these taken in swift succession*
> *will unrevive the corpse again."*

Both *The Café Royal Cocktail Book* (1937) by W.J. Tarling and *The Official Mixer's Manual* (1956) by Patrick Duffy list recipes for a 'Corpse Reviver No. 1, No.2 and No.3'.

Tarling's book listed very different versions of what would be perceived to be the norm at the time as he writes:

> "CORPSE REVIVER
> ⅓ *Brandy.*
> ⅓ *Orange Juice.*
> ⅓ *Lemon Juice.*
> *two dashes Grenadine*
> *Fill with Champagne.*
>
> GODFREY'S CORPSE REVIVER
> ⅔ *Gin.*
> ⅓ *Vodka.*
> *Dash of Grenadine.*
> *Dash of Angostura Bitters.*

NEW CORPSE REVIVER
⅓ Martini Sweet vermouth.
¼ Apple Brandy or Calvados.
½ Brandy."

Duffy's *'No.2'* recipe swaps Swedish Punch in place of Lillet and his *'No.3'* recipe is as follows:

"Place 1 or 2 ice cubes in a highball glass and add the Juice of
¼ Lemon, 1 jigger pernod and fill with chilled Champagne."

A recipe for a pousse-café (an old-school French layered cocktail) style, 'Corpse Reviver No.3' appears in *1700 Cocktails for the Man Behind The Bar* (1934) by R. de Fleury which was made of brandy, maraschino and curacao.

NOTES
- Swapping out the gin for cognac turns this drink into an 'Old McIntyre'.
- Joe Gilmore of The Savoy created a Corpse Reviver with equal parts Brandy, Fernet Branca and white crème de menthe.

CREOLE

50ml Rye
12.5ml Sweet Vermouth
7.5ml Amer Picon
7.5ml Benedictine
Two dashes Peychaud's Bitters

METHOD
- Stirred and strained into a coupe
- Garnished with a lemon peel

Given the name you'd expect this cocktail to stem from New Orleans, and to a degree you'd be correct.

The Creole can be considered a family of cocktail – rather than a singular drink. There are several main branches on the Creole family tree, though only two of those branches have survived into the modern cocktail world.

The two earliest variants that I discovered appeared several years before Prohibition – one from New Orleans, and the other, from Chicago. Firstly, the Creole Cocktail from Chicago comes from Jacques Straub's *Manual of Mixed Drinks* (1913). This variation is absinthe-forward, and this suggests that Straub was trying to highlight the New Orleans lifestyle in Chicago:

> "CREOLE COCKTAIL
> *⅓ jigger absinthe*
> *⅔ jigger Italian Vermouth*
> *Shake well."*

This version tastes as you would imagine, like sweetened absinthe with a highly herbal background.

Evidently, the New York Waldorf Hotel also served absinthe-based variants. In A. S. Crockett's *Old Waldorf Bar Days* (1931) lists that the Creole was on the Hotel's menu in the pre-Prohibition era, similar to Straub's recipe, with the addition of a dash of orange bitters. This variation was not much better, the orange bitters alone does little for the drink.

This branch of the Creole family tree seems to have been weeded out fairly fast, likely a victim of Prohibition and the fact that absinthe was outlawed in the U.S just before Straub's Manual made it to print.

THE NEW ORLEANS VARIANT

The next pre-Prohibition version of the Creole cocktail actually from New Orleans. Dave Wondrich, states that this version actually comes from Henry. C. Ramos, famously known for creating the Ramos Gin Fizz.

Ramos' Creole is a whiskey drink, not a far stretch from the Sazerac:

> *"2oz Whiskey*
> *2-three dashes Curacao*
> *4 dashes Peychaud's bitters*
> *3-4 dashes Angostura bitters*
> *Small lump of sugar*
> *Absinthe to coat the glass."*

Ramos' version reduces the heavy dose of absinthe to a simple wash on the serving glass, and the drink is sweetened with a touch of curacao. It's basically a Sazerac with a hint of orange.

Post-Prohibition, there was an evolution of the Creole. This 1930s branch of the family tree included whiskey, Benedictine, Italian vermouth, and the then-popular, Amer Picon. Harry Craddock was the first to publish this version in the 1930 *Savoy Cocktail Book,* and both Charles Duffy and William Boothby publish it again in 1934, with Boothby dubbing it *"Creole Cocktail No. 2":*

"½ Whiskey
½ Italian Vermouth
two dashes Amer Picon
one dashes Benedictine.

Stir with cracked ice, strain into a chilled
cocktail stem with a twist of lemon peel."

Funnily, this version omits absinthe altogether, and presents a more Manhattan-like format.

Trader Vic's *Bartender's Guide* (1947) lists an equal parts gin, sherry and lemon juice cocktail: that seems to have disappeared as suddenly as it appeared.

CHAMPAGNE COCKTAIL

15ml Cognac
Angostura Bitters soaked sugar cube
Champagne to wash line

METHOD
* Built in a flute and given a short stir
* Garnished with orange peel then discard

The origins of the cocktail are lost to time, as with most drinks. However, drinks historian David Wondrich says *"it dates from the Iron Age of American mixology – that final prehistoric period between the invention of the cocktail, whenever that was, and 1862, when the first cocktail book was published."*

Many believe that it first appears in Jerry Thomas' *The Bon Vivant's Guide or How to Mix Drink* (1862), however this is not the case.

The cocktail is first printed in 1855 in Robert Tomes' book *Panama in 1855: An Account of the Panama Rail-road*. There is an excerpt that shows mentions of the Champagne cocktail originally being served in a tumbler over crushed ice, and made with aromatic bitters, sugar syrup and champagne. Funnily enough there is no mention of brandy – or cognac.

Referring back to Thomas' book, he also speaks of serving the cocktail in a tumbler over crushed ice, and does not include a spirit base with his cocktail either. As a side note, he states to shake the beverage, which is something you should not do.

Cognac came around in the variation denoted in the *Café Royal Cocktail Book* (1937) by W.J. Tarling. His recipe is exactly the same as Harry Craddock's, except at the end he adds:

"A dash of brandy as required"

More in line with what we know as commonplace today.

NOTES
- Champagne at this time would have been on the sweeter side, as brut only came to the market at the end of the 1800s.
- Adding a small amount of sparkling water yields a 'Business Braces'.
- Equal measures cognac and Grand Marnier gives you a 'Prince of Wales'.

CASINO

50ml Gin
10ml Maraschino
15ml Lemon Juice
5ml Simple Syrup (drink can be rather dry without it, but not classic)
Two dashes Orange Bitters

METHOD
- Shaken and strained into a coupe
- Garnished with orange peel then discard

This cocktail turns up in for the first time in Hugo Ensslin's *Recipes for Mixed Drinks* (1917) later appearing in *The Savoy Cocktail Book* (1930) by Harry Craddock, which listed a large number of Ensslin's drinks:

"two dashes Maraschino
two dashes Orange bitters
two dashes lemon juice
1 drink of Tom Gin
Cherry"
ENSSLIN, 1917

"2 dashes Maraschino.
2 dashes Orange Bitters.
2 dashes Lemon Juice.
1 Glass Old Tom Gin."
CRADDOCK, 1930

Interestingly there were a number of drinks in the early stages of the twentieth century that went under this name including one that contained brandy, absinthe and champagne – a slightly more decadent cocktail, fitting of the name.

It has been written that the Casino is an 'Aviation' without the inclusion of crème de Violette, however the drink is meant to be a take on a Martini, the small additions in lemon juice, maraschino and bitters are meant to highlight and accentuate the Old Tom Gin. It screams the mantra of less is more.

COFFEE COCKTAIL

30ml Cognac
40ml LBV Port
10ml Simple Syrup
Whole Egg

METHOD
- Wet and dry shaken then strained into a sours or digestive wine glass
- Garnished with grated nutmeg

A personal favourite of mine due to the education that comes with the cocktail – I imagine I'm not alone in saying that I have had to say there is no actual coffee in this drink.

The drink is fairly undocumented, and so the creator has been lost to the ages however this cocktail makes its first appearance in Jerry Thomas' *Bartender's Guide* (1887) as:

"1 tea-spoonful powered white sugar.
1 fresh egg.
1 large wine-glass of port wine.
1 pony of brandy.
2 or 3 lumps of ice.

The name of this drink is a misnomer, as coffee and bitters are not to be found among its ingredients, but looks like coffee when it has been properly concocted, and hence its name."

As Thomas says, it looks like coffee when named correctly and thus is a delightful after dinner cocktail. I would suggest a young ruby port with plenty of fruit notes for this cocktail.

CLOVER CLUB

50ml Gin
10ml Sweet Vermouth
20ml Lemon Juice
20ml Simple Syrup
Two Raspberries
20ml Egg white

METHOD
* Wet and dry shaken then strained into a coupe
* Garnished with freeze dried raspberry powder

The Clover Club was named after a group of 35 men sharing the same name that met at the Bellevue-Stratford Hotel, Philadelphia. The most apt description of this group actually comes from Albert Crockett's *Old Waldorf Bar Days* (1931) where he lists the cocktail with a little piece of information:

*"A Philadelphia importation, originated, it is said, in the
bar of the old Bellevue-Stratford, where the Clover Club,
composed of literary, legal, finincal and business lights of
the Quaker City, often dined and wined, and wined again.*

Juice one-half Lemon
One-half spoon Sugar
One-half pony Raspberry
One-fourth pony White of Egg
One jigger Gin."

The hotel was the hotspot in Philadelphia at the time, much like
the 'Algonquin Round Table' of New York, the members would host
monthly meetings in which they would consume the cocktail and
indulge in 'social enjoyments'.

The first written recipe appears in Paul Lowe's *Drinks – How to Mix and Serve* (1909) and is listed as:

"½ pony raspberry syrup,
½ jigger dry gin,
½ jigger French Vermouth,
White of 1 egg."

The general take is that Lowe not including lemon juice was a mistake, as by this time the use of citrus juice was widely accepted and popular in making cocktails.

The cocktail was popular right up until the group fizzled out, however it began to fall out of fashion due to the feminine associated to the pink hue and the use of fresh fruit. It was rediscovered and put front and centre at the Brooklyn bar of the same name.

Later we see the cocktail appear in Robert Vermeire's *Cocktails – How to Mix Them* (1922) in which he uses lime juice in place of lemon juice, however this didn't really seem to catch on.

My preference is the use of sweet vermouth with fresh raspberries which closer resembles a recipe from the Hotel Belvedere, Baltimore in 1911, which uses sweet and dry vermouth.

NOTES
- If you add a mint leaf on top of this drink, it becomes a Clover Leaf.
- William Butler Yeats was said to be one of the members of the group.
- The group was made up of all men.
- If you replace the base spirit with rum this turns into a 'Commodore'.

CHARLIE CHAPLIN

35ml Sloe Gin
35ml Apricot brandy
30ml Lime juice

METHOD

Shaken and strained into a coupe

Likely to have been created at the Waldorf-Astoria Hotel, New York in the early 1920s, but not published until Albert Crockett released his *Old Waldorf Bar Days* (1931):

> *"One-third Lime Juice*
> *One-third Sloe Gin*
> *One-third Apricot Brandy."*

Sir Charles Spencer 'Charlie' Chaplin, was a silent movie actor and comedian from England. He would have been at the height of his career when this cocktail was made in celebration for him.

It is recommended to shake this cocktail for slightly longer than usual as dilution is highly important to balance the two liqueurs.

NOTES
• Lemon juice yields a 'sharper' cocktail in place of lime juice.

CAIPIRINHA

60ml Cachaca
One Whole Lime Muddled
Two teaspoons of Brown Sugar/10ml rich simple syrup

METHOD
• Roll a lime, then cut into six pieces
• Put into small tin and add sugar to taste
• Add Cachaca and gently muddle all ingredients together
• Give a hard, quick shake with ice
• Dump into large rocks glass
• Garnished with lime zest

> The best style of ice is if you smash up cubed ice with a rolling pin. Not quite pebbled and not whole, a close definition of 'shaved ice'.

Cachaca is the national spirit of Brazil and it is distilled from fermented sugarcane juice, and has been produced in Brazil from the early 1500s.

One theory claims that the Caipirinha originated in the Brazilian state of Sao Paulo towards the end of WW1. Its original recipe consisted of Cachaca, lime, honey and garlic and was supposedly prepared as a medicine to ease the effects of Spanish flu or Cholera. At some point honey and garlic were exchanged for sugar and the Caipirinha was born. Early adopters of the drink were typically those in more deprived areas of the country.

Another account of this drink comes from a rural part of Sao Paolo in which people were already drinking these ingredients in combination at the end of the nineteenth century and if this holds true, removes the theory of this drink being created at the end of World War I.

Finally the Caipirinha is placed in the city of Paraty, a beautiful coastal town in Brazilian state of Rio de Janeiro. A historian from Paraty, Diuner Mello discovered a document from 1856 which contains a reference to this cocktail discussing an epidemic of cholera in the area:

> *"Because of the concern with cholera and water, by necessity*
> *we began mixing aguardiente with water, sugar and limes,*
> *because it was prohibited to drink straight water."*

Caipirinha seems to come from the word 'caipira' meaning to describe someone from the countryside. Meaning the drink would have found its way into the city, unable to escape glorification. With time the drink spread through Brazil, and in 1922 it went global, and in 2003 Brazilians made the drink the country's official one by law.

The method of making this drink is varied, the muddling aspect has been glorified by one Mr. John Gakuru, the now ex-brand ambassador for Sagatiba Cachaca.

NOTES
- The name of the drink literally translates to "little peasant".

CHRYSANTHEMUM

70ml Noilly Prat
10ml Benedictine
Two dashes Peychaud's Bitters
Two dashes Absinthe

METHOD
* Stirred and strained into a coupe
* Garnished with a lemon peel

The chrysanthemum flower is an edible plant that often finds its way into Asian tea varieties. There is little documented evidence as to why this flower became the namesake for this cocktail, a loose guess is that it was one of the 27 mysterious ingredients within Benedictine.

The first appearance of this cocktail comes from *Recipes for Mixed Drinks* (1916), calling for equal parts dry vermouth and Benedictine. Later, *The Savoy Cocktail Book* (1930) mentions a modern-era version incorporating a 2:1 ratio. This particular variant was made popular among the middle class upon the S.S. *Europa*, a German liner that allowed U.S. citizens a chance to imbibe during prohibition. This cruise liner was built in the 1920s and took its maiden voyage to New York in March, 1930, it was one of the fastest ships of the time and could make the journey to New York in five days.

The vermouth base is the carrier for the more herbaceous delicacies of the absinthe and earthy Benedictine, which mingle extremely well together and are often grouped together. The great thing about this drink is that the garnish can be either orange or lemon peel, and both add their own sense of life to the cocktail.

DAIQUIRI

60ml White Rum
30ml Freshly Squeezed Lime Juice
Two barspoons Caster Sugar
5ml Simple Syrup

METHOD
- Add all ingredients into shaker tin and stir without ice to dissolve sugar
- Long shake with block ice preferably, then strained into a coupe

The recipe hand written in Jenning Cox's dairy is held at the University of Miami Special collections:

"For 6 persons:
The juice of 6 lemons
6 teaspoons of B. sugar
6 bacardi cups – carta blanc.a"

Though written lemons, this seems highly unlikely as lemons were so universally scarce, particularly in Cuba, whilst limes were plentiful on the island.

The initial recipe calls for brown sugar, but a PR representative named Gerry Swinehart, had been employed by Cuban government to promote American tourism, and accidently spread the incorrect recipe stating the use of white sugar.

The classic Daiquiri is rum, lime, and sugar shaken with ice, and takes its name from the place of which it was invented, the mining town of Daiquiri on the south-eastern tip of Cuba. Originally to be called a 'Tum Sour' to rival the whiskey sour, however the fell on deaf ears so they called it the Daiquiri, where it was invented.

During the time of the Spanish-American War in 1898, an American mining engineering by the name of Jenning Cox created the drink to protect his workers from Yellow Fever. According to Bacardi archivist Juan Bergaz Pessino, both the lime and alcohol were thought to protect against the deadly disease, although there are also rumours that cox invented the cocktail when he ran out of gin at a party.

Several decades later, a veteran of the war for Cuban Independence, P. D. Pagliuchi, laid claim to the name, stating:

"On the sideboard of the mine's dining room, there was no
gin or vermouth at all: all we could find was Bacardi rum,

limes, sugar and ice... with this material, Mr. Cox made
up a cocktail, which was so shaken as to be very cold."

Another story comes from chemist Josh Linthicum, who worked with Cox. He states it was named by a bartender who served Cox at San Carlos Club.

Lucius Johnson introduced the cocktail to the U.S. in 1908, when he brought the recipe back from Cuba to the Army and Navy Club, Washington, where a famed plague still exists.

In terms of written book features, the cocktail is highlighted in *Straub's Manual of Mixed Drinks* (1913), and is spelt 'Daiquiri' although it does have double the amount lime to rum in it.

Hugo Ensslin's *Recipes for Mixed Drinks* (1917) lists two cocktails of a similar description:

"BACARDI COCKTAIL AND CUBAN COCKTAIL
A measure of rum, juice of ½ a lime, and
two dashes of gum syrup."

Showing the spread of the cocktail, it was also noted in F. Scott. Fitzgerald's novel *This Side of Paradise* (1920).

The bartender and co-owner of the famous La Floridita bar in Havana, Constantino Ribalaigua Vert further popularised this cocktail by making several variations that would also stick in cocktail canon.

This bar would hold many titles and host many famous characters, who would dub the venue 'Cradle of the Daiquiri'. Several different Daiquiris were served here and labelled by number. More importantly it is here that Hemingway would become coupled with the cocktail served by Constante.

NOTES
Daiquiri No. 2 – Rum, orange curacao, lime juice, orange juice, sugar
Hemingway Daq/ Daiquiri no.3 – Rum, lime juice, Maraschino, grapefruit juice, sugar
Daiquiri No. 4 – Rum, Maraschino, lime juice, sugar
• Adding mint to this cocktail makes it a 'Maison Charles'.

- Swapping the sugar for honey gives you a 'Honeysuckle'.
- Swap light rum and sugar for Jamaican rum and honey, with a dash of Angostura bitters give you a 'Brooklynite'.
- Switching the light rum for aged and the sugar for grenadine, whilst adding mint yields a 'Detroit Daisy'.

PINK DAIQUIRI (DAIQIUIRI NO.5)

50ml White Rum
5ml Maraschino
20ml Lime Juice
7.5ml High Quality Grenadine
5ml Simple Syrup
One dash Angostura Bitters

METHOD
- Shaken and strained into a coupe
- Created by Constantino Ribalaigua Vert at the Floridita bar in Havana.

DARK 'N' STORMY

50ml Gosling's Black Seal Rum
15ml Ginger Syrup
20ml Lime juice
5ml Simple Syrup
Ginger Beer Top

METHOD
- Shaken and strained into a highball
- Garnished with a lime wedge and candied ginger

It's an unproven legend that the drink has a connection to the joys and dangers of seafaring and that the name comes from a sailor whom poured ginger beer over the Gosling's rum and stated:

"The colour of a cloud only a fool or dead man would sail under."

In 1806, the *Mercury*, a charted English ship carrying wines and spirits commanded by James Gosling managed to avoid the 200 square mile coral reef surrounding Bermuda after having been at sea for 91 days on its search for America.

The Goslings would become one of the most prominent families on the island, and started in the rum business in 1857, and realised their first batch in 1860 dubbed 'Old Rum'. They added a ginger beer plant to the site, which became extremely popular with the British Navy. It didn't take long before both two ingredients were combined at the Dark 'N' Stormy was born.

Up until 1914 consumers of Gosling's would refill bottles straight from the barrel. However, during WW1 Goslings distributed rum in champagne bottles at the Royal Navy Officer's mess hall. These bottles were sealed with a distinctive wax that would eventually become the namesake for the rum.

In 1991, Gosling's won two trademarks on the recipe so that the cocktail could only contain their rum if it was to be called a 'Dark 'N Stormy', and this is no small feat. Only three other cocktails have won such trademarks are the Sazerac, the Hand Grenade and the Painkiller.

NOTES
- Swapping rum for Scotch whiskey turns this into a 'Presbyterian'.
- Do the same with sloe gin and you get a 'Cloudy Sky'.
- Using vodka as the base and finishing it with a spritz of rosewater gives you the delicious 'Palma Fizz'.
- Removing the rum and putting in gin instead yields a 'London Buck'. Keeping this theme, dropping the gin slightly and adding 10ml Fernet Branca gives you a 'Late Night Reviver'.

(DE) LA LOUISIANE

45ml Rye
20ml Sweet Vermouth
12.5ml Benedictine
Three dashes Peychaud's Bitters
Three dashes Absinthe

METHOD
- Stirred and strained into a coupe
- Garnished with a cherry

This drink began as the house cocktail of its namesake hotel and Creole restaurant, a once popular French-Quarter spit opened in 1881 by the family that has run the legendary Antoine's since 1840.

The drink celebrates the multicultural heritage of New Orleans by incorporating ingredients the world over. Influenced by the 'Sazerac', Chris Hannah of French 75, goes one step further to describe it as a marriage of a Sazerac (rye, cognac, absinthe, Peychaud's and Angostura) and a Vieux Carré (rye, cognac, sweet vermouth, Benedictine, orange and Angostura bitters).

Paul Gustings, prior head bartender at French quarter institutions Napoleon house and Tujague's, suggests that this drink was created in response to the competition from the hotel around the corner:

> *"The Monteleone had the Vieux Carré so they decided they needed a house cocktail too".*

New Orleans bartending legend Chris MacMillian, insists that the La Louisiane came first by saying *"The restaurant opened in 1881, so it's likely that the drink appeared somewhere in this time period,"* and that the Vieux Carré did not appear until the first few years after the repeal of Prohibition in 1930.

As with many classic cocktails, the truth is often coated in layers of myth. The original spec called for absinthe, a spirit that was banned in 1912 and only made truly legal again 95 years later in 2007.

Both the Vieux Carré and the La Louisiane were first immortalised in 1937 by Stanley Clisby Arthur's books, *Famous New Orleans Drinks and How to Mix 'em.* But cocktails need places to thrive, not simply texts.

The Vieux Carré enjoyed a permanent home at the hotel Monteleone's famous Carousel bar, which eventually spread across the U.S. The 'La Louisiane' found no such luck, and after the restaurant changed hands several times. It fell to the background. However is saw a slight revival in the early 2000s thanks to events like TOTC.

NOTES
- Also works well shaken, but not generally what is expected.

DELICIOUS SOUR

45ml Calvados
10ml Crème de Peche
20ml Lemon Juice
15ml Simple Syrup
10ml Egg White

METHOD
- Wet and dry shaken then strained into a coupe

This cocktail was created by A. William Schmidt, or as he dubbed himself: 'The Only William'. He was the author of the book *The Flowing Bowl* (1891), and he was one of the most celebrated bartenders of his time.

The name delicious sour probably comes from Schmidt's own sense of self, or that it is just truly delicious and is listed in his book as:

"A goblet with the juice of a lime,
A squirt of seltzer,
A spoonful of sugar,
½ of apple-jack,
½ of peach brandy,
The white of an egg."

The peach brandy he speaks about would have been the style used in cocktails like the original 'Mint Julep' cocktail but it is no longer available, modern-day replacement in generally crème de peche.

DELMONICO

25ml Gin
15ml Dry vermouth
15ml Sweet Vermouth
15ml Cognac
One dash Angostura Bitters

METHOD
- Shaken and strained into a coupe
- Garnished with an orange peel

55ml Cognac
20ml Sweet Vermouth
Two dashes Angostura Bitters

METHOD
* Stirred and strained into a coupe
* Garnished with a cherry

Some recipes for this cocktail are simply cognac iterations of the Manhattan, however the addition of gin is what makes this cocktail unique. David Embury's *Fine Art of Mixing Drinks* (1948) states:

> *"The Delmonico is a plain Manhattan with cognac substituted for whiskey. There is also a Delmonico Special which is merely a Medium Martini with 1 teaspoon of brandy to each drink and a twist of orange peel."*

As usual, where the cocktail was exactly created is uncertain, this is because Delmonicos would open, close and move several times over the span of its operation. Dave Wondrich suggests that it stemmed from the original face of the Delmonico in 1876 at Madison Square Garden.

The cocktail first comes to life when two Swiss Brothers – Giovanni and Pietro Del-Monico – opened a pastry shop on South William Street, New York during the 1820s.

In 1831 they opened what was consider to be America's first 'real' restaurant with aid from their nephew Lorenzo who was trained in culinary arts. During this time eating out was not an activity taken in leisure, more a necessity due to the busy nature of the work days. The Delmonico restaurant wanted to change this perception by introducing the 'a la carte' menu concept to the city, going against the norm of serving sandwiches and other snacks typically available. Their first menu was extensive, expanding over 100 pages and listing over 300 offerings.

This perception change was welcomed, but the brothers wanted to further it. It had caught on with neighbouring venues. The Delmonico then began thinking of fine dining, a location in which the wealthy could come to eat and drink, and be seen to be doing so. This new idea brought with it a new menu, listing items such as Lobster and Delmonico steak, Eggs Benedict and Baked Alaska most famously.

The restaurant closed, reopened and moved several times around New York city. The last owned and operated restaurant in the Delmonico name was on 44th Street and Fifth, and closed its doors in 1923.

EAST INDIA (NO.2)

40ml Cognac
15ml Curacao
5ml Maraschino
30ml Pineapple Juice
15ml Lemon Juice
5ml Simple Syrup
Two dashes Angostura Bitters

METHOD
* Shaken and stained into a coupe
* Garnished with an orange peel and nutmeg

The Dutch East India Trading Company was the world's first mega-corporation, operating essentially globally for over 200 years, with its dominance ending in the early nineteenth century.

This drink tends to be associated as a remembrance to such a company, along with coins, architecture and paintings fitting to such an empire.

East India was the name used for the collective lands in Southeast Asia under British and Dutch colonial control including Burma, India, Malaysia and Singapore to name a few.

The ingredients themselves lend homage to trade carried around the world:

* French Brandy exported to the 'New World' and Asia.
* Pineapple juice to showcase tropical fruits brought to Europe from lands undiscovered.
* Curacao brought by a 'New World' settlement, operated by this very company.
* Bitters, showcasing the prominent spice trade.

- Rum, often used in trade for multiple goods, unfortunately a contributing factor to slave trading.

This cocktail first turns up in Harry Johnson's *Bartender's Manual* (1882) and is actually listed with raspberry syrup, which is changed to pineapple syrup in his updated edition in 1900. The pineapple syrup theme would continue for many years, appearing in such texts as Robert Vermeire's *Cocktails And How to Mix Them* (1922), Harry MacElhone of Ciro's *ABC of Mixing Cocktails* (1923) and Frank Meier's *The Artistry of Mixing Drinks* (1936). Of these texts, MacElhone is the only person to credit Harry Johnson as the cocktail's creator.

Two more influential texts in the form of Harry Craddock's 1930 *Savoy Cocktail Book* and W.J. Tarling's *Café Royal Cocktail Book* (1937). Both list pineapple juice as opposed to syrup. The reason for this change is unknown to the best of information provided by additional supporting material.

The use of pineapple syrup versus juice is of no contention in the modern bartending world, however I would suggest using juice in order to yield a consist cocktail each time.

FLORADORA

50ml Gin
20ml Lime Juice
10ml Simple Syrup
10ml Ginger Syrup
Three Fresh Raspberries
Ginger Ale Top

METHOD
- Shaken and strained into a highball over ice
- Garnished with a lime wedge and raspberry

This drink was named after a successful musical comedy that showcased in London in 1889, then in New York City in 1900.

There were six ladies who performed, the Floradora Girls, and one of them (Susie Drake) asked the bartender at an after-party and to make her something special or else she wouldn't drink that evening.

She wanted "something brand new". So the bartender, Jimmy O'Brien, concocted the Floradora that night in the Columbus Avenue restaurant.

One of the oldest print versions of the recipe is from Jacques Straub's *Manual of Mixed Drinks* (1913):

> *"Juice of ½ a Lime.*
> *¼ Jigger Raspberry.*
> *¼ Jigger Dry Gin.*
> *1 Lump Cube Ice.*
> *1 Pint Schweppes Ginger Ale."*

In this book he also has a 'Floradora – Imperial Style' which is a similar cocktail only omitting raspberry syrup and replacing the gin for brandy.

The drink then took home at the original Waldorf-Astoria where it caught on, and remained a mainstay of highbrow New York types for a good half a century. Its run was a lot, lot longer than that of the play – although the latter did see a little London revival in 2006.

NOTES
- All six girls went on to marry millionaires.

FRENCH 75

30ml Gin
15ml Lemon Juice
10ml Simple Syrup
Champagne Top

METHOD
- Shaken and strained into a flute then topped with champagne
- Garnished with a lemon peel

> *Celebrates the firepower of the WWI French 75-millimetre field gun. In recent decades, this has become a potent gin based champagne cocktail with lemon and sugar served in a flute, but it originally consisted of Gin, apple brandy, grenadine and lemon juice.*

Generally cocktails are named after significant people or events in history, this cocktail however is named after a piece of military equipment. It was the 'Canon de 75 Modele', a French 75-mm light field gun that was in the news constantly as a crux of hope against the German forces.

The cocktail first appeared in writing in the *Washington Herald* (1915) with this accompanying piece exported back to America by their war correspondent Alexander Powell.

> *"The Soixante Quinze – the French Seventy-Five.*
> *It is one-third gine, one-third grenadine, one-*
> *third applejack and a dash of lemon juice."*

To little surprise a French bartender in Harry's Bar, Paris (likely Henry Tepe) named a cocktail after the gun also sometime around 1914 therefore spreading awareness of the beverage to those visiting the venue.

The cocktail would have several other appearances before a recipe like those we are familiar with would appear in cocktail texts. In the November edition of *The Sphere* (1916), a London newspaper, it is stated that the cocktail was:

> *"invented by the mixer of the American Bar at Ciro's*
> *called Soixante-Quinze, an agreeable blend of*
> *calvados and other mysterious ingredients."*

The newspaper continues to build a connection between the cocktail and the famous Harry MacElhone as he would later purchase the location of his first bartending role and turn it into Harry's New York Bar, Paris.

In 1922 Robert Vermeire (a well-established French bartender) records the first time that the cocktail was in an industry book. He lists it as the '75' cocktail in his *Cocktails and How to Mix Them* (1922) as:

> *"two dashes of Grenadine.*
> *1 teaspoonful of Lemon Juice.*
> *⅛ gill of Calvados.*
> *⅜ gill of Dry Gin."*

Vermeire goes on to talk about who created the cocktail (meaning that it wasn't him) saying that it *"was introduced by Henry of Henry's Bar."* The easy mistake to make here is misreading this as Harry of Harry's Bar, a much more reputable person in cocktail history, however he is referring to one Henry Tepe of Henry's Bar not three minutes away from the famous Harry's Bar. Many agree that Henry would have created the cocktail and then MacElhone would have brought it to London and popularised it, as he makes no claim to have been the cocktail's creator.

After WWI, MacElhone would move to London to take up residence at Ciro's where he would publish his first *ABC of Mixing Cocktails* (1922). In this book he would print a '75' cocktail as:

*"1 teaspoonful Grenadine, two dashes of Absinthe
or Anis-del-Oso, ⅔ Calvados, ⅓ Gin."*

The cocktails both look fairly similar, with MacElhone omitting lemon juice for absinthe as the prime difference.

This cocktail finally becomes more recognisable in Judge Jr's *Here's How* (1927) book as he lists the 'French 75' as:

*"This drink is really what won the War for the Allies:
2 jiggers Gordon water.
1 part lemon juice:
A spoonful of powdered sugar:
Cracked ice.
Fill up the rest of the glass with champagne!"*

This style of cocktail would later be replicated by Harry Craddock in *The Savoy Cocktail Book* (1930) as he would serve it in a highball over ice (which if you haven't tried is delicious).

David Embury's *The Fine Art of Mixing Drinks* (1948) pays homage to the cocktail being made with a different spirit, notably Cognac. He states that "gin is sometimes used in place of Cognac in this drink, but then of course it should no longer be called French" (in which he has a point).

Stanley M. Jones writes in his *Jones' Complete Barguide* (1977) about the cocktail being made with different spirits and being given different numbers to help identify them i.e. "French 95 being made with Bourbon." He also follows the trend of serving them all over ice in a highball. The change to champagne flute happened in the late 1980s as most cocktails fell victim to a change of glassware in order to stay relevant in the modern era.

OLD FRENCH 75 – Old Tom gin, Calvados, Cognac, lemon juice, grenadine, absinthe, champagne.

FRENCH 95 – Bourbon, lemon juice, sugar, champagne.

FRENCH 125 – Cognac, lemon juice, sugar, champagne (tank-mounted Soviet 2A46 125mm cannon).

FRENCH 76 – Vodka, lemon juice, sugar, Angostura bitters, champagne.

SEAPLANE – Gin, lemon juice, sugar, orange bitters, absinthe, champagne.

BITTER FRENCH – Gin, Campari, lemon juice, sugar, champagne – Grapefruit twist.

MEXICAN 55 – Tequila, lemon juice, sugar, Angostura bitters, champagne.

FORD COCKTAIL

50ml Gin
20ml Dry Vermouth
5ml Benedictine
Two dashes Orange Bitters

METHOD
- Stirred and strained into a coupe
- Garnished with an orange peel

Many would assume this cocktail to be named in honour of Henry Ford and his automobile company that shared his name, however this is not the case as this cocktail predates this titan of industry. Ted Haigh speculates that it may be named after Malcolm Webster Ford, the famous athlete at the time.

The 'Ford' cocktail appears first in George J. Kappeler's *Modern American Drinks* (1895) where he lists it as:

> *"Three dashes Benedictine, three dashes orange bitters, half jigger Tom Gin, half a jigger French vermouth... Add a piece of twisted orange peel."*

Many cocktails at the time were strikingly similar – the Martini, Tuxedo and Turf Club as examples – all using Old Tom gin and perhaps differing on one ingredient and number of dashes of bitters. Some of these cocktails would change, allowing the Ford cocktail to come into its own, however it still is no surprise that it fell out of classic cocktail history due to obscurity.

GIN AND IT (AKA ARTILLERY)

55ml Gin
25ml Sweet Vermouth
One dash Orange Bitters

METHOD
* Stirred and strained into a coupe
* Garnished with a lemon peel

I've thought about this drink a lot lately, staring at its simplicity and the fact it is essentially a cross of a Martini and Martinez. It is the quintessential gin and vermouth cocktail that really showcases drinking culture of its inception. Originally known as a sweet Martini and from what I've read and it was popular during the late 1800s at many New York bars at the time.

The cocktail appears in David. A. Embury's *Fine Art of Mixing Drinks* (1948) as a "Gin and IT" and has a 3:1 gin to vermouth ratio, stating "in Europe the proportions are half and half." This is shown in Frank Meier's *The Artistry of Mixing Drinks* (1936) where he lists it as an equal parts drink with half gin and half Italian vermouth.

At the same time as Prohibition, it seems the drink found its way to London where such people as Harry Craddock would play on the British love of gin at the time. Craddock suggests a drier 2:1 recipe, which would be more agreeable by modern drinking habits.

NOTES
- "IT" is short for Italian, referencing the sweet vermouth aspect.
- The "Gin and Italian" as it was known, until Prohibition when it eventually was shortened to "Gin and IT".

GIN FIZZ

50ml Gin
20ml Lemon Juice
10ml Simple Syrup
Soda Water Top

METHOD
- Shaken and strained into a highball
- Garnished with a Lemon wedge

The term Gin Fizz and Tom Collins are generally interchangeable in the modern cocktail era, however this was not always the case. Both drinks appear in Jerry Thomas' books but the main difference is serve and how they were consumed.

Appearing in Jerry Thomas' *Bartender's Guide* (1876) the original fizz cocktail is listed as a 'Whiskey Fiz' (only one 'Z'):

"4 or 5 dashes of gum syrup
Juice of half a lemon
1 small wineglass of whiskey.
Fill the glass half full of shaved ice, shake
up well and strain into glass.
Fill up the glass with Seltzer water from a
syphon and drink without hesitation."

And following that as drink number 246 is listed a 'Gin Fiz':

"The same as Whiskey Fiz, substituting gin for whiskey."

The next appearance of the 'Gin Fizz' appears in Jerry Thomas' *Bartender's Guide* (1887) differing as it calls for powdered sugar and Holland gin specifically.

"1 tea-spoonful of powdered white sugar.
three dashes of lemon juice.
1 wine-glass of Holland gin.
1 small piece of ice.
Fill up the glass with Apollinaris or Seltzer
water, stir thoroughly and serve."

A 'Fizz' was originally a shorter drink, served in a small highball, without ice, and planned to be consumed quickly (this is how I would still view fizzes, without ice). Thinking of the time period in which they were popularised, 1900–1940, there was a huge push in industry and those involved in it would need to imbibe quickly, and then get moving.

Flip that to a Tom Collins, served in a much larger glass, with plenty of ice, designed to be kept cold for longer periods of time.

NOTES
- Although structurally the same, the main difference between a gin fizz (excluding egg white) and a Tom Collins, is that a Tom Collins would generally use Old Tom Gin.
- Silver fizz – addition of egg white
- Golden fizz – addition of egg yolk
- Royal fizz – addition of whole egg
- Diamond fizz – Additional of champagne rather than soda water
- Green Fizz – addition of green crème de Menthe

A NOTE TO FIZZES

Sours with the addition or carbonated or fizzy ingredients. This category also includes drinks such as the Mojito, which follow the same structure with the addition of herbs, muddled fruits, bitters, etc. Mojitos are a great example of a fizz that you don't realise is a fizz. In the case of white or silver fizz style cocktails, an emulsifier is used.

GIMLET

60ml Plymouth Navy Strength
20ml Lime Cordial

RISE OF THE BARTENDER

- Stirred and strained into a coupe

The Gimlet shows up in *Harry's ABC of Mixing Cocktails* (1922). This recipe lists an equal measure drink of Plymouth gin and Rose's lime cordial specifically.

A note included with the drink by MacElhone:

"Can be iced if desired. A very popular beverage in the Navy."

During the seventeenth century, sailors used citrus fruits to prevent scurvy, a disease brought about by a lack of vitamin C. Experienced Naval officers and surgeons were shown that citrus did prevent scurvy, and Admiral Alan Gardener insisted a daily ration of lemon juice (initially) to be issued on board during a 23-week, non-stop voyage to India in 1794. Once the benefits of drinking citrus juice became known, sailors consumed so much often mixed with their daily ration of rum and water (commonly referred to as 'grog').

The oft-quoted 1867 *Merchant Shipping Act* made it mandatory by law for all British ships to carry rations of lime juice on voyages, due to the serious nature of the disease.

The fruit juice was preserved by the addition of 15% rum but in 1867, Lauchlin Rose, the owner of a shipyard in Scotland, patented a process for preserving fruit juice with sugar and sulphur dioxide rather than alcohol. This product would eventually go on to be called Rose's Lime Cordial.

Legend has it while the sailors drank dark rum, the officers drank gin and so mixed it with Rose's Lime Cordial to make what would soon be Gimlets. So it's creation was circumstance and privilege rather than clever mixing. It was stirred and served over ice at that point.

The story behind the name is that a 'Gimlet' was a small tool used to tap the barrels of spirits which were carried on British naval ships: this is a possibility of the drink's name.

A second story included the Surgeon General of the Royal Navy: Sir Thomas Desmond Gimlette (1857–1943), who is said to have mixed gin with lime "to aid with medicine." Although credible, it is not mentioned in his obituary or memoirs.

NOTES
- Building a Gimlet with gin, fresh lime juice and sugar is more like a gin sour than a Gimlet.
- British soldiers consumed such an abundance of limes they copped the nickname 'Limeys' by people.
- When making your own lime cordial, be sure to include enough lime zest to balance the flavour of bitter to sweet.
- This can also be shaken if preferred.

GRASSHOPPER

35ml Crème de Menthe
35ml Crème de Cacao White
40ml Half and Half

METHOD
- Shaken hard and strained into a coupe
- Garnished with grated dark chocolate

Created at Tujague's the second oldest restaurant in New Orleans, opened in 1856 by Guillaume Tujague. Sometime before he died in 1912, Guillaume sold the restaurant to Philibert Guichet Jr., who in the 1919 won 2nd prize in a prestigious New York cocktail competition. However this timescale is odd it could mean that it was held over Prohibition (1920–1933) which is highly unlikely, particularly for somewhere like New York.

An article from 2014 by Erin DeJusus has found many appearances and references from newspapers and magazines from as far back as 1919. A point she made here is one that really resonated with me, if a cocktail competition had taken place during this time period, it most certainly would not have been written for anyone to find.

Given the sheer popularity of the cocktail in the 1960s–90s, it is not at all surprising that some people thought to add vodka to the mix, and thus the 'Flying Grasshopper' was created.

NOTES

- The original garnish was powered sugar, chocolate rim and a mint leaf.
- This cocktail had a hot streak in the Southern states of American after its inception and was sometimes taken as a blended drink, incorporating ice-cream in lieu of cream.

HARVARD

50ml Cognac
25ml Sweet Vermouth
Two dashes Angostura Bitters

METHOD

- Stirred and strained into a coupe
- Garnished with an orange peel

This recipe has not seen much, if any, alteration from its first appearance in George J. Kappeler's *Modern American Drinks* (1895) listed as such:

*"One Dash gum-syrup, three dashes Angostura
bitters, half-jigger Italian vermouth, half-jigger
brandy in a half a mixing-glass of fine ice. Mix,
strain into cocktail-glass, fill up with seltzer."*

Indeed this cocktail is named after the Ivy League school of the same name as the colour is also a beautiful crimson. In Albert Stevens Crockett's *Old Waldorf Bar Days* (1931) notes that:

*"Named after a school for young men, whose site
is contiguous to the Charles River... Alumni who
drunk it sometimes lost the 'Harvard accent'."*

Two texts deviate from the original recipe, those being Hugo Ensslin's *Recipe for Mixed Drinks* (1917) and David Embury's *The Fine Art of Mixing Drinks* (1948) which call for orange bitters rather than Angostura.

NOTES
- A Harvard served over ice is called 'Flushing Cocktail' – *Jack's Manual* (1933).
- A Dughouse cocktail is a Harvard with a dash of absinthe.
- Generally referred to as a 'Cognac Manhattan'.
- Harvard cocktails nowadays are more modern in style with a 2:1 ratio rather than the original 1:1.

I remember waking up in a friend's house one morning after a night of indulgence and being told to make Harvards with the cognac in the freezer in the afternoon, being hungover and tired, it was a hard proposal to turn down.

HONEYMOON

40ml Calvados
15ml Benedictine
15ml Triple Sec
20ml Lemon Juice

METHOD

* Shaken and strained into a coupe
* Garnished with a lemon peel

The recipe was published in the last major cocktail publication of prior to Prohibition, Hugo Ensslin's *Recipe for Mixed Drinks* (1916). This cocktail played a large of the success of the menu at the Brown Derby restaurant in California in the 1920s.

Both Jim Meehan's *PDT Cocktail Book* (2011) and Ted Haugh's *Vintage Spirits and Forgotten Cocktails* (2004) shed some light on this cocktail that could soon be forgotten describing it as a basic 'Sour' formula but is heightened with the addition of Benedictine, delivering a bright, herbaceous and complex cocktail. Plus Calvados, right?

JACK ROSE

50ml Applejack
20ml Lemon Juice
12.5ml Grenadine

METHOD

* Shaken and strained into a coupe

According to David Wondrich in his always reliable book *Imbibe!* (2015) the Jack Rose was likely invented at Eberline's, a popular Wall Street bar, sometime in the 1880 or 90s. The name was first printed in 1899 by a reporter who had been drinking there.

The first appearance of the Jack Rose in a cocktail book comes from *Jack's Manual* (1908) by J.A. Grohusko and is listed as:

"1 teaspoon sugar
10 dashes Raspberry syrup
10 dashes lemon juice
5 dashes orange juice
Juice ½ lime
75% cider brandy.

Fill glass with cracked ice, shake and strain, fill with fizz water."

Now, the above recipe is different to how we picture the Jack Rose cocktail in modern times. Another appearance that seems to have updated the Jack Rose is written by Jacques Straub in his *Manual of Mixed Drinks* (1913). This omits several of the ingredients from Grohusko's recipe, and streamlines it to be:

"1 Jigger Apple Jack.
½ Lime
¼ jigger Grenadine syrup."

Now this is interesting as it leads to the debate of whether the Jack Rose should have lemon or lime juice as the citrus component. This is dependent on the quality of the grenadine being used or the desired sharpness of the cocktail.

As with many cocktails, and what makes this so interesting, is that there is often a plethora of origin stories. Here are the stories that have been found to have some substance:

1. Named after Jacqueminot rose, which in turn takes its name from French general, Jean-Franois Jacqueminot. According to Albert. S. Crockett's *Old Waldorf-Astoria Bar Book* (1935), it is so called because of its pink colour, exact shade of a Jacqueminot rose, when properly concocted.

2. Some credit this drink's creation to the Colt's Neck inn in New Jersey, which was originally owned by a member of Laird's Family of Applejack distillers. His name was Jack ,and 'Rose' is said to be a reference to the drink's colour. This theory has been discredited by Lisa Dunn, a ninth-generation family ancestor.

3. The *National Police Gazette* in 1905 – *"Frank J. May, better known as Jack Rose, is the inventor of a very popular cocktail by that name, which made him famous. Jack Rose, apparently, also a wrestler, held bar at Gene Sullivan's café, New Jersey."*

4. The most popular theory involves a small-time gangster called Jack Rose who was the informant in a 1912 murder case. 'Bald' Jack Rose, whose favourite drink is said to have been applejack, lemon and grenadine, was heavily implicated in the 1912 shooting of Herman 'Beansy' Rosenthal, owner of several New York gambling

dens. The cocktail supposedly fell out of favour after this case, and many took to calling it a 'Royal Smile'.

5. It could be named after Jack Rose, an early twentieth century brand of cigars which sold for five cents a pack. Interestingly, those cigars became known as squealers after the Rosenthal case.

NOTES
- David Embury lists the Jack Rose as one of his six essential cocktails in his *Fine Art of Mixing Drinks* (1948).
- With the addition of a few dashes of absinthe, this cocktail becomes a 'Pan American Clipper', first listed in Charles H. Baker's *The Gentleman's Companion: Being an Exotic Drinking Book or Around the World with Jigger, Beaker, and Flask* (1939).

JABBERWOCK

25ml Gin
25ml Cocchi Americano
25ml Manzanilla Sherry
Two dashes Orange Bitters

METHOD
- Stirred and strained into a coupe
- Garnished with lemon peel discarded and a cherry

Named after Lewis Carroll's poem 'Jabberwocky', this cocktail's recipe is printed in Harry Craddock's *The Savoy Cocktail Book* (1930) where he lists it as:

"JABBERWOCK COCKTAIL.*
2 dashes Orange Bitters.
⅓ Dry Gin.
⅓ Dry Sherry.
⅓ Caperitif.

" This will made you gyre and gimble in the wabe until brillig all right, all right."*

The notation accompanying the recipe is a nod toward the poem itself, perhaps suggesting that Craddock was a fan of Lewis Carroll's work.

This cocktail evolved a counterpart in the form of the 'Jabberwocky' created by Andrew Meltzer at 15 Romolo, San Francisco. This cocktail replaces the original recipe's Caperitif with the highly accessible Lillet Blanc, meaning you can have both a Jabberwock and a Jabberwocky.

Caperitif is also an aromatised wine but is from South Africa instead of France. It was discontinued until a few years ago when a South African winemaker decided it was time to reintroduce it to market.

NOTES
- Fino sherry also works with this cocktail.
- Manzanilla sherry is produced exactly the same way as Fino, however it is aged by the coast, that add a slightly salinity to the product.

JAPANESE COCKTAIL

60ml Cognac
15ml Orgeat
Two dashes Angostura Bitters
One Lemon Peel in the tin

METHOD
- Shaken and strained into a coupe

This cocktail's first appearance comes from Jerry Thomas' *How to Mix Drinks* (1862) and is said to be one of his few own creations from that book, according to David Wondrich. From research, this cocktail is said to have been made to celebrate the first Japanese diplomatic visit to the United States by Tateishi Onojirou-Noriyuki in 1860.

During their stay in New York City, the visitors were staying in the Metropole Hotel, very close to the bar in which Jerry Thomas tended in 622 Broadway, one block away in fact.

Dave Wondrich's *Imbibe!* (2007) suggests that many a night would have been spent at Thomas' venue, and undoubtedly there would have been various reasons to christen a cocktail after such a visit.

NOTES
- The original recipe calls for the cocktail to be shaken.
- More modern versions call for stirring, if you stir the cocktail reduce the amount of Orgeat used.
- The original cocktail called for 'Bogart's (Boker's) Bitters. A simple misspell in the original text.

JOCKEY CLUB

50ml Bourbon
10ml Maraschino
10ml Sweet Vermouth
One dash Angostura Bitters
One dash Orange Bitters

METHOD
- Stirred and strained into a coupe
- Garnished with a lemon peel

There are two variants of this cocktail, and both come from well-respected texts. Harry Craddock's *The Savoy Cocktail Book* (1930) lists the cocktail as:

"One dash Orange bitters
One dash Angostura bitters
two dashes Crème de Noyau
4 dashes Lemon Juice
¾ Glass Dry Gin."

David Embury's *The Fine Art of Mixing Drinks* (1948) on the other hand suggests it is *"a sweet Manhattan with two dashes of Maraschino"*. But how does this cocktail vary so drastically in appearance?

Different places, people and events laid claim to the cocktail, some of which being horseracing hotspots, where the social elite would gather and drink what was deemed to be acceptable in public eye. Venues such as, The Turf Club, The Jockey Club and the Kentucky Derby is what we are particularly interested in.

An early reference to 'The Jockey Club Cocktail' comes from an article found in the *Sunday Morning Herald* in New York (1882):

"Talking about compounders of drinks reminds me of the fact that never before has the taste for 'mixed drinks' been so great at present and new ideas, and new combinations are constantly being brought forward. It is but a short time ago that a mixture of whiskey, vermouth and bitters came into vogue. It went under various names: Manhattan cocktail, Turf Club cocktail, and Jockey Club cocktail.

"Bartenders at first were sorely puzzled what was wanted when it was demanded. But now they are fully cogizant of its various aliases."

After this article, Jerry Thomas printed a recipe for a 'Manhattan Cocktail' in his *Bartender's Guide* (1887) which more accurately denotes what a widely accepted recipe for what the cocktail looks like today.

No one can deny the mixture of whiskey, vermouth and bitters was a popularised and concoction, however this cocktail went by various names before, and after, it was put into text by authors.

The second recipe, built like a 'Sour' that appears in Craddock's book appears as:

"One dash Orange Bitters.
One dash Angostura Bitters.
2 dashes Crème de Noyau.
4 dashes Lemon Juice.
¾ Glass Dry Gin."

This was updated in Gary Regan's *Joy of Mixology* (2003) in which he swaps out crème de Noyau for Amaretto and removes the orange bitters completely. If you search for this drink, it is highly likely this is the recipe you find most often: gin, crème de Noyau, lemon, sugar, orange and Angostura bitters.

KNICKERBOCKER

50ml Aged Rum
10ml Curacao
20ml Simple Syrup
20ml Lime Juice
Two Raspberries

METHOD
* Shaken and strained into a rocks glass over crushed ice
* Garnished with a mint sprig, raspberry and lime wedge

I enjoy this drink, and not simply because the name is hilarious to say. This history of this drink was quite an interesting discovery.

A gentleman and author, Washington Irving, once produced a book recalling a not so pleasant history of New York and used the name 'Diedrich Knickerbocker' rather than his own. This book layer was known as *Knickerbocker's History of New York* (1809) and the term 'knickerbocker' was used to describe those from New York with Dutch heritage.

Firstly, what is a Knickerbocker? This refers to a style of trousers that were rolled up to slightly below knee-length, a fashion worn by Dutch settlers (and also later shortened to become knickers).

Most would link this cocktail with the grand Knickerbocker Hotel built in New York in 1906, however this drink was first in print in Jerry Thomas' *How to Mix Drinks* (1862). So this leaves quite the gap in which the hotel can lay claim to the cocktail.

Jerry Thomas recipe calls for:

> *"½ a lime, or lemon, squeeze out the juice,*
> *and put rind and juice in the glass.*
> *2 spoon raspberry syrup, 1 wine glass Santa*
> *Cruz rum, ½ teaspoon of Curacao."*

Several years later, William Terrington would release his *Cooling Cup and Dainty Drinks* (1869) and list two differing versions of this cocktail. The 'Knickerbocker a la Monsieur', which was in essence Thomas' cocktail only with the option of orange and the addition of soda water: and a 'Knickerbocker a la Madame', listed as:

"½ pint lemon water ice, ½ pint sherry or Madeira,
1 bottle seltzer and ¼ pint shaven ice."

This would not be the last time this cocktail would appear in a cocktail book. Harry Johnson's *New and Improved Bartender's Manual* (1882) would mimic Thomas' recipe, but with the addition of pineapple and orange to the mix, later.

And finally, where would a cocktail end if not in *The Savoy Cocktail Book* (1930) by Harry Craddock. In here the cocktail is split into two different recipes: one reminiscent of those previously mentioned named 'The Knickerbocker Special', and the other 'The Knickerbocker Cocktail', with the latter being a Martini style drink consisting of gin, sweet and dry vermouth.

LAST WORD

30ml Gin
20ml Lime Juice
20ml Maraschino
20ml Green Chartreuse

METHOD
* Shaken and strained into a coupe
* Garnished with a cherry

> *Created by Frank Fogarty born in Co.
> Tipperary but grew up in Brooklyn*

Securely in the canon of classic cocktails nowadays, but it wasn't always this way. For decades after, the 'Last Word' sat buried in the pages of Ted Saucier's *Bottoms Up!* (1951), that is until the early 2000s, when bartender Murray Stenson came across it and put it on the menu at Seattle's Zig Zag Café.

The original recipe doesn't disclose want colour Chartreuse is used, but green is commonplace nowadays.

A small note comes attached to the recipe in Saucier's book:

> *"This cocktail was introduced here about*
> *30 years ago by Frank Fogarty, who was*
> *very well known here in Vaudeville."*

Records points to it having been invented in Detroit Athletic Club sometime in and around 1916. Soon after that, Frank Fogarty, a well-known vaudeville entertainer, is said to have brought the recipe with him back to New York after trying it on a trip to the motor city.

Few have done more for the 'Last Word' than Audrey Saunders and Phil Ward. Saunders put the cocktail on the list at Pegu Club, and Ward made several variations of the cocktail, including the 'Final Ward' and 'Division Bell'.

NOTES
- Equal parts mean that it should taste the same everywhere you go aside from the gin used (and style of the lime used).

RIFFS ON THE LAST WORD

DUBLIN MINSTREL – Irish whiskey, Green Chartreuse, Maraschino, Lime Juice.

DUTCH/LATEST WORD – Jenever Oude, Green Chartreuse, Maraschino, Lime Juice.

BIRD IS THE WORD – Tequila, Yellow Chartreuse, Apricot Brandy, Lemon Juice.

BIRD IS THE WORD NO. 2 – Grappa, Green Chartreuse, Maraschino, Lime Juice, Chocolate Bitters.

CLOSING ARGUMENT – Mezcal, Green Chartreuse, Maraschino, Lime Juice.

DIVISION BELL – Mezcal, Aperol, Maraschino, Lime Juice.

FINAL WARD – Rye, Yellow Chartreuse, Maraschino, Lemon Juice.

LOOSE TALK – Rye, Suze, Yellow Chartreuse, Lemon and Lime Juice, Maraschino, Benedictine.

MONTE CASSINO – Rye, Yellow Chartreuse, Benedictine, Lemon Juice.

OTHER WORD – Mezcal, Yellow Chartreuse, agave, Maraschino, Lime Juice.

WORDSMITH – Rum, Green Chartreuse, Maraschino, Lime Juice.

LONE TREE

40ml Plymouth Gin
40ml Punt e Mes
One dash Orange Bitters

METHOD
- Stirred and strained into a coupe
- Garnish with orange peel

At first glance this looks to be an original Martini with sweet vermouth, and I would say that most sweet vermouth can be subbed in for Punt e Mes. My suggestion listed is my indication to the closest replication of the cocktail, true to the time.

This drink first appeared in *The Cocktail Book: A Sideboard Manual for Gentlemen* (1900), as well as 1913 edition of *Applegreen's Bar Book*. However it was Jacques Straub who would make this cocktail known after trying it at the Waldorf-Astoria. Straub's *Drinks* (1914) lists the drink as:

" ⅓ jigger Italian vermouth, ⅔ Old Tom Gin and shake well."

Interestingly enough Straub and Oscar Tschirky, who would go on to become one of the Waldorf-Astoria's most famous bartenders, both came to America from Switzerland together and would help popularise the cocktail.

Albert Steven Crockett's *Old Waldorf Bar Days* (1931) has a similar story:

"After the that-time equivalent of what was a 'nine-teenth hole' – a tree which stood alone in a secluded part of a golf course near Philadelphia. Recollections of that tree inspired a group of Philadelphian's so to Baptize cocktail especially created for their now nourishment.

Dash of orange bitters
One-half jigger Italian Vermouth
One half Jigger Plymouth Gin."

Old Tom gin becomes Plymouth gin, orange bitters have been added, and the ratio has been taken from 2:1 to 1:1 – gin:vermouth.

It appears to have been a very popular with the social elite, and perhaps an already established cocktail that went under local guise. Drinks at the time were likely taken by word of mouth between establishments, and so this is why it likely lacked consistency and did not spread like other classics.

Several years before the *Old Waldorf Bar Days* was published, in *Barflies and Cocktails* (1927) by Harry MacElhone, you have another recipe listed as:

> *"⅓ Gin, ⅓ Italian Vermouth, ⅓ French Vermouth.*
> *Squeeze orange peel into shaker."*

Quite the difference with the addition of a new ingredient, perhaps a commonplace mistake as it was retold by someone who had consumed one too many.

Five years after the cocktail was initially published, Frank Meire working in Paris, provided this recipe in *The Artistry of Mixing Drinks* (1936) with an ever-so-slightly altered recipe:

> *"One-third Italian vermouth, two-*
> *thirds Gin, serve with an Olive."*

Luckily, whatever the story, and whatever the recipe you prefer it is a delicious mix of vermouth and gin, garnish it as you please.

MARTINI

60ml Gin or Vodka
10ml Dry Vermouth

METHOD
- Stirred and strained into a Nick and Nora
- Garnished with a lemon peel, olive or pickled onion

This cocktail is one enjoyed by so many around the world, yet remains one of the most mysterious drinks available. As with many classic cocktails, the origins of the Martini are unknown but the accepted tale is that it evolved from the 'Martinez' which was inspired by the 'Manhattan'.

As for where the Martini dawns its name from, well there are several sources that are called upon. The most realistic assumption is that it comes from the brand Martini & Rossi that was doing heavy marketing at the time the cocktail was extremely popular. However other theories that are thrown around is that it was a spin on the Martinez, there was also a town in California that was also called Martinez where people claim the was invented.

The evolution is complicated as many variants of the original drink begin to appear with additions of things like gum syrup, maraschino and bitters. This spawned a family tree of drinks like no other including the Margurite, Martina and Bradford a la Martini.

HISTORY OF THE MARTINI

Here we will go through the many appearances and variations of the Martini in early books, to get a feel for what was being consumed then, and how it developed. The first thing to note is that the original Martini was a cocktail compromising of equal parts gin, specifically Old Tom, and sweet vermouth garnished with a lemon peel.

Recipes appear as early as O. H. Byron's *The Modern Bartender* (1884) listing of a Martinez cocktail, saying that *"Same as a Manhattan, only you substitute gin for whisky."* I should note that his Manhattan cocktail used gum syrup and Angostura bitters.

Wehman's Bartender's Guide (1891) specifically lists a Martini cocktail as:

> *"2 or three dashes of Gum Syrup.*
> *2 or three dashes of Bitters.*
> *one dash of Curacoa.*
> *⅓ wine glassful of Old Tom Gin:*
> *½ wine glassful of Vermouth.*
> *Squeeze lemon peel on top."*

George J. Kappeler's *Modern American Drinks* (1895 and 1906) give a recipe for a 'Martini Cocktail':

"Three dashes orange bitters, one-half jigger Tom gin, one-half jigger Italian vermouth, a piece of lemon peel."

Following this Harry Johnson's *Bartender's Manual* (1900) does contain a drink named 'Martini Cocktail' with the recipe:

"2 or three dashes of Gum Syrup:
2 or three dashes of bitters: (Boker's genuine only.)
one dash of Curacao or absinthe if required:
½ wine glassful of Old Tom Gin:
½ wine glassful of Vermouth."
Squeeze lemon peel on top."

In this edition he similarly lists the 'Bradford a la Martini' which is looks more like the modern day cocktail than the 'Martini Cocktail' that appears in his book:

"BRADFORD A LA MARTINI
3 or 4 dashes of orange bitters:
The peel of one lemon into the mixing glass:
½ wine glass of Tom gin:
½ wine glass of vermouth:
Put a medium-sized olive into it and serve."

All of the predecessors seem very similar, and it is only in Harry Johnson's book that a new contestant enters the fold, the Marguerite cocktail:

"2 or three dashes of orange bitters:
2 or three dashes of anisette
½ wine glass of French vermouth:
½ wine glass of Plymouth gin:
Squeeze a piece of lemon on top."

In one story, this is the cocktail that is believed to be the origin of the Martini, it was named Marguerite after the vermouth that was used in its making.

The Martini starts to step in a drier direction in Tim Daly's *Bartender's Encyclopedia* (1903) in which he has a 'Martini Cocktail' and a *"bottle of Martini cocktail"*. The bottle of Martini is the interesting recipe as it splits the cocktail into *"1/3 bottle of French vermouth"* and *"2/3 bottle of Tom gin"* which is different from the usual equal parts style cocktails seen before.

The dry Martini most likely appeared with the emergence of the London Dry style of gin and was helped by Martini & Rossi running newspaper ads in the U.S. towards the end of the nineteenth Century and at the beginning of the twentieth century for their recently launched Dry Martini Vermouth with the tagline, *"It's not a Martini unless you use Martini."*

The first known written recipe for a drink actually called a 'Dry Martini Cocktail' appears in 1904 French book *American-Bar Recettes des Boissons Anglaises* Frank. P. Newman, bartender at the Ritz in Paris. Also John Applegreen's *Bar Book* (1904) lists a Martini and a Dry Martini recipe:

"two dashes orange bitters
two dashes syrup
½ jigger Tom gin
½ jigger Italian Vermouth
Piece lemon peel.

MARTINI COCKTAIL, DRY
Same as above except to omit the syrup."

However in this book there is also a 'Crisp Cocktail' that looks strikingly similar to a 50-50 dry Martini:

"two dashes orange bitters
½ jigger Plymouth gin
½ jigger French Vermouth
Piece of lemon peel."

This trend is continued in *Stuart's Fancy Drinks* (1904) as he splits the ratio to 2/3 Plymouth gin to 1/3 French vermouth. Louis Muckensturm's *Louis' Mixed Drink* (1906) changes this again by listing both a 'Martini' and a 'Dry Martini' using different types of bitters for each and only garnishing the dry Martini with lemon peel.

This would carry into the future, and by the time Hugo Ensslin released *Recipes for Mixed Dinks* (1916) the 2:1 ratio of gin and vermouth seemed to be the norm, as also shown by Harry Craddock in *The Savoy Cocktail Book* (1930), and by this time bitters had been removed completely.

The Martini continues to appear, showing its popularity, over the years and in two very important texts: Robert Vermeire's *Cocktails and How to Mix Them* (1922) and *The Savoy Cocktail Book* (1930). Both call for sweet vermouth but Harry Craddock actually omits bitters and simply has a 2:1 gin to sweet vermouth ratio as his Martini.

The Martini turns progressively drier. Remember, the Martini, like the Martinez was initially sweet, hence the need to distinguish its descendant as a 'Dry Martini'. As the years went one, people began to realise that they simply couldn't consume multiple sweet drinks and opted for drier cocktails.

As time went on even vermouth started to feel the sting of being ejected as Ted Saucier's *Bottom's Up!* (1951) lists a Martini that is four parts gin to one part dry vermouth. Some places, like Duke's of London, decide to rinse the glass with vermouth then throw it away. Ted Saucier also has a Vodka Martini among his recipes which follows the same 4:1 ratio of vodka and vermouth (this is the first time vodka Martini is listed in a cocktail book), and is called a 'Vodkatini'.

A mention to the vodka Martini, which was likely made famous by Ian Fleming's character James Bond. The famed line "Shaken not stirred" from fictional character has stuck with many when they think of the cocktail. The steady rise of vodka from the 1970s right through to the late 90s made vodka the spirit pf choice for many, and thus would find its way into many a Martini glass.

VARIATIONS ON THE MARTINI

KANGAROO: The name David Embury gave to a Vodka Martini in his *The Fine Art of Mixing Drinks* (1948) book.

MONTGOMERY: a 15:1 spirit to vermouth ratio Martini named after a British Field Marshal who would attack only if he had a 15:1 advantage on the battlefield.

GIBSON: a dry Martini with pickled onion brine and a pickled onion garnish.

SMOKY MARTINI: Rinse with Scotch in place of vermouth.

BUCKEYE: Garnished with a black olive.

RICHMOND: Switches dry vermouth with Cocchi Americano, garnished with a lemon peel.

GIBSON: Garnished with two pickled onions.

DIRTY MARTINI: Add olive brine to mixing glass to taste preference.

MILLIONAIRE NO. 1

20ml Sloe Gin
20ml Apricot Brandy
20ml Jamaican Rum
20ml Lime Juice
5ml Grenadine

METHOD
* Shaken and strained into a coupe

There is no beautiful backstory to this cocktail, however there are several cocktails that fly the flag of the 'Millionaire' name, varying from gin to rum. The recipe provided is one that I would say is most commonly associated with the moniker in modern drinking,

The first text to reference a Million cocktail appears in Hugo Ensslin's *Recipes for Mixed Drinks* (1917), in which he lists a No. 1 and 2. While the Millionaire cocktail 1 is listed as:

"⅓ Jamaica Rum
⅓ Apricot Brandy
⅓ Sloe Gin

one dash Grenadine
Juice of 1 Lime."

The 'Millionaire Cocktail' No. 2 varies wildly, appearing as gin, white absinthe, egg white and a dash of anisette, with no reasoning to the huge difference.

There is another appearance of the Millionaire No.1 and No.2 in *The Savoy Cocktail Book* (1930) that follows suit from Ensslin's book, and in the *How and When* book (1937) as Millionaire no. 4. So more numbers, but no explanation as to differences in recipes.

Jacques Straub's aptly named *Drinks* (1914) notes another different Millionaire cocktail as:

"one dash orange bitters.
6 dashes curacao.
¾ jigger rye whiskey.
two dashes grenadine syrup.
1 white of egg."

There are numerous cocktails that go by the name Millionaire, the recipe based on rye, curacao, grenadine, egg white and lemon juice is thought to have predated 1925, and this is validated by its appearance in Harry McElhone's *Barflies and Cocktails* (1927) where it is credited to London Ritz Hotel.

NOTES
• Employees Only, NY spawned their own take on this cocktail that has been hugely successful for them:

BILLIONAIRE (EMPLOYEES ONLY)

Bourbon
Lemon juice
Sugar
Grenadine / Campari
Absinthe Bitters

METROPOLE

55ml Cognac
20ml Dry Vermouth
5ml Simple Syrup
One dash Orange Bitters
One dash Peychaud's Bitters

METHOD
- Stirred and strained into a coupe
- Garnished with an orange peel

The Metropole first appears in George Kappeler's *Modern American Drinks* (1895) as:

> *"Two dashes gum-syrup, two dashes Peyschaud bitters,*
> *one dash orange bitters, half a jigger brandy, half a jigger*
> *French vermouth, a mixing-glass half-full fine ice. Mix,*
> *strain into cocktail-glass, add a maraschino cherry."*

The cocktail was named after the Hotel Metropole which was situated just off Times Square, New York. This was the first hotel in city to have running water in each room, and so was a luxury location for those with money to spend. The hotel had an adjoining café with a less than desirable reputation. Located on street-level, Café Metropole was privy to an all-night license meaning that it attracted some shady characters throughout service and as Albert Crockett mentioned in *The Old Waldorf Bar Days* (1931):

> *"Attributed to a once well-known and somewhat*
> *lively hotel, whose bar was a long centre of life*
> *after dark in the Times Square district."*

Not exactly the comments you want to hear about your establishment, however this venue plays host to a famous story about Herman Rosenthal, who owned several New York gambling dens. Rosenthal was murdered as he left the bar one night (this tale is retold in the story of the Jack Rose Cocktail also) and one week after Hotel Metropole went bankrupt before being reborn as Hotel Rosoff.

There is a similar drink named the Metropolitan, which is also named after a New York hotel. This cocktail actually appears in text (1884) before the Metropole, and it is likely that the Metropole is a simple riff on this as the hotel wanted its own signature serve. The Metropolitan appears in O.H. Byron's *The Modern Bartender* (1884) as:

"METROPOLITAN COCKTAIL
½ pony brandy.
1 pony French vermouth.
three dashes Angostura bitters.
three dashes gum syrup."

MORNING GLORY FIZZ

50ml Single Malt Scotch
20ml Lemon Juice
20ml Simple Syrup
Three dashes of Absinthe
15ml Egg White
Soda Water

METHOD

- Add a small amount of soda water to the bottle of an empty highball.
- Dry and wet shake the other ingredients and strain into highball.
- Top with more soda water until optimal wash-line.
- Garnish with star anise

The whiskey used should be a single malt as it wasn't until the late nineteenth century that blended scotch even turned up in America.

This cocktail belongs in the hair-of-the-dog canon of hangover recipes and was first written about by Harry Johnson in his *New and Improved Bartender's Manual* (1882) in which he lists it as:

"3 or 4 dashes of lemon juice:
2 or three dashes of lime juice:
3 or 4 dashes of absinthe:
1 egg (the white only)
1 wine glass of Scotch Whiskey:

*The author respectfully recommends the above drink
as an excellent one for a morning beverage, which
will give a good appetite and quiet the nerves."*

It is mentioned several years later in both O.H. Byron's *The Modern Bartender's Guide* (1884) and George Kappeler's *'Modern American Drinks' (1895).*

Byron lists it as:

*"Mix 3 or 4 dashes absinthe in a little water.
three dashes lime juice
4 or 5 dashes lemon juice.
1 table-spoon sugar.
The white of 1 egg
A wine-glass of Scotch whisky.*

*To be drank immediately, or the effect will be lost. It is
a morning beverage, a tonic and a nerve quieter."*

Kappleler's book is similar but he omits the lime juice from the cocktail and doesn't advocate drinking it immediately. I'm not entirely sure, but having a section dedicated to hangover remedies certainly showcases old drinking habits, everyone must have had a state of perpetual drunkenness. Some life.

NOTES
• One of Sasha Petraske's favourite jobs was separating the
  perfect start anise from the broken ones. Every detail counts.

MARTINEZ

50ml Old Tom Gin
25ml Sweet Vermouth
7.5ml Maraschino
One dash Orange Bitters

METHOD
• Stirred and strain into a Nick and Nora glass
• Garnished with an orange peel

Drinks historians broadly agree that the Martinez evolved from the Manhattan and preceded the (dry) Martini. That's a whole lot of drinks beginning with M, and all extremely important. Pretty much every bartender I've met has had their own recipe for making this cocktail, which is interesting seeing as it is a four-ingredient drink.

The first known recipe emerged in O. H Byron's *The Modern Bartender* (1884), where it was listed as a riff on a Manhattan *"only you substitute gin for whisky."*

"MANHATTAN COCKTAIL NO. 1.
1 pony French vermouth.
1 pony whiskey.
3 or 4 dashes Angostura bitters'
three dashes gum syrup.

MARTINEZ COCKTAIL.
Same as Manhattan, only substitute gin for whisky."

The original Martinez was most likely based on jenever and not Old Tom or London dry gin as this book would suggest as this type of gin was not readily available in America until the 1890s. David Wondrich's *Imbibe!* (2015) says that

"in the 1850s New York Port was clearing between 4500–6000
120 gallon pipes of Genever a year (2.7-3.6 750ml bottles)
a year, as opposed to the 10–20 pipes of English Gin."

Gin being produced in America at the time followed a more malt-forward approach (not dissimilar to jenever) rather than the lighter English style gin. French dry vermouth was much more commonplace than sweet vermouth at the time, so it's possible it was used in the early life of this drink.

The next appearance that gives life to Martinez is Jerry Thomas' *Bartender's Guide* (1887) but not in his 1862 cocktail book. Thomas lists the cocktail as:

"one dash of Boker's bitters.
two dashes of Maraschino.

1 pony of Old Tom gin.
1 wine-glass of Vermouth."

This recipe looks incredibly similar to a modern day one, however Thomas does not disclosure what style of vermouth he uses. It is likely to be sweet as it was the most commonplace in America at this time.

Thomas is often credited as the cocktail's creator, and made it whilst in San Francisco in the early 1860s for a guest headed to the town of Martinez. However as it only appears in his book from 1887, and was being made prior to this, it is unlikely that this is the case.

MANHATTAN

60ml Rye Whiskey
25ml Sweet Vermouth
Two dashes Angostura Bitters

METHOD
- Stirred and strained into a Nick and Nora glass.
- Garnished with a cherry

N.B Please don't drink dry Manhattans.

One thing that is known for certain regarding this colossal cocktail, is that it predates other great vermouth cocktails like the Martinez, Rob Roy and Bobby Burns. It is likely that this cocktail started to pop up around the 1850s under another guise. Like many great cocktails, the origin stories regarding the Manhattan are numerous.

One tale that makes for a good story but doesn't hold much credibility, is that it was created at New York City's Manhattan Club in the 1870s. The story goes that Jennie Jerome, aka Lady Randolph Churchill mother of Winston Churchill, was hosting a party to celebrate Samuel Tilden, who had just been elected governor and was on track to become a presidential candidate. One of the guests, Dr. Iain Marshall, became concocting drinks and landed on a mix of whiskey, vermouth and bitters that was such a hit that people began requesting it after the party, giving it the name of the club in which it was created. Dave Wondrich in his book *Imbibe!* (2007) fact-checks this story only to bust

it open and come to the realisation that Jennie Jerome was actually in Oxfordshire, giving birth to little Winston.

The best lead on the origin of the Manhattan is from a story written by William F. Mulhall, a bartender who spent more than 30 years at the famed Hoffman House, New York starting in 1882. In the *Valentine's Manual of New York* (1923) Mulhall says:

> *"The Manhattan cocktail was invented by a man*
> *named Black, who kept a place ten doors below*
> *Houston Street on Broadway in the sixties – probably*
> *the most famous drink in the world in its time."*

To be fair to this tale, Dave Wondrich also researched this and found a George Black in New York, this man also operated a venue at 493 Broadway below Houston called The Manhattan Inn. Coincidence, I think not.

Parts of these stories may be true, and it is likely that the Manhattan Club made the cocktail famous however by this time the Manhattan was already known as a hugely popular cocktail, as we get written reference of the cocktail in 1882 in the New York, *Sunday Morning Herald* where it is described as:

> *"It is but a short time ago that a mixture of whiskey,*
> *vermouth and bitters came into vogue. It went*
> *under various names – Manhattan cocktail, Turf*
> *Club cocktail, and Jockey Club cocktail".*

The earliest written recipe for the Manhattan appears in Harry Johnson's *The Modern Bartender's Guide* (1884), where he lists:

> "MANHATTAN COCKTAIL NO.1
> *1 pony French vermouth.*
> *½ pony whisky.*
> *3 or 4 dashes Angostura bitters.*
> *three dashes gum syrup.*
>
> MANHATTAN COCKTAIL NO.2
> *two dashes Curacoa.*
> *two dashes Angostura bitters.*

½ wine-glass whisky.
½ wine-glass Italian vermouth."

So essentially a dry and a sweet variant of the same cocktail. In the same year *How to Mix Drink: Bar Keeper's Handbook* by George Winter who uses equal parts whiskey and vermouth (unspecified) coupled with gum syrup and Peruvian bitters. Perhaps the bitters we to add a touch of difference from other recipes at the time, perhaps it was due marketing as many of his cocktails use bother Peruvian and Orinoco bitters.

The cocktail was so popular that it was included in both Jerry Thomas' *Bartender's Guide* (1887) and Harry Johnson's *Bartender's Manual* (1888). The variations that appear here are rather similar to those from previous texts, however Johnson suggests adding "absinthe if required" like he did with a few of his stirred cocktails. He adds "The drink is very popular at the present day."

From here we begin to see the Manhattan take a modern-day formula with William Schmidt in *The Flowing Bowl* (1891), as he lists it as:

"two dashes of gum,
two dashes of bitters,
one dash of absinthe,
⅔ drink of whiskey,
⅓ drink of vino vermouth.
(A little maraschino may be added.)"

Disregarding the absinthe and gum, we see the more standard 2:1 ratio of whiskey and vermouth here, showing evolution of the cocktail within a few years.

I think it rude not to include The Manhattan Club's own recipe from 1916 when talking about this cocktail, they speak of it as *"equal portions of vermouth and whiskey, with a dash of orange bitters."*

Whiskey is rarely specified in this book, however it is easily to believe that a majority of bartenders would be using rye at this time, New York in particular. Rye, or Canadian whiskey, was particularly easy to come by during this time and was cost-effective to use.

NOTES
- The Manhattan is claimed to have had several names over its live such as the *Jockey Club and Turf Club* cocktail.
- The Manhattan is a cocktail that has had several riffs on it such as 'Carroll Gardens' which adds Punt e Mes, Nardini Amaro and Maraschino.
- A 'Bensonhurst' adds maraschino, Cynar and replaces sweet vermouth for dry.
- Simply adding a dash of absinthe to this cocktail with change it to a 'Meteor'.

MARGUERITE

45ml Plymouth Gin
45ml Dry Vermouth
Two dashes Orange Bitters

METHOD
- Stirred and strained into a coupe

Not to be confused with the Margarita, the Marguerite is the precursor to the Dry Martini cocktail.

This lesser-known cocktail is essentially a Dry Martini with orange bitters. The Marguerite first appeared in *Cocktails... How to Make Them* (1898) by Livermore and Knight Co. and was printed long before a 'Dry Martini Cocktail' was listed in a book. They list the cocktail as:

> *"Three dashes of orange bitters, one-half jigger of*
> *Plymouth gin, one-half jigger of French vermouth...*
> *place an olive in the bottom of the glass."*

Two years later the Marguerite reappears in another text from Harry Johnson in his *Bartender's Manual* (1900) which reads:

> *"2 or three dashes of orange bitters:*
> *2 or three dashes of anisette:*
> *½ wine glass of French vermouth:*
> *½ wine glass Plymouth gin:*
> *Cherry, squeeze a piece of lemon peel on top."*

Lastly, before the popularity of the Marguerite began its downward slope, it pops up in Thomas Stuart's *Stuart's Fancy Drinks and How to Make Them* (1904) in his section "New and up-to-date drinks" showcasing there had been a change in flavour appreciation over the course of only a few years:

"one dash of orange bitters
⅔ Plymouth gin.
⅓ French vermouth."

The cocktail takes a drier turn, perhaps leading the way for the new structure of the soon to be Dry Martini. The one thing that is consistent with the cocktail is that it always calls for Plymouth gin, which was commonplace at the time. Plymouth is comprised of seven botanicals including orange peel making it a great partner for the soft vermouth.

The Martini and Marguerite would often appear next to one another in cocktail texts, showing that one did not automatically replace the other. It looks to have been a slow transition, with the Martini finally winning out due to marketing.

NEGRONI

30ml Gin
25ml Campari
25ml Sweet Vermouth
Two dashes Orange Bitters

METHOD
* Stirred and strained into a rocks glass over block ice
* Garnished with an orange peel

Some debate this is the perfect aperitif, and more than a handful of my close friends and colleagues swear by this cocktail. And why wouldn't they, this is certainly one of the most popular cocktails in modern history and is the same the world over.

The most widely reported version of this drink's origin is that it was invented at Caffe Casoni (nowadays Caffe Giacosa) in Florence, Italy 1919–20. This tale states that one Count Camillo Negroni asked the bartender, Forsco Scarselli, to further lace his cocktail of choice, the

Americano. This was achieved by adding gin in place of soda water. A second addition was that Scarselli replaced the typically lemon wedge with an orange and the rest is history. Or at least, so we thought.

Whether this story is true or not is fairly difficult to recover, there are tales of Camillo Negroni travelling around America (and being a cowboy no less), living in London, and with its raging gin scene at the time may have contributed to the creation of the cocktail. However other stories have unfolded about the origins of this drink, and to not explore them would be an injustice.

Count Camillo is rumoured to have fled a dry America and returned to Florence when Prohibition was enacted. It seems a shame to squash a romantic story but Colonel Hector Andres Negroni, against popular belief, claims that there is *"no count Camillo Negroni in the Negroni family genealogy, which dates back to the 11th century... The true inventor of the Negroni cocktail was General Pascal Oliver Comte de Negroni."*

This new information is backed by Luca Picchi, head bartender at the Caffe Rivoire in Pizza Della Signora, round the corner from Caffe Giacosa and *"knows more about the Negroni's history than anyone else"* according to Alice Lascelles, in her book *Ten Cocktails* (2015).

He recalls of a story about a gentleman named General Pascal Olivier Comte de Negroni, who created it whilst based in Senegal, Africa, 1857. Pascal was a Frenchman and fought in the Franco-Prussian War of 1870, and during this time at a party *"introduced the Luneville Officier's club to his signature vermouth-based cocktail."*

Following from these tales of two Counts, the latter also has some holes within the story. The main being that Campari wasn't even brought to market until 1860, several years after the Frenchman laid claim to the cocktail. So how close was that version of the Negroni to the one in the story we all hold so dear?

Furthermore Robert Hess, co-founder of the Museum of the American Cocktail, has offered evidence suggesting that the Italian Count did exist, including a picture of his birth certificate and travel records.

Either way, the world got a delicious cocktail of out the mix, and a great story to share.

Unsurprisingly, the Negroni makes many appearances in cocktail books throughout time. The earliest perhaps being a cocktail named a 'Mussolini' in *L'Heure du Cocktail* (1927) as:

"½ gin, 3/10 Italian vermouth and 2/10 Campari."

This cocktail is garnished with a lemon peel, and in a later print there is a 'Campari Mixte' in *L'Heure du Cocktail Recetted pour 1929* made with equal parts, that also has a lemon peel garnish.

A cocktail under the name Negroni actually appears in a book called *Cocktails Portfolio* (1947) by Amedeo Gandiglio and this was only very recently uncovered by bartender Paulo Ponzo. In it, there are two listed variations for a Negroni:

"NEGRONI: ⅓ Campari , ⅓ sweet vermouth (Grassotti Rosso), ⅓ gin, splash soda, orange twist garnish. Served in a rocks glass with one piece of ice.

ASMARA O NEGRONI: a few drops of Campari, ⅔ Gordon's Gin, ⅓ white vermouth (Grassotti Bianco), orange twist garnish. Served straight up in a cocktail glass."

Jim Meehan in his PDT book writes that:

"The combination of gin, sweet vermouth and Campari, showed up in French and Spanish cocktail books such as J. S. Brucart's 1943 Cien Cocktails and L'Heure Du Cocktail before universally being recognised as the Negroni."

There is an earlier reference to the Negroni called the 'Camparinette' in Boothby's *World Drinks and How to Mix Them* (1934) in which the familiar recipe states it is garnished with a lemon peel.

NOTES
- Several variations of the Negroni exist including a white variant made of gin, Lillet Blanc and Suze.
- Lucien Gardens is looking at a Negroni through a French lens as it implores gin, dry vermouth, Campari, Cointreau. Inspired by a French fencer who won gold medals at both the 1924 and '28 Olympics.

- Adding two dashes of Absinthe to your Negroni cocktail makes it into a 'Quill' cocktail.
- Topping your Negroni cocktail with sparkling wine gives you a 'Famiglia Reale'.

NEGRONI SBAGLIATO

40ml Campari
40ml Cocchi Torino
Prosecco to washline

METHOD
- Stirred briefly and strained into a rocks glass over ice.
- Add Prosecco to washline
- Garnished with an orange wedge

As a reference, sbagliato means mistake in Italian.

Cocktail folklore describes this drink as a mistake, or a messed up take on a classic 'Negroni'.

Mirko of the Stocchetti family, head bartender of Bar Basso, Milan is credited with its creation in 1968 where he mistakenly grabbed a bottled of sparkling wine instead of gin, and thus the Sbagliato was born.

I would call this less of a mistake and more a happy accident, however 'Negroni Contento' isn't almost as interesting a name.

NEW YORK SOUR

50ml Rye Whiskey
25ml Lemon Juice
20ml Simple Syrup
15ml Egg White
15ml Malbec Float

METHOD
- Wet and dry shaken, then strained into a rocks glass over ice
- Float the red wine as garnish – even make a design if you wish

It is generally accepted that this cocktail was invented in Chicago around 1880, and not in New York. It went by several other names during its inception: the 'Continental Sour', 'Southern Whiskey Sour', 'Brunswick Sour', and 'Claret Snap'. It wasn't until the early 1900s that it finally dawned the New York Sour title, and thus it has stayed until this date. The most intriguing of these names is the 'Claret Snap' – claret being the term prescribed for any red wine being poured in saloons during this time. This tale is unlikely to be true as David Wondrich has pointed out there is evidence of a written cocktail menu dating back to 1856 in Toronto which lists the cocktail.

PISCO PUNCH

50ml Pisco
40ml Pineapple Juice
20ml Lime Juice
10ml Simple Syrup
5ml Falernum
Prosecco top

METHOD
* Highball and strained into a highball
* Garnished with grated nutmeg

In the late 1800s, the Pisco Punch wasn't just a cocktail, it was a status symbol, and spoke volumes about the Gold Rush happening in San Francisco at the time.

Every cocktail needs a birthplace, and this one just so happens to be a place called Bank Exchange and Billiard Saloon, an extravagant venue that was a testament to the West coast of America. There was a section even where 'non-working' women could drink unimpeded as equals to men making it the first American lounge to allow this, showcasing the forward-moving nature of the city.

Said to have been invented by bartender Duncan Nicol at Bank Exchange, who later in 1887 who purchase the bar for himself, securing the intellectual rights to the recipe

But why was pisco was popular and how could Nicol charge such a price for the cocktail? Peruvian traders had been bringing pisco to

San Francisco, which then was part of Mexico, for some time. As more gold was discovered in this region, more Peruvians made their way to the city with their mining skills, and brought more of the national brandy with them. Once the city got a taste for it, it took a sweeping grip. Some would go as far as to compare it to the London 'Gin Craze' that occurred in the eighteenth century.

The other reason was pineapples. Pineapples came on these same ships carrying pisco, and so they ended up in the cocktail. The city was so wealthy due to the gold that they could afford to put the luxurious fruit in the cocktail, as saloon owners would take whole fruits and place them in window fronts. This made the pineapple the *"international symbol of hospitality."*

Bank Exchange would suggest there was another ingredient in the Pisco Punch, asides from the two above, lime juice and sugar, but would never let anyone know what it was. Several people would guess, including Mark Twain and Rudyard Kipling, suggesting it was *"composed of the shavings of Cherub's wings."*

Another writer assumes it may have been a fortified wine from Bordeaux called Vin Mariani, and the lead ingredient in that was coca leaves from Peru, in other words cocaine. This suggestion comes from the style of writing coming out of San Francisco in that era, a lot of angry and hyperbole in their prose. Quite the deduction if that is the case.

Sadly, the craze would come to a bleak end when Nicol would have to close the bar due to the enactment of Prohibition, and would later to the Pisco Punch recipe to the grave.

In 1937, founder of the *New Yorker* magazine, Harold Ross wrote:

> *"In the old days in San Francisco there was a famous drink called Pisco Punch, made from Pisco... Pisco Punch used to taste like lemonade but had a kick like vodka."*

NOTES
- It was said that the recipe is handed down from owner to owner in secrecy.
- Duncan Nicol owned the hotel for 32 years 1887–1919.

- Mark Twain would drink with a man he met whilst working as a reporter in the city. The man's name was Tom Sawyer and these tales would inspire the adventures in his later books.

PEGU CLUB

50ml Gin
20ml Dry Curacao
15ml Lime Juice
5ml Simple Syrup
One dash Orange Bitters
One dash Angostura Bitters

METHOD

- Shaken and strained into a coupe
- Garnished with a lime coin

The Pegu Club is named for the bar it was invented in, which was built in Rangoon, Burma (now Yangon, Myanmar) in 1880 to serve British Army officers during their time away from home, however it was off-limits to locals of the area.

The cocktail has had several appearances in cocktail book, first being Harry McElhone's *Cocktails and Barflies* (1927) as:

"PEGU CLUB COCKTAIL
one dash Angostura Bitters, one dash Orange Bitters,
1 teaspoonful Lime juice (Rose's), ⅛ Curacao (Orange), ⅔ Gin."

It appears it two other texts by bartenders whom actually worked with one another at some point, both at Ciro's of London. Perhaps this was the venue that popularised this drink in Europe, yet that is purely speculative.

Both *Cocktails by "Jimmy" Late of Ciro's* (1930) and *The Savoy Cocktail Book* of the same year list the Pegu Club among their main recipes. The primary difference is that "Jimmy" used equal measures of lime juice and curacao, resulting in a less sweet drink overall:

PEGU CLUB BY "JIMMY"
"4 parts Gin
1 part Curacao
1 part Lime Juice
one dash Angostura Bitters per cocktail
one dash Orange bitters per cocktail."

While the drink may have disappeared from memory in present day Myanmar, it ventured far and wide. In *Harry Craddock's The Savoy Cocktail Book* (1930), Craddock wrote:

"One of the favourite cocktails of the Pegu Club, Burma, and
one that has travelled, and is asked for, around the world.

One dash Angostura Bitters.
One dash Orange Bitters.
1 Teaspoonful Lime Juice.
⅓ Curacao. ⅔ Gin."

The drink owes its popularity to Audrey Saunders, the advocate of revitalising forgotten classic cocktails, when she opened the now-closed Pegu Club, New York in 2005.

NOTES
• MacElhone used lime cordial instead of the recognised lime juice we would assume today, so there is an ongoing debate as to what classes as an authentic recipe.

PISCO SOUR

60ml Pisco
20ml Lemon juice
20ml Simple Syrup
15ml Egg White

METHOD
• Wet and dry shaken and strained into rocks glass over ice or coupe
• Angostura bitters dropped on foam of finished dink

The Chilean story of the Pisco Sour attributes it to a man called Elliot Straub in 1872. Straub is claimed to have created the cocktail in Chile and then have brought it to Peru, as he was a steward on a travelling ship, however after much research it seems that Straub was referring to the 'Whiskey Sour' (which he also did not create), not the Pisco Sour.

On the first Saturday in February, Peruvians raise a glass to their country's most well-known cocktail: the Pisco Sour. Since 2003, this simple twist on the classic whiskey sour has had its own national holiday. But whilst the drink evokes a sense of pride in Peru, the Pisco Sour is heavily attributed to a Mormon man from Salt Lake City named Victor. V. Morris.

Morris co-ran a floral shop with two of his brothers. Sadly in 1900 Morris' brother Burton was on a date and was killed leaving Morris to continue to operate the flower shop for a few more years before selling the business to take a position with a local railroad company. He may have stayed in this position and never left the U.S. if not for the business venture of a well-known Salt Lake City resident named A. W. McCune. McCune would later run for Mayor and Senate, he also owned the *Salt Lake Herald* and half the Utah power company. A powerful man indeed.

McCune would embark on a mining project, something to which Salt Lake City was accustomed, however this would take place in Peru. In the late 1800s, a scouting expedition led McCune to rediscover mines first excavated by Spanish Colonists in the town of Cerro de Pasco. The town had been a source of great riches for the Spanish, according to one local legend, the rocks around Cerro de Pasco's campfires 'wept silver'. McCune signed a mining agreement with the Peruvian government, and by 1902, he had broken ground. The project transformed Peru's economy and kickstarted its mining industry. This mining town would see the creation and popularisation of Peru's signature cocktail.

Many residents joined the mining venture and in 1902, Victor Morris travelled to Cerro De Pasco as one of the early arrivals from Utah to join the project. However the mining project wasn't McCune's only endeavour, he was also planning to build a railroad to a close by town with a port in which to export metals.

The town was booming and soon, Cerro de Pasco was the second largest city in Peru, losing only to Lima. Tourists, expats and investors expected the world at their fingertips, and had the mining dividends to pay for such luxuries. This highlighted the need for luxury saloons to pop up all over the city, and it is here that Morris would discover Pisco.

Now, Morris was a member of a well-respected Mormon family, so would he succumb to the success of the town and its luring pleasures?

It wasn't just a mining town, Salt Lake City was bustling with alcohol production, from breweries to distilled, owned by members of the Mormon Church. One Brigham Young, apostle and church leader of Latter-day Saints owned the first bar and winery in Salt Lake City in fact, and it wasn't until 1921 that the church made temperance church law. This action seemed to line up with the looming onset of Prohibition that was spreading across the United States, and even dispute that killed Morris' own brother was fuelled by poorly crafted mint juleps. Morris knew his way around a bar to say the least.

Dr. Jose Antonio Salazar Mejia, a Peruvian historian, suggests that this may have been where Morris discovered a traditional Peruvian drink that would act as a base for the soon to be Pisco Sour. In 2012, *Nuevo Manual de Cocina a la Criolla (New Manual of Creole Cooking)* by S. E. Ledesma from 1903 was discovered with a similar recipe to the Pisco Sour, providing some evidence to this possibility. This manual contained a recipe called 'Cocktail' and was listed as:

> *"An egg, a glass of pisco a teaspoon of fine sugar and a squeeze of lime."*

Clearly there are similarities between this and what is a known Pisco Sour, so Morris may have brought the drink to life, but didn't create it.

Another story, one by Morris himself, tells a different version of events regarding the discovery of the Pisco Sour. An all-day party took place after the completion of the railroad in 1904, in which Morris replaced whiskey with pisco in the sours being consumed, as the whiskey had been depleted.

Regardless of the claim, the precise year of the cocktail's creation is still debated, mainly because it did not achieve the mass popularity until Morris moved to Lima with his family and opened his own venue, Morris's Bar.

THE PISCO SOUR WAS MORE OF A COLLABORATIVE EFFORT

Morris' bar became a major hub of intellectual, political and celebrity activity. Pisco Sours were his signature drink. Famed American aviator and soldier of fortune, Dean Ivan Lamb noted the strength of the drink in his memoir *The Incurable Filibuster*, writing:

"In Morris' Bar I ordered a pisco sour. It tasted like a pleasant soft drink and I ordered another, to which the bartender objected, informing me that one was usually sufficient."

By the 1920s, some of Morris's bartenders had taken the Pisco Sour recipe to other Lima bars such as Hotel Bolivar and Grand Hotel Maury. This both help to spread the drink, and change it, adding to the difficulty in pinpointing who exactly 'invented' the cocktail.

Mario Bruiget, a one-time employee of Morris' Bar, brought the drink to the Grand Hotel Maury, where it is believed he added egg white and bitters today. This site claims to be the original site of the modern day Pisco Sour.

After Morris's passing in 1929, the drink only grew in popularity. By the 1930s, the drink had reached San Francisco, and by the 1960s it was in New York. In Lima, the drink became the signature cocktail of high-end hotel bars. A popular legend from the Grand Hotel Bolivar describes Ava Gardner dancing around the hotel bar after an evening consuming pisco sours and then being carried to her room by John Wayne himself.

NOTES
- Chuncho bitters are based on several Amazonian barks and herbs found from that part of the world.
- It is noteworthy that a Pisco Sour normally has three drops on Angostura bitters on top as a garnish.
- Traditionally a Chilean Pisco Sour omits egg white and bitters from the mix completely.

PENDENNIS CLUB

50ml Gin
20ml Apricot Liqueur
20ml Lime Juice
5ml Simple Syrup
Two dashes Peychaud's Bitters

METHOD
• Shaken and strained into a coupe

The actual Pendennis Club is in Louisville, Kentucky and is named after a character, Arthur Pendennis, who was the eponymous lead in a nineteenth-century novel by William Thackeray. The club was seen as the prominent social club in the state, and one of the most lavish in the country.

The earliest known mention of this cocktail was found in a 1915 supplement to William Boothby's *The World's Drinks and How to Mix Them* (1908). Highlighted here is an adaptation of the recipe published in *Vintage Spirits and Forgotten Cocktails* (2004).

A source of mine tried to contact the club but was directed to a gentleman named William Hinkebein, the acclaimed most knowledgeable source on club history.

There is little access to information surrounding this cocktail, as the club itself has said that the cocktail's narrative has been lost to time. The cocktail wasn't even available in the club's own bar until 2014, when the food and beverage director Jeff Watts-Roy cited the recipe in Charles Baker's *Gentleman's Companion* (1939).

Hinkebein referenced The Juniper Club, which was a private fishing and hunting club founded in 1897 by members of the Pendennis Club who served their own signature cocktail concocted with gin, Cointreau, lemon juice and Peychaud's bitter. At first glance this is a 'White Lady' with Peychaud's, but it isn't a far stretch from the Pendennis cocktail.

NOTES
• The club is famously credited with the creation of the Old Fashioned, yet no one is sure as to who called it that.

PINK LADY

45ml Gin
15ml Applejack
20ml Lemon Juice
15ml Simple Syrup
5ml Grenadine
20ml Egg White

METHOD
• Wet and dry shaken then strained into a coupe.

It is rather difficult to verify the origins of this cocktail as it appears in several books under different names and has a host of different recipes listed under its classic name.

Although the cocktail's inventor is unknown, the drink is credited to American actress and interior decorator, Elsie de Wolfe, who was known for the movement that championed lighter designed over heavy Victorian styles of the time.

One story as to the cocktail's name is that it gets it from the 1911 Broadway musical starring Hazel Dawn, who was known as 'The Pink Lady'. It was an extremely popular show thus it could have commanded a liquid homage.

This cocktail was widely known during Prohibition and was popular at the Southern Yacht Club in New Orleans where it went under the guise of 'Pink Shimmy'. During the Prohibition-era, when cheap alcohol was abundant and extremely unpleasant, the Pink Lady seems to be the embodiment of masking these flavours with other ingredients.

Much like the 'Jack Rose' it also first appeared in *Straub's Manual of Mixed Drinks* (1913) as:

"½ Jigger Lime Juice.
½ Jigger Gin.
½ Jigger Apple Jack.
5 dashes Grenadine."

This recipe does have Applejack as one of the components, though it does not have egg white. Without the Applejack, the cocktail would be strikingly similar to a *'Clover Club'*.

Harry Craddock notes a recipe in his *The Savoy Cocktail Book* (1930) as:

> *"The White of 1 Egg.*
> *1 Tablespoon of Grenadine.*
> *1 Glass Plymouth Gin."*

Oddly enough he has removed the Applejack and citrus juice from the equation, similar to the recipe in W.J. Tarling's *Café Royale Cocktail Book* (1937).

Sadly the Pink Lady caught quite a lot of bad press in texts from people such as *Esquire's Handbook for Hosts* (1949), in which they put a message across that it was a feminine cocktail, and that it looked unapproachable by inexperienced drinkers.

QUEENS

50ml Gin
12.5ml Sweet Vermouth
12.5ml Dry Vermouth
30ml Pineapple Juice
10ml Simple Syrup

METHOD
* Shaken and strained into a coupe.

This cocktail is a riff on a 'Perfect Martini' with the addition of pineapple juice to the mix. Similar to the 'Bronx' (a perfect Martini with orange juice), I imagine a bartender on the other side of the river decided they needed their own signature cocktail and swapped out the flavoured juice component, yielding a cocktail they could call their own.

The Queens is made with pineapple, the fruit that is synonymous with the borough of New York. For generations in New York, pineapples were accepted as a form currency from Astoria to Flushing.

The Savoy Cocktail Book (1930) lists a drink called 'Queen's Cocktail', whether that is in reference to the area or the Queen herself is unknown, however the recipe reads:

"½ Slice of Crushed pineapple.
¼ French Vermouth.
¼ Italian Vermouth.
½ Gin."

Pineapple and dry vermouth automatically connect me to the 'Algonquin' cocktail, and the hotel which also happens to be in New York. Perhaps it was British sailors returning home to England years before bearing pineapples as gifts, and then having it be mixed with the abundance of gin on hand. So many stories.

RAMOS GIN FIZZ

50ml Old Tom Gin
10ml Lime Juice
10ml Lemon Juice
25ml Simple Syrup
30ml Double Cream
20 Egg White
Three dashes Orange Blossom Water
Soda Water to top

METHOD
* Add soda to a highball
* Shake with one large block ice and two small cubes
* Strain into highball primed with fresh soda water
* Rest drink in freezer for 1 minute
* Add more soda to the tin, then strain into glass and let head rise
* Straw should sit directly in the middle of drink

Created by Henry. C. Ramos in 1888 at the Imperial Cabinet Saloon in New Orleans, the cocktail was originally named the New Orleans Fizz. Ramos would eventually move his bar to a much larger location when he bought over The Stag Saloon, in which the cocktail only grew in popularity.

One of the most popular stories in regards to the Ramos Gin Fizz is that on Mardi Gras of 1915 there were 20 bartenders and 'shaker boys' on site to make and shake cocktails that were order. Even with this additional help, if that's what it was, they venue still struggled to meet demand.

In his book *Famous 'New Orleans Drinks and How to Mix 'Em* (1938), Stanley Clisby Arthur says:

> *"The corps of busy shaker boys behind the bar was one of the sights of the town during Carnival, and in 1915 Mardi Gras, 35 shaker boys near shook their arms off."*

Vanilla extract was said to be the secret that meant the cocktail could not be replicated, however the original recipe had no mention of this ingredient, nor had any other book since. Clisby's book mentions that it is an optional component, however this may have been his best guess.

With the onset of Prohibition, 27th October 1919, at midnight, Henry Ramos announced, *"I've sold my last Gin Fizz"*. There was an excerpt from New Orleans Tribune from 1928 in which Henry had supposedly handed over his recipe on the night he sold his final cocktail:

> *"One and Only One Ramos' Original Gin Fizz Recipe: One tablespoonful powdered sugar, Three or four drops of Orange Flower water, One half lime (juice), One half lemon (juice), One jigger of Old Tom Gin (Old Gordon may be used but a sweet gin is preferable), The white of one egg, One half glass of crushed ice, About 2 tablespoonful of rich milk or cream. A little Seltzer water to make it pungent."*

After the repeal of prohibition, The Roosevelt Hotel trademarked the cocktail's name in 1935, and helped to promote the cocktail beyond New Orleans. Clearly they did a great job.

NOTES
- There is a rumour that the cocktail needs to be shaken for 12 minutes in order to achieve the desired texture. This is never the case, however having both cream and egg white makes the drink extremely difficult to emulsify.
- You can use a blender to achieve the desired texture.

VARIATIONS ON A RAMOS

ANTIQUE FIZZ

40ml Citron Vodka
20ml Ricard
20ml Double cream
20ml Simple Syrup
12.5ml Lime
12.5ml Lemon juice
Egg white
Soda Water

PEACHBLOW FIZZ (STRAWBERRY RAMOS)

50ml Gin
20ml Half and half
25ml Simple Syrup
15ml Lemon juice
15ml Egg white
Two Strawberries
Soda top

ROB ROY

50ml Scotch whiskey
20ml Sweet Vermouth
Two dashes Orange Bitters
One dash Angostura Bitters

METHOD

* Stirred and strained into a coupe
* Garnished with a cherry

In essence, the Rob Roy is a Scotch Manhattan.

Unlike other classic cocktails, the history of the Rob Roy is rather well-known, but of course has a few contesting tales.

The cocktail is named after Robert Roy MacGregor, who was a Scottish outlaw who lived in the highlands. Despite being an outlaw, Roy became known as a Scottish Robin Hood and inspired much local folklore.

The tales of Roy go beyond his death in 1734, as in 1894 two high-profile composers and lyricists, Harry B. Smith and Reginald De Koven, named an opera after him that opened in New York. The theatre was situated around the corner from the Waldorf-Astoria, and so a bartender felt it fitting to promote the musical, and created the Rob Roy cocktail for the opening night.

The Rob Roy appears in various texts, the earliest of which seem to be from the *New York Herald* in 1897 and states:

> *"Of course, the Rob Roy is made of Scotch whiskey. It is completed by vermouth and orange bitters."*

The first creation of a Rob Roy, prior to being written about, may perhaps lay in the hands of a bartender named Henry A. Orphal. He worked at Duke's House, New Jersey during 1895 and is said to have mixed up a Manhattan with Scotch for a whiskey salesman who could not drink anything but his own company's product.

This is in contrast to Dave Wondrich's version that he uncovered in *The Banquet Book* (1902) which he believes to be the earliest written reference to a cocktail named a 'Rob Roy' with a recipe. This cocktail called for two dashes of aromatic bitters, rather than orange.

It appears in several other texts, notably *Applengreen's Bar Book* (1904) with orange bitters again, alongside Scotch whisky and Italian vermouth.

The Rob Roy is consistently served with sweet vermouth, whether you wish to use dry vermouth or serve it with both is a personal choice. The point of contention is the style of bitters used, and from tasting and popular vote, I must say the use of both seems to yield the better cocktail.

NOTES
- Lemon peel is used in almost every recipe in classic book, whilst the maraschino cherry seems to be a more modern addition.
- Cutting the scotch whiskey slightly and replacing the 10ml with Islay whiskey turns this cocktail into a Fitzroy.

- Rinsing the glass with Drambuie makes this cocktail the disco special Holiday Style Rob Roy.

SARATOGA COCKTAIL

30ml Rye
30ml Cognac
30ml Sweet Vermouth
Two dashes Angostura Bitters

METHOD
- Stirred and strained into a coupe
- Garnished with a lemon peel

This cocktail first appears in Jerry Thomas' *The Bartenders Guide* (1887) however it does not appear in prior books.

> *"two dashes Angostura bitters.*
> *1 pony of brandy.*
> *1 pony of whiskey.*
> *1 pony of Vermouth."*

It is likely the cocktail's name stems from the Saratoga Springs, a popular resort town in New York State which had the popular Saratoga and Schenectady Railroad running through it. Eventually, a number of hotels and hospitality venues began to open there and it became a famed gambling getaway location, much like the Las Vegas of its time.

Be sure to pick a full-bodied vermouth for this cocktail, you want it to match up against the two hearty spirits.

SARATOGA BRACE UP

50ml Cognac
20ml Lemon Juice
20ml Simple Syrup
One Whole Egg
Two dashes Absinthe
Soda Water Top

METHOD
- Wet and dry shaken and strained into a highball over ice

The Saratoga Brace Up appears for the first time in text as the Saratoga cocktail, in Jerry Thomas *The Bartenders Guide* (1887) as:

"1 table-spoonful of fine white sugar.
two dashes of Angostura bitters. 4 dashes of lemon or lime juice.
two dashes of Absinthe.
1 fresh egg.
1 wine-glass of brandy."

In 1882 Harry Johnson wrote of the Morning Glory Fizz cocktail, Thomas created a riff on this by subbing scotch or cognac, dialling down the absinthe and using the whole egg.

SOUTHSIDE

60ml Gin
30ml Lime Juice
15ml Simple Syrup
Six Mint Leaves

METHOD
- Shaken and fine strained into a coupe
- Garnished with a single mint leaf

The Southside history is muddled, in fact there are three variations of the origin.

The earliest story to mention the drink comes from the Southside Sportsmen Club in Long Island during the 1890s when fizzes were still at their peak popularity. The 'Southside Fizz' was known to have been consumed here, no wonder – minty and refreshing, it would have been the perfect post sports beverage.

Harry Craddock's *Savoy Cocktail Book* (1930) featured a recipe for a 'Southside' but it does not use soda, meaning the fizz style was the first to come forward.

A similar cocktail was consumed on the south side of Chicago in the 1920s, hence another reason for the name.

At this time, Chicago was a gang-ruled area. Joe Saltis, Frank McErlane and Al Capone were three major bootleggers controlling the south of the city. A line between the north and the south were distinctly drawn and one of the many distinctions was the way drinks were served: North side mobsters had better access to premium spirits – i.e. gin and ginger ale. While south side mobsters used lemon juice and sugar to sweeten the black-market booze.

The final origin story from which the southside comes from is the 21 Club in New York. The club established by Jack Kreindler and Charlie Berns, was one of the greatest speakeasys during prohibition and was designed so that the bar and all of its booze could be covered quickly by a maze of levers and chutes should the police show up. The pair were never caught and the club still exists today.

The cocktail first appears in Hugo Ensslin's *Recipes for Mixed Drinks* (1917), and as this predates Prohibition it is unlikely that the 21 Club or the mobsters created the cocktail.

FRENCH PEARL – Gin, lime juice, sugar, mint, absinthe

EASTSIDE – Gin, lime juice, sugar, mint, cucumber slices

NORTHSIDE – Gin, grapefruit liqueur, lime juice, sugar, cucumber slices

WESTSIDE BY EMPLOYEES ONLY   Lemon vodka, lemon juice, sugar, six mint leaves, soda water, served in a coupe.

STINGER

50ml Cognac
25ml Crème de Menthe Blanche

METHOD
* Stirred and strained into a Nick and Nora

The Stinger first appears in William Schmidt's *Flowing Bowl* (1892) under a different guise, 'The Judge':

"three dashes of gum,
⅓ crème de menthe
⅔ of brandy."

The 'Stinger' catches bad press due to its hosting crème de menthe which only recalls poor memories, however the cocktail does have an interesting point of origin.

The story is that it was created by Reginald 'Reggie' Vanderbilt (father of fashion designer Gloria Vanderbilt) an American socialite. Reggie was keen into cocktails and even had a bar in his 5ᵗʰ Avenue mansion, he claims to have created the cocktail *"a short drink with a long reach."* David Wondrich suggests these rumours to be true after recalling a newspaper article from 1923 which credits Reggie to the cocktail.

However it was perhaps created before this as it was said that air force pilots drank it in WW2 as the mint liqueur covered the low-quality liquor and made their breath smell good.

The 'Stinger' also appears in George J. Kappeler's *Modern American Drinks* (1895) with a dash of Angostura bitters. It is called the 'Brant', before being called the Stinger by Jacques Straub in his *Manual of Mixed Drinks* (1913) in which he called for a lemon peel to be shaken with the cocktail.

NOTES
- The cocktail appears in the 1956 move *High Society* in which Bing Crosby suggests how it got its name: *"It's a Stinger. It moves the sting."*
- It also appears in the James Bond novel *Diamonds are Forever.*
- Simply switching port for cognac gives you a 'Port Stinger'.
- Adding a dash of absinthe yields a 'Midnight Stinger'. Having this cocktail on the rocks is called a 'Stinger Royal'.

TOM COLLINS

60ml Gin
25ml Lemon Juice
15ml Simple Syrup
Soda Water Top

METHOD
* Shaken and strained into a highball over ice
* Garnished with a lemon wedge and cherry

The earliest known history of the Tom Collins involves a gentleman from New York, Richard Price. Price left New York's Park Theatre to move to London's Covent Garden Theatre. Sadly it didn't go as planned and after several years he took up mantle at the Garrick Member's Club. As the name might suggest it was a rather classy venue in contrast to Price's more rough exterior. His pocket ace was his gin punch that he had originally served in New York – gin mixed with cold soda water. Punches in London were served with ice whilst Price's was not and he also included things like citrus peel and maraschino, which was uncommon at the time.

Another popular, and likely story about this cocktail is that it is derived from a gin punch served at Limmer's Hotel, London. The creation of the Collins is credited to John Collins, bartender and head waiter at Limmer's. The 'Coffee House' of the hotel was made famous for its exciting drinks and buzzing atmosphere during the nineteenth century. According to the 1860s memoirs of Captain Gronow, the hotel became a prime attraction for celebrities due to gin punch as early as 1814, and this punch became linked to John Collins suggesting he only changed the name due to the use of Old Tom gin. This cocktail's fame rose and the name soon spread to Canada in 1864 (it was on the menu at Dolly's Tavern, Montreal), and then into America by the 70s.

The interesting differentiation is when did the drink turn into the Tom Collins from the John Collins?

It had to have happened prior to 1876 as this is when it appears in text written by Jerry Thomas. It likely happened as the John Collins was being made with genever, and the Tom Collins with Old Tom gin.

Genever was highly popular in America at the time, so perhaps they wanted to separate their cocktail from that of English descent.

The Tom Collins begins its written life in Jerry Thomas' *Bartender's Guide* (1876) as he lists three kinds of Collins cocktails:

"TOM COLLINS WHISKEY.
5 or 6 dashes of gum syrup.
Juice of a small lemon.
1 large wineglass of whiskey.
Fill up the glass with plain soda water
and imbibe while it is lively.

TOM COLLINS BRANDY.
The same as Tom Collins Whiskey,
substituting brandy for whiskey.

TOM COLLINS GIN.
The same as Tom Collins Whiskey, substituting gin for whiskey."

Most of Jerry Thomas' fizzes are stirred with a small lump of ice, and I can't help feeling that this represents the American style rather than a true difference in the cocktail itself. As for the Tom Collins, it gets its name from two places – a bartender named John Collins, who was known to some degree for fabulous gin punch that he made, and the Old Tom brand of gin. It is quite possible that the drink began its life as Collins' punch or sling, then slowly became a Collins with Old Tom, then the Tom Collins we know today. The other aspect of the drink worth mentioning is that it is essentially a Gin Sour with soda water added. Soda water was first created in 1767, but it wasn't until 1800 that its use outside of medicine began. By the mid-1800s, when the Tom Collins begins to appear, soda water would have been quite common, and a Gin Sour topped with soda water and drunk quickly would have been a sensation.

Genever started to disappear from the American cocktail scene and the John Collins adapted a whiskey base instead, however this would change with the 'Tom Collins Hoax' of 1874 in New York. The hoax, as the newspapers would report it, was a man would enter a bar and say to someone that another person was making negative comments about them in a bar some distance away. The victim would likely be sent into a rage and upon arriving at the next venue he would be told that *"he just missed him."* This would continue for some time until the victim caught on that Tom Collins did not exist. Some joke.

However, the drink is almost certainly named after Old Tom Gin, a sweetened style popular in the mid-nineteenth century England. The drink is identical to a gin fizz, except for numerous rules of thumb about one having ice and the other not, one being stirred and the other shaken. The only real difference between these two drinks is that the Gin fizz began its life in America and the Tom Collins in England. The gin Fizz uses dry gin, and the Tom Collins a sweetened style.

So did the Collins spiral from the early gin punch or was it from elsewhere?

Another story attributes the drink's creation to a Mr. Collins who started work at a New York tavern called the Whitehouse in 1873 and made thirst-quenching gin drinks and punches. A final tale identifies a different Tom Collins, who worked as a bartender in New Jersey and New York. There are supposedly versions attributing its creation to San Francisco and Australia, and it is not impossible that the drink evolved in two or more places at the same time.

Originally there were two 'brothers' – Tom and John – however numerous other brothers and cousins have appeared in recent years:

Captain Collins – Canadian Whiskey
Colonel Collins – Bourbon
Sandy Collins – Scotch
John Collins – London Dry Gin
Pedro Collins – White rum
Pierre Collins – Cognac
Joe Collins – Vodka
Mike Collins – Irish whiskey

NOTES
- Add a dash of absinthe to this drink and you get a *Hayes Fizz* cocktail.
- This cocktail is covered in-depth in David Wondrich's *Punch* (2010).

TUXEDO

50ml Gin
20ml Fino Sherry
Two dashes Orange Bitters

METHOD
- Stirred and strained into a Nick and Nora
- Garnished with a lemon peel

First documented in Harry Johnson's *Bartender's Manual* (1900) the Tuxedo, basically an equal parts 'Dry Martini' and is one of those classic cocktails which, over the decades, acquired different variations on the same theme.

Harry Johnson's listed recipe is:

> *"1 or two dashes of maraschino:*
> *one dash of absinthe:*
> *2 or three dashes of orange bitters:*
> *½ wine glass of French vermouth:*
> *½ wine glass Sir Burnett's Tom gin."*

This leads onto the discussion of separation, as there are two schools of thought as to what the cocktail actually consists. One side of the coin is that it looks something similar to that of what Johnson listed, and the other is that it is a simpler Martini style cocktail with sherry and orange bitters.

The cocktail draws its name from the Tuxedo Club, a private members country club near Tuxedo Park, slightly north of New York. The club opened in 1886 and it is assumed by many that the cocktail came to be in the 1890s. The club, unsurprisingly, is credited with being the birthplace of the tuxedo jacket. Given how only the elite could afford to live here, it isn't a farfetched thought.

The Tuxedo is one of many Martini-style drinks that appear to be popular in the late 1800s, with the first Martini recipe appearing in Harry Johnson's *Bartender's Manual* (1888). However 12 years later he would print a new book containing a recipe for the Tuxedo and Marguerite cocktails with very few differences between them.

I believe it would be best to break down the Tuxedo cocktail recipes to what they are and where they appear:

The 'original' recipe consists of equal parts Old Tom Gin and dry vermouth with two dashes of maraschino, one dash of absinthe ad two dashes of orange bitters.

TUXEDO NO. 1: equal parts gin and dry vermouth, two dashes of absinthe with expressed lemon in the mixing glass.

TUXEDO NO. 2: equal parts gin and dry vermouth, one dash maraschino, one dash absinthe, two dashes orange bitters.

TUXEDO NO. 3 (LOWE AND STRAUB'S RECIPE): gin, dry vermouth, 5ml fino sherry, one dash maraschino, one dash absinthe, three dashes Angostura bitters.

TUXEDO NO. 4: 50ml Gin, 20ml Fino sherry, two dashes orange bitters.

TUXEDO NO. 1

This version of the cocktail is actually not the first recipe to have been chronologically created. This appears in Craddock's *The Savoy Cocktail Book* (1930) and due to the influence of the book, the consensus was that this was the actual recipe, even though there is an 'No.2' listed beside that closer resembles the original:

"TUXEDO COCKTAIL NO. 1
1 Piece Lemon Peel.
2 dashes Absinthe.
½ French Vermouth.
½ Dry Gin.

TUXEDO COCKTAIL NO. 2
One dash Maraschino.
One dash Absinthe.
2 dashes Orange Bitters.
½ Dry Gin.
½ French Vermouth."

Several years later, Patrick Duffy's *The Official Mixer's Manual* (1934) copies these two cocktails and their naming for his text, therefore reinforcing this idea. Note these recipes are equal parts gin and vermouth.

TUXEDO NO. 2

This cocktail draws from *The Savoy Cocktail Book* (1930) yet again, only it has one major change from the 'original' recipe. As with all accounts for cocktails of this nature, tastes took a particularly dry turn and thus the use of Old Tom gin was no longer going to be applicable. Both Craddock's and Duffy's 'No.2' are identical to Harry Johnson's 1900 recipe, except the change of the style of gin used.

TUXEDO NO. 3

The prior recipes have all been rather similar, calling for equal parts gin and vermouth, with additions of absinthe and bitters. This recipe first shows up in Paul Lowe's *Drinks as they are Mixed* (1904) as:

"Angostura bitter, one dash.
Sherry Wine, 1 barspoonful.
Vermouth, Italian, ½ jigger.
Tom gin, ¾ jigger."

Taking a step back in time from the No.1 and No.2 this cocktail is still using sweeter Old Tom gin and actually calls for Angostura bitters over orange. The main distinction here is the split of gin and vermouth, with a heavier gin ratio. This ratio is repeated in *Straub's Manual of Mixed Drinks* (1913) where he also includes sherry wine and two more dashes of Angostura.

However, also included in this book is the recipe for a drink named *"Tussetto Cocktail"* which is:

"⅓ Jigger Sherry Wine.
⅔ Jigger Dry Gin.
2 dashes Orange Bitters."

A recipe much closer to the standard version today.

TUXEDO NO. 4 AND THE TUSSETTO

The final iteration of this cocktail comes with the inclusion of sherry, therefore I am a fan. It wasn't a popular trend apart from at the Old Waldorf-Astoria where the cocktail was made very similarly to Straub's version of 1913:

"TUXEDO

After a settlement on the Erie R. R. where many
customers of the bar had country places.

Dash of Orange Bitters
Two-thirds Plymouth Gin
One-third Sherry Wine."
(The Old Waldorf-Astoria Bar Days, 1931)

Even though this was printed as *a* 'Tussetto' before, Albert Crockett lists it as simply a 'Tuxedo'. Perhaps the two drinks are not so interchangeable. The note that accompanies the cocktail is interesting, it references the Erie Railroad, and the settlement was where the Tuxedo Club (the place that created the cocktail) was located. Due to the clientele and reputation of the Waldorf-Astoria, it is likely that this version was created at the hotel as it differs rather drastically from the others.

TO SUMMARISE DIFFERENCES

1900 HARRY JOHNSON – BARTENDER'S MANUAL (equal parts Old Tom gin, dry vermouth, two dashes maraschino, one dash absinthe, two dashes orange bitters)

1903 DALY'S BARTENDER'S GUIDE (equal parts maple gin and dry vermouth, two dashes maraschino, two dashes orange bitters)

1904 DRINKS AS THEY ARE MIXED (PAUL. E. LOWE) equal parts old Dry gin, jigger sweet vermouth, one dash Angostura bitters, one barspoon Fino sherry)

1910 JACK'S BAR MANUAL (equal parts Old Tom gin and dry vermouth, one dash maraschino, one dash absinthe, three dashes Angostura)

1912 HOFFMAN HOUSE BARTENDER'S (equal parts Old Tom and dry vermouth, one dash maraschino and absinthe, three dashes orange bitters)

1914 DRINKS (JACQUES STRAUB) ⅔ dry gin, ⅓ dry vermouth, one dash maraschino, one dash absinthe, one dash Angostura and one barspoon dry sherry)

1927 BARFLIES AND COCKTAILS (HARRY MCELHONE) equal parts Old Tom and dry vermouth, one dash maraschino and absinthe, two dashes orange bitters.

1930 SAVOY COCKTAIL BOOK equal parts dry gin and dry vermouth, two dashes absinthe, one lemon peel expressed in the mixing glass.

1931 OLD WALDORF-ASTORIA BAR DAYS (ALBERT STEVENS CROCKETT) ⅔ Dry Gin, ⅓ dry sherry, one dash orange bitters

NOTES
- The Tuxedo (gin, dry vermouth, absinthe, maraschino, orange bitters) predates the Tussetto (sherry, gin, orange bitters) but they have become interchangeable nowadays.

TIPPERARY

40ml Bushmills ten-year Irish Whiskey
20ml Sweet Vermouth
12.5ml Green Chartreuse
Two dashes Orange Bitters

METHOD
- Stirred and strained into a coupe
- Garnished with a lemon pest

I'd feel like I let my country down if I didn't include this Irish tipple.

County Tipperary is where homesick Irish soldiers sang about during their deployment during in WW1. The song they sang was 'It's a long way to Tipperary' written by Jack Judge, and the reason for it becoming so associated with the war is that a news reporter heard an Irish regiment signing the song as they marched through northern

France in 1914. From there the song became extremely popular, thus it would not have been a far stretch for it to be known by the time a cocktail of the same name surfaced.

The drink first appears in Hugo. E. Esselins *Recipes for Mixed Drinks* (1917) as:

> *"⅓ Bushmills Irish Whiskey*
> *⅓ Chartreuse*
> *⅓ Italian Vermouth."*

Like most cocktails of this time using Chartreuse, it is unspecified as to whether it is green or yellow, although the use of green is accepted for modern recipes.

A cocktail of the same name appears in Harry MacElhone's *ABC of Mixing Cocktails* (1923) but is something completely different:

> *"⅙ Orange Juice, ⅙ Grenadine, ⅓ Noilly Pratt French*
> *Vermouth, ⅓ Gordon's Gin, 2 springs of Fresh Mint."*

Nothing close to the recipe from several years prior, however the song and would have spread far and so inspiration and ingredients would have differed.

Famously, Harry Craddock in The Savoy Cocktail Book (1930) lists both of these recipes as Tipperary Cocktail No.1 and Tipperary Cocktail No.2 respectively. I can only wonder which wonder have been more popular.

NOTES
- The cocktail is classically listed as equal parts, however this yields an unbalanced result and that which I have provided has been the best tasting one I have produced.

TURF COCKTAIL

50ml Gin
20ml Dry Vermouth
7.5ml Maraschino
Two dash Orange Bitters
One dash Absinthe

- Stirred and strained into a coupe
- Garnished with a lemon peel

This cocktail is popularised as being related to both the Martinez and the Martini, and is likely the first time that gin and vermouth make a combined appearance in text, as highlighted in George Winter's *How to Mix Drinks* (1884).

A Turf Club originally was a gentleman's venue set up by a group of wealthy investors as a place in which they could gather, eat, drink and gamble. Horseracing was a sport of choice for the wealthy and thus they always had a 'turf accountant' (bookmaker) on site to facilitate this hobby.

The drink in question is likely to have been coined at the most famous of these clubs which stood on the corner of Madison Avenue and 26th Street, overlooking Madison Square Park.

Like other classic cocktails this drink goes through several iterations, and is depicted in different ways. Here we have several interpretations of the drink appearing in chronological order:

As previously mentioned, George Winter's 1884 listed the cocktail for the first time with equal parts Old Tom gin and sweet vermouth:

> *"Two or three dashes of Peruvian Bitters:*
> *One-half wine glass of Tom gin:*
> *One-half Italian Vermouth:"*

He also calls for the use of Peruvian bitters, which aren't as common nor do they yield a drink as good than if you were to use Angostura bitters today.

George Kappeler's *Modern American Drinks* (1895) omits vermouth entirely and adds three dashes of orange bitters, he also calls in 'Turf Cocktail', not 'Turf Club':

> *"One dash Angostura bitters, three dashes*
> *orange bitters, one jigger Tom gin."*

> Both recipes call for Old Tom gin in their making.

Another style of the same cocktail with the inclusion of genever and appears in William Boothby's *American Bartender* (1891) where his 'Turf Cocktail' is listed as:

> *"One-quarter teaspoonful of bar sugar – three drops of Angostura bitters, half a jiggerful of Holland gin and half a jiggerful of vermouth. A small dash of orange bitters may be added."*

Jacques Straub and his *Drinks* (1914) book also list the exact recipe as Boothby, but lists it as 'Turf Cocktail No.2'. It was actually Albert Crockett and his *Old Waldorf Bar Days* (1931) book that was credited with this 2:1 genever and sweet vermouth cocktail, but that is because of the influence and popularity that book held.

The final style is the one most commonly associated with being the 'correct' version of the Turf Club. It famously appears in Harry Johnson's *Bartender's Manual* (1900) where he changes the Old Tom to dry gin and the sweet vermouth to dry, signifying a change in guest palate during this time. He also adds maraschino, absinthe and makes orange bitters a staple in place of Angostura:

> *"TURF COCKTAIL.*
> *2 or three dashes of orange bitters:*
> *2 or three dashes of maraschino:*
> *two dashes of absinthe*
> *½ wine glass of French vermouth:*
> *½ wine glass of Plymouth gin."*

This cocktail would go on to be adapted into cocktail culture and be replicated in many texts including Harry MacElhone and Craddock's books. Even Charles Baker Jr's *Gentleman's Companion* (1946) adapts this cocktail and goes into detail as to the Turf club in which he drank one.

WALDORF COCKTAIL

50ml Rye
25ml Sweet Vermouth
Two dashes Orange Bitters
Absinthe rinse

METHOD
• Stirred and strained into a coupe
• Garnished with a lemon peel

Similar to the 'Manhattan', and created at the Old Waldorf (now the Waldorf-Astoria) in New York. The original recipe appears in *Straub's Manual for Mixed Drinks* (1913) as:

"WALDORF COCKTAIL
⅓ *Jigger Rye Whiskey.*
⅓ *Jigger Italian Vermouth.*
⅓ *Jigger Absinthe.*
2 dashes Orange Bitters.
Shake."

Later, Albert. S. Crockett's *The Old Waldorf-Astoria Bar Book* (1931) would repeat the cocktail as:

"Dash of Manhattan Bitters
One-third Whiskey
One-third Absinthe
One-third Italian Vermouth."

There was a cocktail, not given in the book from which these recipes were translated, but which came into considerable favor among customers, who sometimes tired of the ordinary Bronx cocktail. It was called the WALDORF BRONX. According to Solon, it was composed of two-thirds gin, one-third orange juice, and two slices of fresh pineapple."

Perhaps Crockett was looking for a new signature serve for the newly reconstructed and renamed version of the famed hotel.

Even though the original hotel no long exists, the cocktail was brought back to the spotlight thanks to Dale DeGroff's adaption for the modern-day palate.

DeGroff's variant restructures the cocktail the look similar to a Manhattan only with an absinthe rinse rather than the heavy alcohol equal parts cocktail that was originally listed. I mean, could you imagine an equal parts absinthe cocktail?

NOTES
- Angostura bitters is also a choice here, however classically speaking orange is 'correct'.

WARD 8

50ml Rye Whiskey
20ml Lemon juice
10ml Simple Syrup
5ml Grenadine
Two Orange Wedges (15ml orange juice)

METHOD
- Shaken and strained into a coupe

When you think of America's cocktail culture, Boston is unlikely to be the first place that comes to mind, however it did give the world the coiled Hawthorne strainer named after a saloon in the city.

A step prior to being published in what would become a famed cocktail book, the Ward 8 came up in *A Bachelor's Cupboard* (1906) by Amy. L. Phillips in which she writes about the use of grenadine and that it

> *"is used notably in the concoction of the 'Ward Eight' of Boston's Winter Place Hotel."*

This would become Boston's answer to the rapidly growing cocktail culture that was spreading across the United States. Ward Eight was a voting district of Boston, and famed for the political corruption that occurred there. Martin Lomasney was running a political campaign for a seat at the General Court of Massachusetts that represented the district.

Modern myth suggests the cocktail is said to have been created by Tom Hussion in 1898 at Boston's Locke-Ober Café (the former name of the Winter Place Hotel) in celebration for Lomasney after securing political victory. Seems fitting as the politician also owned the café, so it would have been a safe environment to celebrate.

This cocktail then appears in Robert Vermeire's *Cocktails: How to Mix Them* (1922) as:

> *"1 teaspoonful of Grenadine.*
> *⅛ gill of Orange Juice.*
> *⅛ gill of Lemon Juice.*
> *¼ gill of Rye Whisky."*

Another source found in *The Boston Sun* newspaper regarding its origin is that bartender, Charlie Carter, who worked at Puritan Club in 1903 created the cocktail, not Hussion.

WIDOW'S KISS

50ml Calvados
15ml Benedictine
15ml Yellow Chartreuse
Two dashes Angostura Bitters

METHOD
- Stirred and strained into a coupe
- Garnished with a cherry

A classic cocktail that been grouped into the 'forgotten classics' category, this complex cocktail yields herbaceous and dangerous elegance.

It is imperative to take notice of the relationship between the rise of mixed drinks and the business of apothecary. The flavour profile of the Widow's Kiss reflects these influences very impressively.

During the late nineteenth century, pharmacies, released numerous tinctures based on herbs that contributed to everyday life. Many of these bitters were attributed with having healing benefits and so they tried to sell them on the market. The best examples of these are Angostura and Peychaud's bitters which started at medicine and made their way into mixed drinks. French herbal liqueurs also were also used in this fashion, and both the Benedictine and Chartreuse monasteries were releasing products to alleviate illness.

Created in the early 1890s by George J. Kappeler, head bartender at Holland House Hotel, Manhattan. It would later be released in his book *Modern American Drinks* in 1895 as:

> *"Two dashes Angostura bitters, one-half*
> *a pony yellow chartreuse, one-half a pony*
> *Benedictine, one pony of apple brandy."*

YALE COCKTAIL

50ml Gin
20ml Dry Vermouth
10ml Maraschino
10ml Crème Yvette
One dash Orange Bitters

METHOD
• Stirred and strained into a coupe
• Garnished with a lemon peel

The Yale Cocktail has undergone several iterations and made many appearances in cocktail texts, and the drink falls into a family of drinks that are named after Ivy League schools such as the 'Princeton' or 'Harvard'.

The cocktail first crops up in *Modern American Drinks* (1895) by George J. Kappeler who lists at as:

> *"Three dashes orange bitters, one dash Peyschaud*
> *bitters, a piece of lemon peel, one jigger Tom*
> *gin... add a squirt of siphon seltzer."*

Jacques Straub writes in *Straub's Manual of Mixed Drinks* (1913) of a the 'Yale Cocktail' as a similar beast, but has altered it slightly:

> *"One dash Orange Bitters.*
> *One dash Absinthe.*

> *1 Jigger Dry Gin.*
> *1 Lemon Peel."*

The Peychaud's bitters have been swapped for absinthe and the Old Tom gin for London dry. This would have made for a less sweet and more complex style of cocktail, perhaps more in line with the tastes at the time.

Harry's ABC of Mixing Drinks (1923) and *The Savoy Cocktail Book* (1930) are the last books to follow the recipe of simply gin and bitters as they both call for:

> *"3 dashes of Orange Bitters.*
> *One dash of Angostura Bitters.*
> *1 Glass Dry Gin."*

The cocktail would later evolve to include dry vermouth and Crème Yvette which was discontinued in 1969 due to lack of popularity, until 40 years later when it would be revived by Robert Cooper. Where these additions came from remains a mystery, a best guess would be that it occurred at the actual Yale College in which a proud student decided to take the cocktail under their wing and make it the school's own. The end result that ended up in *Yale Alumni Magazine* is reminiscent of an Aviation, and that tends to be the accepted version for the classic nowadays.

ZAZA

40ml Gin
40ml Dubonnet
One dash Angostura Bitters

METHOD
* Stirred and strained into a coupe
* Garnished with a lemon peel

Zaza was a French-language play that was first shown in Paris, 1898. The cocktail takes its name from this play after it took to Broadway several years later.

There are numerous stories to this cocktail as there is debate as to what this cocktail actually named. There is a cocktail called 'Jack Zeller' which is first listed in Jack Grohusko's *Jack's Manual* (1908) as:

"50% Booth's orange gin.
50% Dubonnet."

This book also lists a 'Zaza Cocktail' containing Gordon's gin and Dubonnet, but no bitters. One other cocktail worth noting in this book is the 'Dubonnet Cocktail' which reads:

"½ Jigger Dry Gin.
½ Jigger Dubonnet.
One dash orange Bitters."

Jacques Straub in his *Straub's Manual of Mixed Drinks* (1913) updates the Zaza to use Old Tom gin instead, and also includes Angostura bitters:

"½ Jigger Dry Gin.
½ Jigger Dubonnet.
One dash Angostura Bitters."

It's safe to say to say that these cocktails have their places and own names, but have been so mismatched and forgotten that they almost have become interchangeable.

To break it down – Aromatic bitters is a Zaza, orange bitters is a Dubonnet cocktail, and neither is a Jack Zeller. Glad we cleared that up.

Dubonnet begins in 1846 when chemist Joseph Dubonnet, attempted to make a quinine drink to help French Foreign Legionaries battle malaria in Northern Africa. In amid to make it less bitter, he blended it with herbs and fortified wine, thus Dubonnet was born.

NOTES
• Gary Regan said a flamed orange peel balances this cocktail.

THE NOBLE
EXPERIMENT/
PROHIBITION
(1920–1935)

The 18th Amendment to the U.S. Constitution – which banned the sale, manufacture and transportation of intoxicating liquids – began a period in history that would become known as Prohibition. Although there was talk of such a law coming into place for several years, Prohibition became realised on 17 January 1920 after the passing of the Volstead Act.

Many would think why would such a movement occur and what was its purpose. It began in the 1830s when religious revivalism was sweeping America led to increased calls for temperance or 'perfectionism' movements. As early as 1838 states such as Massachusetts passed temperance laws, only for them to be repealed several years later, then in 1846 Maine passed the first state-wide Prohibition law.

By the turn of the century temperance movements seemed common fixtures across America, with large roles being filled by women as they viewed alcohol as a destructive force within families. Soon after more attack came in the form of the Anti-Saloon League and the rise in evangelical Protestantism and its views on saloon culture as ungodly. Even factory owners supported Prohibition as it would decrease accidents at work and increase productivity in an era of heightened industrialism.

Post-World War I, President Wilson called for a temporary Prohibition in order to save grain for food manufacturing and in that same year Congress submitted the 18th Amendment. Initially this was meant to have a seven-year lead time, however the Amendment received the necessary three-quarters majority support in just 11 months. Congress put forward a National Prohibition Act and provided guidelines for the Federal enforcement of Prohibition in light of 33 states already enacting their own legislation.

As would be assumed, Prohibition was difficult to enforce and led to an increase in illegal production and sale of alcohol (soon to be called "bootlegging"), the birth of speakeasies with coupled gang violence and criminal activity. The most notable example was Al Capone who earned around $60 million annually from bootleg operations and speakeasies, this money would fuel gang activities such as the St. Valentine's Day Massacre in Chicago, 1929.

Speakeasies had replaced saloon culture and the some 100,000 venues stretched from Canada to Florida. Names such as blind tiger and blind pig became common as visitors would pay an entry fee to view and exotic animal and be able to fill a bottle with illicit booze out of sight. The rise of such establishments and their secrecy meant that they could not afford to segregate by sex any longer, and for the first time both men and women could sit next to one another and order themselves a drink.

During the latter part of the 1920s the high price with bootleg alcohol and the health issues associated with bathtub booze meant that America's working class and poor were much less well off than before, the cost of the legal system spiralled upwards and support for Prohibition waned. With the country amid the 1932 Great Depression the appeal of revenue form legalising alcohol sales seemed huge, and Franklin Roosevelt ran for President that year with a main campaign aim to repeal the 18th Amendment. All these factors led Congress to propose a new solution and thus the 21st Amendment to the Constitution would repeal the 18th. This Amendment was put into effect 5 December 1933, and even though this was the case it wasn't until 1966 when all states abandoned the ban of alcohol sales.

President Hoover once called Prohibition "the great social and economic experiment, noble in motive and far reaching in purpose" in his campaign against Franklin Roosevelt, a noble sentiment but highly impractical.

ARMY NAVY

50ml Gin
20ml Lemon juice
15ml Orgeat
One Lemon Peel in Tin

METHOD
- Shaken and strained into a coupe
- Garnished with lemon peel

Created by occasional *New York Sun* contributor Carrol Van Ark.

This drink was submitted to G. Selmer Fougner's *Along the Wine Trail* (a drink column in the *New York Sun*) in 1934 and this is the first time this cocktail was recorded in print.

The most notable appearance is *in The Fine Art of Mixing Drinks* (1948) by David Embury, which calls for a simpler 2:1:1 recipe, stating the original is *"horrible"* and:

> *"If made with my 1:2:8 formula it is merely a Gin*
> *Sour with orgeat used in place of sugar."*

The complexity lies in the balancing of balance with the orgeat as it in itself is a highly complex syrup. When made correctly (as the recipe given) this cocktail is a delightful floral, citric and nutty character.

AVIATION

45ml Gin
12.5ml Maraschino
7.5ml Violette
20ml Lemon Juice
5ml Simple Syrup

METHOD
- Shaken and strained into a coupe
- Garnished with a cherry

AVIATION #1

50ml Applejack
5ml Crème De Cassis
15ml Lime Juice
15ml Simple Syrup
Two dashes Absinthe

METHOD
- Shaken and strained into a coupe
- Garnished with a lemon peel

Like many classic cocktails it isn't clear who invented this drink, however the first Aviation recipe appears in Hugo Ensslin's *Recipe for Mixed drinks* (1916), and as such he is credited for the creation.

Hugo Ensslin, a German born bartender, took mantle as head bartender of the Wallick House hotel in Times Square, New York, at

30 years old. Aside from this, there is little information regarding him and his life.

The cocktail is said to pay homage to the dawn of commercial aviation, having the small sky-blue tint stemming from the Violette within the cocktail. Cocktails were generally named after people or events in history, and few others would have been deemed worthy like the ability for people to travel by plane.

In the early days of the cocktail renaissance this drink travelled the globe as a modern day 'bartender's handshake'. A cult favourite of the cocktail-insider's at the time.

After this, the drink found its way into Harry Craddock's *The Savoy Cocktail Book* (1930) however this version omitted the Violette, and for years this became the industry standard.

The cocktail was subject to a moment in the spotlight when several bartenders and authors spearheaded the modern-day revival of classic cocktail culture. This group had several books amongst them including Dale DeGroff's *The Craft of the Cocktail* (2002) which followed *The Savoy Cocktail Book* (1930) recipe of simply gin, lemon juice, and maraschino.

All this changed when drinks historian, David Wondrich (author of '*Punch*') began to replicate his copy of Ensslin's book. He recounts how he almost destroyed his copy of the book in a bowl of soup upon seeing the inclusion of Crème de Violette. This recipe was:

> *"½ Lemon Juice*
> *⅔ El Bart Gin*
> *two dashes Maraschino*
> *two dashes Crème de Violette"*

Ensslin lists another cocktail called 'Blue Moon Cocktail' which has the ingredient Crème Yvette. For a time bartenders would interchange these components however, crème Yvette is typically made with violets along with berries and citrus whilst Crème de Violette is the violet flower only.

A prime reason as to why this cocktail fell out of favour was that crème de Violette was almost impossible to come by for a long time. It wasn't until around 2006 that Eric Seed, founder of Haus Alpenz – a company that creates and distributes no-longer available alcohols – asked Dave Wondrich what he should be making. His reply was that there were no Violettes in America and within a year the liqueur was on the market again.

ACACIA

45ml Gin
15ml Benedictine
12.5ml Kircsh

METHOD
• Stirred and strained into a coupe
• Garnished with lemon peel

Benedictine replaces vermouth in this Martini variation, which also calls for kirsch, or kirschwasser, a cherry eau de vie. (You might have cooked with it if you've ever made a traditional fondue.)

According to author David Embury, this cocktail took first place at a cocktail competition in Biarritz in 1928, he also suggests adding more gin and a dash of lemon juice to yield a more balanced cocktail.

NOTES
• The lemon zest is essential in tying this cocktail together, it is critical to making this drink.

APEROL SPRITZ

60ml Aperol
90ml Prosecco
30ml Soda Water

METHOD
• Built in a wine glass over ice, then given a short stir
• Garnished with an orange wedge

Italy has many famous and delicious beverages. There's wine like Bardo, Chianti, and Super Tuscans. Beer like Peroni. However, few things have as strong a claim to being an 'Italian drink' as the 'low-ABV' Aperol Spritz. Built from the 11% aperitif from Northern Italy.

The drink goes back to 1805 and the Napoleonic wars. In the Aftermath of the wars, Austria-Hungary took ownership of the Vento region of northern Italy, where Venice is located.

For the next 50 years, Austrians took the local Italian wine and added a splash, or in German 'spritz' of water. Over time (and two world wars) the water turned into sparkling water, and the still wine morphed into fortified wine with liqueur. The liqueur of choice quickly became Aperol.

In 1919 Aperol was born and the Barbieri brothers launched the product in the Venetian city of Padua. It was an instant hit and gain further popularity in the 1920s and 30s due to creative and extensive marketing on part of the brothers.

Aperol had a lower alcohol percentage that existing competitors at the time, and thus already had and advantage. They began targeting athletes and women and used the slogan *"for women and sportive people"* – a rather exclusive corner of the market at the time.

It wasn't until the 1950s that Aperol capitalised on the spritz. The 3:2:1 recipe of Prosecco, Aperol and soda water became an important part of the advertising campaign in America as it heightened the ease of making and the 'do-it-yourself' attitude.

Then in the 2000s the Aperol Spritz became the worldwide phenomenon that it is today as in 2003, Gruppo Campari bought the Aperol brand and used its global distribution to make the product the ever-popular cocktail it is today.

ADONIS (THE DRIER THE SHERRY, THE BETTER)

50ml Fino Sherry
25ml Sweet Vermouth
Two dashes Orange Bitters

METHOD
- Stirred and strained into a Nick and Nora
- Garnished with an orange peel

The 'Adonis' named after the 1884 Broadway burlesque by William Gill, often credited as the first Broadway musical ever, and starred Henry. E. Dixon and ran for over 600 showings.

Of the stirred aperitif drinks of the nineteenth century that involve sherry, there are really two archetypes that are riffed on: 'Bamboo' and 'Adonis'.

While the show enjoyed its popularity, the Waldorf-Astoria Hotel New York created this sherry-based aperitif drink in its honour, and this can be seen in the *Old Waldorf-Astoria Bar Days* (1931) with a comment regarding the cocktail:

> *"Named in honor of a theatrical offering which made at least two persons famous. One was Henry E. Dixey, a handsome and talented actor, long on Broadway: the other was Fanny Ward.*
>
> *Two dashes Orange Bitters*
> *One-half Sherry*
> *One-half Italian Vermouth*
> *Stir"*

One widely contested aspect to this cocktail is the ratio of vermouth to sherry in the drink. Jacque Straub lists this cocktail for the first time in text in his *Straub's Manual for Mixed Drinks* (1913):

> *"2 dashes Orange Bitters.*
> *⅓ Jigger Sherry.*
> *⅔ Jigger Italian Vermouth.*
> *Stir."*

Interestingly, in *The Savoy Cocktail Book* (1930) Harry Craddock reverses this ratio by listing:

> *"One dash Orange Bitters.*
> *⅓ Italian Vermouth.*
> *⅔ Dry Sherry."*

As above, Albert Crockett uses an equal-parts cocktail. From this I have listed a 2:1 sherry to vermouth recipe for your enjoyment.

NOTES
- Manzanilla sherry also works well here.

ALFONSO

20ml Dubonnet Rouge
Three dashes Angostura Bitters
One Cube Caster Sugar
Topped with Champagne

METHOD
- Built in flute and given a short stir
- Garnished with a lemon peel

Named after the deposed Spanish King Alfonso XIII, who first tasted the drink while exiled in France in 1931, the year of the King's exile.

This story doesn't quite line up with the cocktail's printing in industry texts as it first shows up in *Harry's ABC of Mixing Cocktails* (1922) as:

> *"Put one lump of sugar in a medium-sized wine-glass, two
> dashes of Secrestat Bitter poured on to the sugar, one lump
> of ice, one quarter of the glass Dubonnet, and fill remainder
> with Champagne, and squeeze lemon peel on top.
> The above cocktail was very popular at Deauville
> in 1922, during his Majesty the King of Spain's
> stay at that popular Normandy resort."*

Harry himself wrote of the year 1922, in which the King actually did visit France before his exile nine years later. So it is true that King Alfonso may have tried the drink whilst in France, but it would not have been at his year of exile.

The cocktail is repeated in *Barflies and Cocktails* (1927) with the same note about the King's trip to Normandy.

Diamond Reef Co-owner Dan Greenbaum's interest in this drink, was sparked by an entirely different take on the drink which appeared in Frank Meier's *Artistry of Mixing Drinks* (1936) which reads:

*"Equal parts fino sherry and Dubonnet,
served up with a lemon twist."*

THE ALGONQUIN

50ml Rye Whiskey
25ml Dry vermouth
30ml Pineapple Juice
5ml Simple Syrup

METHOD
- Stirred and strained into a coupe
- Garnished with a lemon peel

This cocktail was named after the historic hotel that graced the New York skyline from 1919 until 1929, and home of the famous Algonquin Round Table. Some of the greatest literary minds, celebrities and artists sat at this table daily to discuss the goings-on within their industries.

The table hosted people such as Harpo Marx (an actor and comedian), Dorothy Parker (poet and writer), Harold Ross (founder of the *New Yorker),* and Robert Benchley (author and actor). It is likely to assume that when people of this social circle gathered, even during Prohibition, there were plenty of drinks being passed around. Ironically, this cocktail was likely never consumed at the table as they generally preferred Martinis as Robert Benchley would say:

"Why don't you get out of that wet coat and into a dry Martini?"

Interestingly, the Algonquin Hotel was dry before the Temperance Movement swept the nation due to the hotel's owner Frank Case supporting this cause. The cocktail was likely created elsewhere as it didn't appear in print for the first time until 1935 when it would come up in G. Selmer Fougner's *Along the Wine Trail,* a column piece in the *New York Sun.*

NOTES
- There is a drink sharing the same name made from Rum, Blackberry brandy and Benedictine.
- I was given another recipe that included pineapple syrup if you already have some or you wanted to try another version of the cocktail;

50ml Rye
20ml Dry vermouth
15ml Pineapple syrup
One dash Peychaud's Bitters
Stirred and strained into a coupe

BENTLEY

50ml Calvados
25ml Sweet Vermouth
One dash Absinthe
One dash Angostura Bitters

METHOD
- Stirred and strained into a coupe
- Garnished with a lemon peel

Over the course of the 1920s and 30s, a group of engineers, race car drivers and gentleman known as the 'Bentley Boys' became famous over the world for their play-hard, self-indulgent attitudes.

The Bentley Boys became household names overnight due to their appearance at Le Mans, a famous car race held in France since the early 1920s. Their success led to five trophies in eight years.

The cocktail is supposed to have been created when the Bentley Boys came to the Savoy Hotel to celebrate a race win in 1927. The group were able to bring a Bentley racing car into the hotel's dining area where they then enjoyed an 11-course meal, and many bespoke cocktails created by Harry Craddock himself.

Founder of Bentley W.O. Bentley stated that the public liked to depict the Boys lifestyle as:

> *"Living in expensive Mayfair flats, drinking champagne in nightclubs, paying the horses and the Stock Exchange, and beating furiously around the racetrack at the weekend. Of several of them, this was not such an inaccurate picture."*

A recipe identical to the one in Craddock's Savoy appears in the *Buckstone Book of Cocktails* (1925) Robert Buckby and George Stone.

In 1926, *The Atlanta Constitution* published a dispatch from Craddock, taunting readers in the then-dry U.S with parts of the Savoy menu, and the Bentley is among them.

NOTES
• The original iteration of this cocktail contained Calvados and Dubonnet only, crafted at the Savoy Hotel.

BETWEEN THE SHEETS

25ml Cognac
25ml White Rum
20ml Cointreau
20ml Lemon juice

BETWEEN THE SHEETS (DALE DE GROFF)

35ml Cognac
15ml Benedictine
15ml Triple Sec
20ml Lemon juice

METHOD
• Shaken and strained into a coupe
• Garnished with a lemon peel

First appearing in *The Savoy Cocktail Book* (1930) by Harry Craddock but likely created in the early 1920s by Harry MacElhone at his New York, Paris, derived from the 'Sidecar'. MacElhone's arsenal of cocktails were no stranger to unusual names such as the 'Monkey Gland' and 'Scofflaw'.

There remains another origin story, that its inventor was a Mr. Polly – the bar manager of the Berkeley Hotel, London 1921. Sadly both stories carry little evidence but the credit normally lays with Harry MacElhone.

NOTES
• Some also refer to the drink as a *'Maiden's Prayer'*.

BOULEVARDIER

30ml Rye Whiskey
25ml Campari
25ml Sweet Vermouth
One dash Orange Bitters

METHOD
* Stirred and strained into a coupe
* Garnished with an orange peel

A rye-laced take on a 'Negroni' this cocktail appears in Harry MacElhone's *Barflies and Cocktails* (1927). Supposedly, two years before the Negroni came to be, this cocktail was created for Erskine Gwynne when he came to visit Harry's New York Bar, Paris. This is further backed by Harry's written piece in the book regarding the cocktail:

> *"Now is the time for all good barflies to come to the aid of the party, since Erskinne Gwynne crashed with his Boulevardier Cocktail: ⅓ Campari, ⅓ Italian vermouth, ⅓ Bourbon whisky."*

Much like Harry, Erskine was an American expat, also known to dabble in writing and was nephew of railroad tycoon Alfred Vanderbilt. Erskine would go on to edit a monthly magazine called the *The Boulevardier* hence the name of the cocktail, which would feature in Harry's cocktail book.

In recent years, Ted Haigh as actually increased the whiskey base stemming from his ideas in *Vintage Spirits and Forgotten Cocktails* (2004) and as such the world can thank him from bringing the drink back into the spotlight. I am in the same camp as Haigh and I don't believe may cocktails truly benefit from being equal parts.

BLINKER

50ml Rye
35ml Pink Grapefruit Juice
10ml Lemon Juice
10ml Grenadine

METHOD
* Give a short shaken and strained into a coupe

The Blinker is an odd one. It resides in the same line of classics as the 'Between the Sheets' and 'Japanese Slipper': recipes that don't particularly make sense on paper – but work well enough in a glass.

Perhaps a better comparison may be the 'Lion's Tail', since both of these drinks contain a whiskey element, and are both rather quite good.

Originally published in *The Official Mixer's Manual* (1934) by Patrick Gavin Duffy the Blinker might have drifted off into history had it not been illuminated by Ted 'Dr. Cocktail' Haigh in 2009 book *Vintage Spirits and Forgotten Cocktails:*

"1 jigger Rye, 1½ jiggers Grapefruit juice, ½ jigger Grenadine."

He made one significant change in which raspberry syrup was subbed in for grenadine. He stated that in the 1930s grenadine and raspberry syrup were often interchangeable, but raspberry syrup made for a better cocktail.

BLOOD AND SAND

30ml Scotch
25ml Sweet Vermouth
25ml Cherry Heering
20ml Orange Juice

METHOD
* Shaken and strained into a coupe
* Garnished with orange zest and discard

This cocktail is supposed to be able to convince someone who does not like Scotch that they can enjoy it in a cocktail. It remains unknown who exactly created this cocktail, but it first appears in *The Savoy Cocktail Book* (1930).

At first glance the combination of ingredients in this cocktail may not seem to work as a symphony, but once mixed together they become an oddly harmonious band.

It is based on a film from 1922 of the same name, which takes the plotline from a 1909 Spanish novel called *Sangre Y Arena* by Vicente

Blasco Ibanez. It is the tale of a love story between one of Spain's greatest matadors and an affair with a wealthy widow.

BROWN DERBY (HOUSE DRINK OF THE NOW DEFUNCT HOLLYWOOD RESTAURANT OF THE SAME NAME)

50ml Bourbon
25ml Grapefruit Juice
12.5ml Honey Syrup
One Lemon Rind

METHOD
* Shaken and strained into a coupe
* Garnished with grapefruit peel and discard

There are two competing origin stories. The first is that the eponymous signature cocktail at the Brown Derby, a restaurant-chain in L.A. The original location was shaped like an actual derby hat, and its Vine Street outpost was a popular hangout for Hollywood movers and shakers. And the other story claims that the cocktail was created nearby at the Vendome Club on the Sunset Strip and named, for some reason, in honour of the Brown Derby restaurant.

Interestingly enough, the Brown Derby cocktail wasn't even close to appearing in Hollywood during the 1930s, in fact it was being consumed in New York – and consisted of rum, maple, sugar and lime – not similar to today's incarnation.

The West coast story is highlighted by serval drinks writers and the cocktail is identical to what Harry Craddock listed as *'De Rigueur'* in the *Savoy Cocktail Book* (1930):

> *"½ Whiskey*
> *¼ Grape Fruit Juice*
> *¼ Honey*
> *Shake well and strain into a cocktail glass."*

Craddock seems to have taken the recipe from Judge Jr.'s *Here's How* (1927). This version calls explicitly for "Scotch Whisky", while Craddock's more generically lists "whisky".

Did the Rigueur over across the pond and make its way to Hollywood, perhaps by globetrotting movie star. Or maybe a bartender had a copy of the Savoy cocktail book, and naturally used bourbon instead of scotch?

The answer seems to be even simpler than expected, and it stems from an odd book named *Hollywood Cocktails* (1933). It was the work of George Buzza, Jr., an artist and entrepreneur who established the Buzza company, that once he sold it, he moved to Hollywood to retire. Once there he opened up a greeting card and novelty books business, one of these books was *Hollywood Cocktails*.

Listed on page 17 was the recipe for the *'Brown Derby Cocktail'*, looking exactly like Harry Craddock's De Rigueur Cocktail. In fact, it is word for word the same as Craddock's recipe, except that Buzza closes up 'Grape Fruit' and omits cracked ice from the ingredients.

This is no coincidence. Buzza didn't roam all over Hollywood asking for recipes from celebrities and bartenders alike. Instead, the first recipe is (The Absinthe Cocktail) and the very last (The Zazarac) are lifted directly from *The Savoy Cocktail Book,* word for word.

There is no evidence to suggest that the Brown Derby was served at either the restaurant or the Vendome or anywhere else in Hollywood. In fact the Brown Derby's signature cocktails seem to have been Brandy-based, as confirmed by Ted Haigh listing on of their drinks as *"The Honeymoon"* consisting of Calvados, Benedictine, orange curacao and lemon juice.

THE EAST COAST DERBY

In New York City, there were people drinking a cocktail called the Brown Derby in the 1930s. Dave Wondrich turned up this variant in the files of *Esquire* and wrote about it back in 2002. Aside from similar proportions, it doesn't seem to relate to the De Rigueur. It first appeared in *Esquire*'s 'Painting the Town' column in 1935. In which the unsigned author wrote:

> *"Amen Corner of Fifth Avenue Hotel gave me my chance to imbibe a Brown Derby amid politicians and litterateurs."*

Four years later, the magazine published an actual recipe for a Brown Derby in Murdock Pemberton's 'Potables' column:

"2 parts dark rum
1 teaspoon maple sugar
Juice of one lime"

This rum-based drink appears to have a brief appearance in New York. In 1941, a *House and Garden* article on rum included a picture of a bartender that was captioned *"Mixing a rum Brown Derby at the Waldorf's Palm Bar."* it makes other appearances in various books in the following years, Like *Esquire*'s *Handbook for Hosts (1957)* and Seagram's *New Official Bartender's Guide (1995)* but they look to be recycled recipes for a drink that was no longer popular.

BEE'S KNEES

60ml Gin
20ml Lemon
20ml Honey syrup

METHOD
• Shaken and strained into a coupe

This cocktail is associated with the late Sasha Petraske, a real driving force behind the modern era speakeasy revival and fine-tuned hospitality.

A gin-based cocktail with honey and lemon to mask the flavour and odour of the often-unpleasant bathtub gin being used at speakeasys during Prohibition.

Like most classic drinks, the origin is lost to the wind however it was apparently created by Frank Meier at the Ritz in Paris during the 1920s, and this is backed by Georges Gabriel Thenon's *Cocktails de Paris* (1929).

Then I found a 1929 article – a 22 April 1929 *Standard Union* article from Brooklyn, NY, page two, to be precise – about a new phenomenon in Parisian nightlife: 'women's bars' where men were prohibited and concoctions of gin and honey was being served.

The phrase 'bee's knees' (a common saying at the time) which initially was used to indicate something small or insignificant, predates the cocktail by more than a century. As the phrase evolved it began to become applied to people or things that were considered rare or extraordinary.

The cocktail would also appear in William Boothby's *World Drinks and How to Mix Them* (1934) and would have the inclusion of orange juice also. If these timelines are accurate then Boothby was the first to list the cocktail as Meier's book wouldn't be released for another two years, this is not to say he still couldn't have created the drink.

BLACK ROSE

30ml Bourbon
30ml Bourbon or Cognac
7.5ml Grenadine
Two dashes Peychaud's Bitters

METHOD
- Stirred and strained into a rocks glass over block ice
- Garnished with a lemon peel

Said to have been created by Frank Meier at the Ritz Hotel, Paris. This cocktail came back to life when it was touched upon by Dale DeGroff in his *The Essential Cocktail* (2008).

It can be served either like a classic 'Old Fashioned', or like a 'Sazerac' with no ice. This Sazerac style is reflected in the recipe as it can have a split or full spirit base.

BLOODY MARY

50ml Vodka
70ml Tomato Juice
30ml Spice Mix
15ml Lemon Juice
Malbec Float

METHOD
- Built in a highball over ice and given a short stir
- Garnished with lemon wedge, olive and black pepper

Of all the cocktails that have complicated or multifaceted histories, the Bloody Mary is among a top contender. The cocktail stories include a ruined dress, a Monarch, a comedian, a famed bartender and many more.

If you want to go into further detail Brain Bartel's *The Bloody Mary* (2017) offers much more details and clarification surrounding this drink.

> *"The good news is, the Bloody Mary was invented... the answer to the question of how it originated, however, is a murky one."*

I'll take several theories in turn as lay them out:

- A popular theory points to a gentleman named Fernand 'Pete' Petiot as the creator of the cocktail. He bartended at Harry's New York, Paris during the 1920s where he would mix vodka and tomato juice for American guests. Drinking tomato juice was a trend during the early twentieth century, and throughout Prohibition.

- Following this, a comedian named George Jessel was an advocate of drinking tomato juice at this time and one night found himself sat at a hotel bar in Palm Beach, 1927. He found a bottle labelled 'vodkee' to pour into his tomato juice, soon after Mary Brown Warbuton walked in and Jessel handed her the same drink, spilling it all over her white dress – She proclaimed "Now you can call me Bloody Mary" (referencing Queen Mary I of England). Jessel would recall this beverage in Lucius Beebe's column of the 1939 *New York Herald*.

- Jessel would later appear in a Smirnoff vodka advert in the March edition of the *Collier's* magazine, 1956, stating "*I think I invented the Bloody Mary.*"

Interestingly, an article from eight years later gives an interview had with Petiot in which he says:

> *"I initiated the Bloody Mary of today. George Jessel said he created it, but it was nothing more than vodka and tomato juice when I took it over."*

Petiot then goes on to detail his recipe which included salt, pepper, Worcestershire sauce, cayenne pepper and lemon.

- Early cocktail books make no mention of the drink, even those written by the bar owner where it was meant to have been created. Petiot would later move to New York, where he would tend bar at King Cole Bar in 1934. Post-Prohibition he introduced the 'Red Snapper', the gin-laced version of the 'Bloody Mary'. He wanted to call it by is usual name, but the hotel's owner Mr. Astor had a wife named Mary, so this didn't go down well. The drink was an over-whelming success an saw printing in Crosby Gaige's *Cocktail Guide and Ladies Companion* (1941).

Even after all these theories, there exist more but with less depth. Some believe that it is named after a waitress named Mary who worked at the infamous Bucket of Blood Saloon, Chicago, whilst others claim that it takes its name from Mary Tudor of England. A theory that I have grown to enjoy is that a guest that Petiot used to serve when in Paris was waiting for a suitor that never turned up to meet her, a sad tale indeed.

COMMODORE

45ml Bourbon
15ml Crème de Cacao
10ml Lemon Juice
5ml Grenadine

METHOD
- Shaken and strained into coupe

This cocktail most relevantly appears in Albert Crockett's *Old Waldorf Bar Days* (1931) with an original and a 'No.2' version, in which I will be focusing on here. The cocktail was attributed to a man who was a ranking officer in the New York Yacht Club or Larchmont Yacht Club, this is likely why there were two variants.

The Commodore No.2 is listed as:

"One-third Lemon Juice
One-third Bourbon Whiskey
One-third Crème de Cacao

Dash Grenadine Syrup
Frappe in a champagne glass."

The original 'Commodore' is essentially a 'Clover Club' with a rum base, however this is different drink entirely, and is likely based on the preference of the creator. Another recipe appears in Harry MacElhone's book from 1922 and 1927 listed as:

"1 teaspoonful Gomme Syrup, two dashes Orange
Bitters, Juice of half a Lime, glass of Rye Whisky."

With this recipe, MacElhone credits a bartender by the name of Phil Gross from Cincinnati, meaning this cocktail would have been popular enough to travel to Europe – even if it doesn't look great on paper.

CAMERON'S KICK

30ml Irish Whiskey
30ml Smokey Scotch Whiskey
20ml Lemon Juice
15ml Orgeat
One Lemon Peel in shaker

METHOD
- Shaken and strained into a coupe
- Garnished with a lemon peel

I'm in the camp of saying that on paper this cocktail should not work, on the flipside of that argument I also love this cocktail.

The drink first appears in Harry MacElhone's *ABC of Mixing Cocktails* (1922) as:

"⅓ Scotch Whisky, ⅓ Irish Whisky,
⅙ Lemon Juice, ⅙ Orgeat Syrup."

Several years later the cocktail is repeated in *The Savoy Cocktail Book* (1930) but that also provides no clarity as to the origin of the name. The closest connection I made is a well-known Scottish Clan, the Cameron Clan, whose chief Donald Dubh was forced into exile in Ireland after the battle of Inverlochy, 1431.

CHAMP-ELYSEES

45ml Cognac
15ml Green Chartreuse
12.5ml Lemon Juice
5ml Simple Syrup
Two dashes Angostura Bitters

METHOD
* Shaken and strained into a coupe
* Garnished with a cherry

This cocktail is said to first appear in *The Savoy Cocktail Book* (1930) but it actually replicates the recipe from another book: *Drinks – Long and Short* (1925) by Nina Tote and A.H. Adair. Harry Craddock would go on to list the cocktail in his book as a group serve, which would popularise the drink in that century:

> *"3 Glasses Cognac, 1 Glass Chartreuse, 1½ Glasses Sweetened Lemon Juice, One dash Angostura Bitters."*

Named after the famous central Paris Boulevard that runs into the Arc de Triomphe. The name, which translates to 'Elysian Fields' is depiction of heaven in Greek mythos.

The street is a symbol for the French: it's the last leg of the tour de France, it's the site of the National bastille day parade, and where allied forces marched in celebration of the liberation of the city from Nazi rule.

DEATH IN THE AFTERNOON

15ml Absinthe
5ml Simple Syrup
Champagne top

METHOD
* Built in flute and given a gentle stir
* Garnished with lemon peel then discarded

Ernest Hemingway claimed to have invented the Death in the Afternoon, a risky pairing of absinthe and champagne, himself. His exact instructions

suggested adding iced champagne to a jigger of absinthe until it attained *"the proper opalescent milkiness. Drink 3 to 5 of these slowly."*

The title of Ernest Hemingway's 1932 novel is both a direct reference to the gruesome finale of Spanish bullfights, and a more oblique one about his medication and morality.

This cocktail was his addition to a 1935 collection of cocktails created by celebrities titled *So Red the Nose, or Death in the Afternoon.*

EL PRESIDENTE

40ml White Rum
40ml Chambery Demi-sweet Vermouth
10ml Dry Curacao
5ml Grenadine

METHOD
* Stirred and strained into a coupe
* Garnished with an orange peel

Although the 'El Presidente' originated as Cuba's tip of hat to whiskey drinks, Americans craved it during it Prohibition. The drink became far more than just a stand-in.

The drink was first invented in Havana during the 1910s for Cuban president Mario Garcia Menocal, who ruled from 1913 to 1921.

The cocktail was refined and popularised by American bartender Eddie Woelke, who arrived in Havana in 1919 to run bar at Sevilla Biltmore Hotel.

According to drinks historian Anastasia Miller and Jared Brown's book, *Cuban Cocktails* (2012), the libations fresh cachet caught attention of Cuba's new president, Gerardo Machado, who took over in 1925. Naturally he demanded his own version, which simply added a few dashes of Curacao.

Cuban Cantinero Constante Ribalagigua Vert guised up the El Presidente at legendary Havana bar, El Floridita. He garnished the drink with cherry and orange peel.

One of the earliest written recipes for the El Presidente comes from John B. Escalante's *Manual del Cantinero* (1915):

"Curacao, a few drops
Angostura bitters, a few drops
Grenadine or simple syrup, ½ barspoon
Orange, 1 twist
Chambery vermouth, 2 parts
Bacardi Rum, 1 part

Mix with spoon, stir and strain into cocktail glass, garnish with a cherry."

As the drink progressed, grenadine seems to have been omitted from the pages, likely due to the nature of vermouth used at the time. However with it becoming more scare, a sweetening agent would be required:

LEON PUJOL AND OSCAR MUNIZ,
MANUAL DEL CANTINERO (1924):
"½ Bacardi Rum
½ Chambery
A little grenadine, or better, curacao.
Serve with Carbonated water, orange peel and a cherry."

Post prohibition, the American bartending industry needed to regain footing due to the 13-year dry spell. Bartenders went back to books and saw that the drink calls for French vermouth, they used the same stuff they used in Martinis.

RIBALAIGUA'S RECIPE, BAR LA FLORIDA (1934):
"½ Chambery Bermouth
½ Bacardi Gold
½ teaspoon of Curacao
Crushed Ice
Serve with cherris and a peel of orange."

It was Dave Wondrich who rescued the El Presidente from decades of obscurity by taking another look at the drink and the vermouth aspect. In 2012, he discovered that a semisweet blanc-style vermouth from the French town of Chambery – and not dry vermouth was required. This made the cocktail much more complex by adding a rich mouthfeel to the combination of rum and vermouth.

There is a question as to whether the classic 1:1 Ratio may be outdated in favour of a 2:1 ratio, however I believe the cocktail is best represented when the rum and vermouth are mixed in equal proportions rather than as a rum Manhattan.

HANKY PANKY

45ml Gin
45ml Sweet Vermouth
7.5ml Fernet Branca

METHOD
- Stirred and strained into a Nick and Nora
- Garnished with an orange peel

Ada Coleman's father had a professional relationship with the soon to become Chairman of the Savoy, Rupert D'Oyly Carte. He was the one to give Ada Coleman the position at the American Bar in 1903, where she would make the bar, and herself, a London landmark. The Hanky Panky cocktail is credited to Ada Coleman, head bartender at the American Bar at The Savoy Hotel until her retirement in 1924.

Ada Coleman would make cocktails for some of the most well-known and influential figures of the time period, but she created the Hanky Panky for actor Sir Charles Hawtrey who was a leading comedian and actor of the time. Coleman told the story behind the creation of the Hanky-Panky to England's *The People* newspaper in 1925:

> *"The late Charles Hawtrey ... was one of the best judges of cocktails that I knew. Some years ago, when he was overworking, he used to come into the bar and say, 'Coley, I am tired. Give me something with a bit of punch in it.' It was for him that I spent hours experimenting until I had invented a new cocktail. The next time he came in, I told him I had a new drink for him. He sipped it, and, draining the glass, he said, 'By Jove! That is the real Hanky Panky!'*

In 2010 there was a trend of adding 1.5ml of fresh pressed orange juice as the drink as it would uplift the heavy Fernet with slight-fruity notes. However it did make the drink cloudy and unsightly, so it didn't last long

NOTES
- The original version of the cocktail was shaken.

LONG ISLAND ICE TEA

15ml Vodka
15ml White Rum
15ml Gin
15ml Tequila
15ml Dry Curacao
10ml Lemon Juice
10ml Simple Syrup
Cola

METHOD
- Add all ingredients except Cola to tin
- Shaken with ice
- Pour Cola into bottom of a highball with ice
- Strain the contents over the back of a barspoon and layer on top of the Cola.

There are two competing stories for the creation of this drink. The most widely known is that the drink was created by Robert Rosebud Butt, in the early 1970s at the Oak Beach Inn, Long Island, New York.

The other story, with less proof, is that the drink was created in the 1920s by 'Old Man' Bishop, who passed his recipe on to his son Ransom Bishop. 'Old Man' Bishop was a bootlegger was operated during Prohibition and produced high-quality distillate in Long Island, Tennessee. The proportions weren't as streamlined as they are today and they were initially balanced out with maple syrup.

Ransom Bishop would modify the recipe with the addition of lemon, lime and cola.

Whatever the truth is, the recipes are almost identical, with Mr. Bishop preferring soda to cola and a drop of maple syrup. However this range of spirits who not have been easily available during Prohibition.

In 2019 both Tennessee and New York representatives met to discuss the legitimacy claim to the cocktail, and Tennessee was declared the victor in this matter. There's a fact for you the next time you're in New York ordering the 'Long Island Iced Tea'.

NOTES
- This cocktail without the Cola is called a 'Baptist's Redemption'.

LEAP YEAR COCKTAIL

50ml Gin
12.5ml Sweet Vermouth
12.5ml Grand Marnier
10ml Lemon Juice

METHOD
- Shaken and strained into a coupe
- Garnished with a lemon peel then discarded

Harry Craddock created this cocktail in celebration of the 1928 leap year and listed the recipe in his *The Savoy Cocktail Book* (1930).

Harry Craddock must have been a romantic, as this cocktail is highly requested on February 29th when it is a tradition that women can propose to men.

The Leap Year Cocktail is listed in the Savoy book as:

"One dash Lemon Juice
⅔ Gin
⅙ Grand Marnier
⅙ Italian Vermouth.

This cocktail was created by Harry Craddock, for the Leap Year celebrations at the Savoy Hotel, London, on February 29th, 1928. It is said to have been responsible for more proposals than any other cocktail that has ever been mixed."

A leap year is an occurrence once every four years (the next leap year whilst I write this book is 2024 falling on Thursday, February 29th). This additional day on these years aid to synchronise our human-created calendars with the Earth's orbit around the sun, and the actual passing of the seasons. Without them, February would be a summer month for the Northern Hemisphere.

MARY PICKFORD

50ml Bacardi Carta Blanca
30ml Pineapple juice
5ml Grenadine
5ml Lemon juice
5ml Simple Syrup
5ml Maraschino

METHOD
* Shaken and strained into a coupe

Created in the during Prohibition in the 1920s by Fred Kaufman at the Hotel Nacional de Cuba, for silent movie star, and wife of Douglas Fairbanks Sr., Mary Pickford.

Mary was filming a movie in Cuba with her husband and Charlie Chaplin, and this is recounted on page 40 of Basil Woon's book *When it's Cocktail Time in Cuba* (1928), in which the cocktail is listed with a note as:

*"Two-thirds pineapple juice, and one-third
Bacardi, with a dash of grenadine.*

*The Mary Pickford, invented during a visit to Havana
of the screen favourite by Fred Kaufman."*

This is the accepted story in the modern cocktail world, however the drink appears in an earlier text, *Manual del Cantinero* (1924) with Gordon's Gin in place of Bacardi:

*"1 cup Gordon's Gin
1 teaspoon pineapple juice
½ teaspoon maraschino
½ teaspoon grenadine"*

Maraschino was solidified as a staple later in Harry Craddock's *The Savoy Cocktail Book* (1930), and would remain that way.

NOTES
- Mary Pickford was actually from Toronto, but was known as 'America's Sweetheart'.

MONKEY GLAND

50ml Gin
30ml Orange Juice
7.5ml Grenadine
5ml Simple Syrup
Two dashes Absinthe
10ml Lemon Juice

METHOD
- Shaken and strained into a coupe
- Garnished with an orange peel

Fighting for increased tourism due to Prohibition has clouded the origin of this drink, and two men lay claim to its creation, Harry MacElhone and Frank Meier.

Created in the late 1920s by Harry MacElhone at his New York Bar, Paris and is first printed in *Harry's ABC of Mixing Cocktails* (1922) followed by another appearance in *Cocktails and Barflies* (1927) several years later. For a drink with such an interesting name, it must have had some success to have two successive printings.

Cocktails and Barflies lists it as:

"MONKEY GLAND COCKTAIL
one dash of Absinthe,
1 teaspoonful of Grenadine,
1/2 Orange Juice,
1/2 Gordon Gin.
Shake well, and strain into cocktail glass.

(Invented by the Author, and deriving its name from
Voronoff's experiments in rejuvenation.)"

The Monkey Gland takes its name from the work of Dr. Serge Voronoff in France, 1920 who convinced that testosterone was vital to a long and healthy life, transplanted monkey testicles onto an elderly Frenchman. Unsurprisingly he had few volunteers for such experiments, but the world got this drink from it.

Frank Meire of the Paris Ritz bar, also claims to have created the drink, and a 1923 *Washington Post* article backs this up as a *"special cable dispatch"* from Paris was sent to the Washington Post that read:

> *"Frank, the noted concoctor behind the bar of the Ritz, has devised a new series of powerful cocktail, favourite of which is known as the monkey gland"*

And continues to read to be served *"only with a doctor handy."*

The cocktail would go on to be printed in *The Savoy Cocktail Book* (1930) securing itself entirely in cocktail canon:

> *"3 dashes Absinthe.*
> *3 dashes Grenadine.*
> *⅓ Orange Juice.*
> *⅔ Dry Gin.*
> *Shake well and strain into cocktail glass."*

MIMOSA & BUCK'S FIZZ

Orange Juice
Champagne

METHOD
• Built in flute and given a gentle stir

The Buck's Fizz is said to have been created in 1921 by Pat McGarry, the first bartender at the Buck's Club (a members-only club) on Clifford Street in Mayfair, London. The theory was that this drink would discreetly allow members to drink before noon, without drawing any attention. While the Mimosa is said to have been created four years later by Frank Meier at the Ritz Hotel, Paris, and draws its name from a native Australian flower 'Acacia dealbata' commonly known as mimosa. However in his own book *The Artistry of Mixing Drinks* (1936) published 11 years later, he makes no claim to have created the drink. There is a small mark beside the drinks he claims to have made, and the Mimosa has no such mark.

Meier's recipe calls it a "Champagne Orange" and lists it as:

> *"In a large wineglass: a piece of ice, the juice of one-half Orange: fill with Champagne stir and serve."*

Both *The Savoy Cocktail Book* (1930) and Frank Meiers' book also include a cocktail called the 'Valencia' which is similar to both of these drinks but is shaken and has the addition of *"one-half glass of apricot brandy."*

The next notable mention of the Buck's Fizz is in W.J. Tarling's *Cafe Royale Cocktail Book* (1937) with the recipe, *"Pour into a tumbler, 2 tablespoons of orange juice, fill with champagne."* Tarling makes no mention of the Mimosa in this text.

However, across the board and various book appearances, the consensus is that the Buck's Fizz has a higher proportion of champagne (generally 2:1 is a good bet) than the Mimosa and is served straight up. While the Mimosa is typically served in a 1:1 ratio with ice. Although, nowadays it is likely when you ask for either of these cocktails they will come straight up.

The Buck's Fizz was a fizz made at the Buck's Club, and it lives in the fizz family of drinks, not the 'buck' family (the buck family of drinks being that given to cocktails with a spirit, citrus, and lengthened with ginger ale or ginger beer).

If you wanted to separate the drinks it could be done in several ways:

BUCK'S FIZZ generally has a 2:1 ratio of champagne to orange juice and came straight up.

THE MIMOSA has equal parts and was initially served in a wine glass with ice.

OLD PAL

25ml Rye
25ml Dry Vermouth
25ml Campari

METHOD
- Stirred and strained into a coupe
- Garnished with a lemon peel

Leading bartender to the lost generation was Harry MacElhone, born in Dundee in 1890, he traversed many a city with his equipment, most notably Paris, New York, and London before purchasing his own venue, Harry's New York Bar, Paris in 1923.

These drinks, at their time, would have been dubbed Campari-laced Manhattan riffs, something relatable to the American who has travelled to avoid Prohibition and quench one's thirst. But where did they come from and why are they named as such?

Two individuals, both regulars at Harry's New York Bar, came to be credited with these 'Negroni' twists.

The first was William Harrison 'Sparrow' Robertson. Official sports editor for the Paris office of the *New York Herald Tribune*. Sparrow is credited with the 'Old Pal', being rye, dry vermouth, and Campari, which was named as such as it was his way of addressing all manner of people.

Next is Edward Erskine Gwynne Jr. Grandnephew of railway baron Cornelius Vanderbilt II, and joint founder of the *Boulevardier* magazine.

Dave Wondrich has weighed in on the topic as to where the cocktail was first printed. Interestingly, Wondrich states that the main body of the *Barflies and Cocktails* book (1927) is an exact reprint of the current *Harry's ABC of Mixing Drinks* (1922). The 1927 book contain an additional section toward the book's end named "Cocktails around town" which was written by Arthur Moss, and recounts drinks from the bar's most notable guests at the time:

> *"Here's the drink I invented when I fired the pistol the first time at the old Powderhall foot races and you can't go wrong if you put a bet down on 1/3 Candian Club, 1/3 Eyetalian Vermouth and 1/3 Campari. And then he told the Writer that he would dedicate this cocktail to me and call It, My Old Pal."*

I read articles and tried searching for copies of earlier editions of *Harry's ABC of Mixing Drinks* (1922) and tried to get in touch with Isabelle MacElhone, current owner of Harry's Bar, to no avail. As per usual, Dave Wondrich was on hand to point me the right direction. Wondrich confirms it is not in either the 1919 or 1922 edition of *Harry's ABC of Mixing Cocktails*, the Old Pal makes a formal appearance in 1929, calling for dry vermouth, and not the originally listed Italian, or sweet, vermouth.

The cocktail also appears in *The Savoy Cocktail Book* (1930) and is the same as prior recipes. Campari was only beginning to enter British cocktail culture, and so this is the only mention of Campari within this book as not even the Negroni gets mentioned.

NOTES
- A Boulevardier is comprised of rye whiskey, sweet vermouth, Campari and orange bitters.
- The Boulevardier is listed with The Old Pal in the appendix/joke section of the *Barflies and Cocktails* book, accompanied by a written piece by journalist Arthur Moss.
- Canadian Club was the rye whiskey of choice as it was relatively cheap to use at the time.
- A friend of mine from a famed Parisian bar swears by a recipe of 45ml whiskey, 15ml Campari, 15ml dry vermouth – I do love some competition.

OLYMPIC

30ml Cognac
25ml Grand Marnier
25ml Orange Juice
Two dashes Orange Bitters

METHOD
- Shaken and strained into a coupe
- Garnished with an orange peel

Created at Ciro's of London around 1922 and draws its name from the *Olympic* ocean-liner, sister to the *Titanic*.

The *Olympic* was also a sister, but to a cocktail, and that cocktail was the 'Sidecar'. However, much like the ocean-liner the cocktail was pushed into the background and only one would be remembered.

Interestingly, this cocktail does not appear in *Harry's ABC of Mixing Drinks* (1923) and later goes on to be listed in *The Savoy Cocktail Book* (1930) with no reference to exactly who created it.

POET'S DREAM

50ml Gin
20ml Dry Vermouth
7.5ml Benedictine
Two dashes Orange Bitters

Originally listed in *The Old Waldorf-Astoria Bar Book* (1935) by A.S. Crockett as:

"One-third Benedictine
One-third French Vermouth
One-third dry Gin
Lemon Peel squeezed on top"

So, similar to a more modern recipe, just omitting orange bitters from the mix. This recipe looks almost like a 'white' bijou cocktail, in which it would most likely be on the sweet side rather than balanced.

Interestingly, this cocktail closely resembles the make-up of the 'Ford Cocktail' which uses Old Tom gin in G.J. Kappeler's *Modern American Drinks* (1895).

A cocktail we would see as a modern-day variant appears two years later in *The Café Royale Cocktail Book* (1937) by W. J. Tarling reading more as Martini-style cocktail:

"⅓ French Vermouth
⅔ Gin
two dashes Orange Bitters
two dashes Benedictine
Stir."

NOTES

- During my research I uncovered a poem by Percy Bysshe Shelley that shares the same name as this drink, however it is from 1875, a good 50 years before this appears in industry text.
- Swapping out the Benedictine for yellow Chartreuse changes this cocktail into one called a 'Puritan'.

QUEEN'S PARK SWIZZLE

60ml Demerara Rum
25ml Lime Juice
20ml Simple Syrup
Eight Mint Leaves
Five dashes Angostura Bitters
Splash of soda water

METHOD

- Muddle rum, mint, lime juice, sugar and a scoop of crushed ice.
- Add more crushed ice and swizzle until the glass gets a light frost.
- Add crushed ice, add straw and layer the Angostura Bitters on top.
- Cap off with crushed ice.
- Garnish with large mint bouquet.

Swizzles are made using wooden sticks that are created from the Bois lélé

tree in the Caribbean. A highly desirable variant is dubbed the 'swizzle-stick tree' or *Quararibea turbinate*, originating from Martinique.

To swizzle a cocktail is to take the swizzle stick between the palm of your hands and place it at the bottom of your glass (generally this will be a crushed iced drink), then you rub your hands together to agitate the ice and bring together your ingredients, adding dilution in the process.

This is the signature cocktail of the Queen's Park Hotel in Trinidad, and was created at the grand hotel in the 1920s.

The Queen's Park Hotel was built in 1893 and by 1895 it had electricity as well as other well-to-amenities, making it a prime spot for well-off holiday makers to eat and drink their trip away.

The cocktail's popularity had been so widespread that Trader Vic even stated in his *Book of Food and Drink* (1946):

"The most delightful form of anaesthesia given out today."

Unfortunately the hotel has been closed for some time now, however the cocktail endures. In 2017, the House of Angostura has been attempting to make the Queen's Park Swizzle the national drink of Trinidad and Tobago, and seeing as the drink of course features Trinidad's most famous concoction angostura bitters, I say continue the push.

NOTES
- A variation on this cocktail is called the 'Maloney Park Swizzle' in which angostura bitters are swapped out for Peychaud's.
- Switching out the rum for gin and you get a Hayes Park Swizzle.

QUILL

30ml Gin
25ml Campari
25ml Sweet Vermouth
Two dashes Absinthe

METHOD
- Stirred and strained into a rocks glass over block ice.
- Garnished with an orange peel.

What is essentially a herbaceous cousin to the Negroni, the Quill is the lesser known of the two (perhaps because people don't want to sully their Negroni).

The name of this cocktail stems from a man named Frank C. Payne, a theatrical press agent in the early 1900s. Payne was the founder of

the 'Theatrical Press Agents of America' for whom he published *The Quill* magazine to promote the agenda of the organisation.

McElhone was known to dedicate drinks to favoured patrons, however whether Payne encouraged this drink's creation or Harry was feeling generous enough to name this after him is unknown. This cocktail doesn't appear in *Barflies and Cocktails* (1927) or *Harry's ABC of Mixing Drinks* (1930), yet it does make an appearance in much later editions of *Harry's ABC of Mixing Drinks*, notably in the 1996 printing.

REMEMBER THE MAINE

50ml Rye Whiskey
20ml Sweet Vermouth
7.5ml Cherry Heering
Three dashes Absinthe
Two dashes Angostura Bitters

METHOD
- Stirred and strained into a coupe
- Garnished with a lemon peel then discarded

The name of the drink refers to the sinking of the U.S.S *Maine*, an American Battleship, off the coast of Cuba in 1898. This led to the Spanish-American war, and in turn, Cuban Independence.

There was a rallying chant amongst the people was then picked up by newspapers that truly inspired this cocktail's name:

"Remember the Maine, to hell with Spain!"

First appearing in Charles. H. Baker's *The Gentleman's Companion, Around the world with Jigger, beaker and Flask* (1939) as:

"1 jigger of good rye whiskey, ½ jigger Italian vermouth, 1 to 2 tsp of cherry brandy, ½tsp absinthe or Pernod Vertias."

Charles Baker was a respected writer who worked with such magazines as *Gourmet*, and *Esquire*, before writing his own book. He was a real advocate for detail, in fact, in the case of the 'Remember the Maine', a drink he sampled during the 1933 uprising in Havana, he instructed that it must be stirred *"briskly in a clockwise fashion."*

According to his book, when he sipped this drink:

> *"Each swallow was punctuated with bombs going off on the Prado,*
> *or the sound of 3-inch shells being fired at the Hotel Nacionale."*

Not one to shy away from adventure in the name of drinking it seems.

ROSE

45ml Noilly Pratt
25ml Kirsch
5ml Cherry Heering
5ml Raspberry syrup

METHOD
• Stirred and strained into a coupe
• Garnished with a lemon peel

Kirsch is a colourless brandy traditionally made from double distillation of morello cherries.

According to Harry MacElhone, owner of Harry's New York Bar in Paris, and Frank Meier, head bartender at the Ritz Hotel, the Rose was Giovanni "Johnny" Mitta's invention and was created in 1920 by him at the Chatham Hotel, Paris.

Robert Vermière would confirm this in 1938 as he wrote:

> *"This cocktail has a truly exceptional particularity, in*
> *that it is never made the same way anywhere."*

The details of Mitta's career are unusually sparse, considering that he was a sort of celebrity in Paris. He was at the helm of the Chatham between 1893, and 1898 (when he was thanked for a tip on a horse).

The cocktail first appeared in a Parisian newspaper, *Le Figaro* in 1910, however Mitta had been bartending in Paris since 1890 so it is likely this cocktail was known by the time of printing. Later, he was linked to the

Rose in 1912 when the Paris correspondent for the *Sporting Times of London* found it remarkable that the author Maurice Maeterlinck could pop into the Chatham without having Johnny be there and get one.

The drink began to suffer as cheap gin started to become popularised and some would try and replace the kirschwasser completely in the cocktail. The recipe started to become recast as a spirit-forward bracer, whilst others would cheapen it and use as little as they could. According to Vermiere, the originally component that gave the drink its red hue was *sirop de groseille*, a French redcurrant syrup, with some early adaptations using cherry brandy also. Later on, it is either all cherry brandy or some mix of cassis and grenadine, which lessened the quality of the drink even more.

Sadly the Rose started to become an outdated Martini and as such, was thrown to the wayside.

It is unclear when Johnny left the Chatham or, why he did, but the last time he can be placed there is in 1916. Perhaps he was still there in 1922, when MacElhone included the Rose in his *ABC of Mixing Cocktails*, published just before he came from London to take over the New York Bar.

NOTES
- Be careful using kirschwasser in this drink, it can overpower anything it is in, much like maraschino-flavours.
- Noilly Pratt is a great vermouth choice here as it is light and subtle.
- *Sirop de Groseille* is a tough find, so a homemade raspberry syrup works well here, although an additional splash of cherry brandy is not a bad addition.

ROYAL BERMUDA YACHT CLUB

50ml Barbados Rum
10ml Triple Sec
10ml Velvet Falernum
20ml Lime Juice

METHOD
- Shaken and strained into a coupe
- A spiced and richer variation of a classic daiquiri.

This cocktail is named after, well, the Royal Bermuda Yacht Club, which at the time was a private British yachting club dating back to 1844. The club, and subsequently the cocktail, only got the prefix 'Royal' after the Prince of Wales, Prince Albert, decided to become a patron of the Bermuda Yacht Club. If a cocktail deserves the royal treatment, so do you.

The club played host to a series of highly-competitive races in Bermuda over the course of the century, and eventually settled in the capital city of Hamilton in 1933, soon developing into a permanent residential community.

This cocktail first appears in Crosby Gaige's *Cocktail Guide and Ladies' Companion* (1941) witty read that puts drinks across in an entertaining manner. He lists it as:

"3 parts Barbados rum and 1 part lime juice."

The rest of the cocktail is without much regard, simply stating ½ parts of both falernum or sugar, and Cointreau or brandy.

Trader Vic, whom popularised a more contemporary take on this cocktail in his *Bartender's Guide* (1947) which would often lead to misinformation about him being the original creator, but this is not the case.

The interesting part is why is there Barbados rum in a cocktail named after an establishment in Bermuda. A simple theory, is that the bartender themselves may have been from Barbados, and so better acquainted with that style of rum.

ROYAL SMILE

30ml Gin
20ml Applejack
20ml Lime Juice
10ml Simple Syrup
5ml Grenadine

METHOD
• Shaken and strained into a coupe

First printed in *Jack's Manual* (1933), and in further editions of his book, the Royal Smile is in essence, an egg white-less 'Pink Lady' cocktail. Jack lists his cocktail as:

"1 tablespoonful of grenadine
50% dry gin
50% applejack
Juice of one lemon"

By adding an egg white, you have a spirit-forward riff on a Clover Club.

Two more texts several years after this printing would edit the proportions of the Royal Smile, and thus this must have been a fairly popular tipple of its time.

The Waldorf- Astoria Bar Book (1935) by Albert S. Crockett interestingly amends the cocktail to be equal parts as:

"One-fourth Gordon Gin
One-fourth Applejack
One-fourth Grenadine
One-fourth Lemon Juice"

This seems a little odd as it is very different from the original printing, and the equal measures of grenadine lend to be particularly sweet. Finally, the 'Royal Smile' cocktail appears in W.J. Tarling's *Café Royal Cocktail Book* (1937) in which he doesn't credit the drink's creator, unlike many other cocktails in his book (likely because it is unknown):

"Two dashes Grenadine.
three dashes Lemon Juice.
⅓ Calvados.
⅔ Dry Gin."

There is an apparent debate as to whether it is correct to use Calvados or Applejack in this cocktail. Seeing as this drink rarely sees the light of day, I'm not exactly sure who is debating it. For flavour purposes, and historical accuracy, Applejack gets my support.

NOTES
- The U.K.B.G (1937) book lists a recipe identical to that of Tarling's, using Calvados in place of Applejack.

RATTLESNAKE

50ml Rittenhouse Rye
20ml Lemon Juice
20ml Simple Syrup
20ml Egg White
Three dashes Absinthe

METHOD
- Wet and dry shake, then strained into a coupe
- Angostura Bitters dropped on top of finished drink

A rye-based whiskey sour with dashes of absinthe, it is truly that simple. I remember in my early bartending days I could never remember what was in this cocktail. I always had my friend Jack Turner to remind me however, and this one cocktail is dedicated to him.

This cocktail first appears from *The Savoy Cocktail Book* (1930) but more recently made famous by Maison Premier, Brooklyn. The glassware for this cocktail is extremely important and it needs to be one that heightens the smell of the absinthe. Harry Craddock, he lists it as a cocktail for six people:

"4 Glasses Rye Whisky.
The Whites of 2 Eggs.
1 Glass Sweetened Lemon Juice.
A few dashes Absinthe."

Craddock leaves with it a note so to speak, perhaps a warning:

"So called because it will either cure Rattlesnake bite,
or kill Rattlesnakes, or make you see them."

Rye whiskey was most likely used for the same reason it was used in cocktails in this book, it was a cheaper product at the time (and likely played well with the herbaceous absinthe).

SIX CYLINDER

12.5ml Tanqueray
12.5ml Cherry Heering
12.5ml Dubonnet
12.5ml Dry Vermouth
12.5ml Sweet vermouth
12.5ml Campari

METHOD
- Stirred and strained into a coupe
- Garnished with a lemon peel

A cocktail that looks like it shouldn't work on paper due to the sheer variety of components involved.

The cocktail comes from a gentle man named Raymond Latour, he won the 1928 Paris Cocktail Championship on December 2nd with a drink made of the same ingredients and dubbed it the 'Six Cylinder'.

SINGAPORE SLING

40ml Gin
10ml Dry Curacao
10ml Cherry Herring
10ml Benedictine
40ml Pineapple Juice
20ml Lemon Juice
One dash Angostura Bitters
Soda top

METHOD
- Sling glass
- Shaken and strained into a large highball
- Garnished with a lemon wedge and cherry

A cocktail whose tale has been told many times over, but some details have been misplaced.

The story we all know and love is that the cocktail was created by Ngiam Tong Boon at Raffles Hotel in Singapore, 1915 (the hotel was named after the Coloanal founder of Singapore – Sir Stamford Raffles). I doubt many disagree with this fact, however the exact timing when the cocktail was created may be amiss.

Boon unfortunately passed away when he left the hotel to return to his hometown in China in 1915. This is where the timeline is foggy, you see there were cocktails similar to that of the Singapore Sling being consumed in the colony for many years prior to its creation. Many believe that Boon simply adapted this recipe to his own tastes to give the hotel bar its signature serve.

At this point Singapore was part of the 'Straits Settlements' – a group of four British trade centres in Southeast Asia including Penang, Singapore, Malacca and Dinding. In these regions there were popular cocktails called slings and this is listed in many book appearances, firstly Robert Vermeire's *Cocktails and How to Make Them* (1922):

"STRAITS SLING

½ gill of Gin, ⅛ gill of Benedictine, ⅛ gill of Dry Cherry Brandy, The juice of half a lemon, two dashes of Angostura bitters, two dashes of Orange bitters. Shaken... topped with soda.

A well-known Singapore drink."

This is a much more simplistic recipe than the Singapore Sling we know today, but is similar to the popular versions being consumed at the end of the nineteenth century. Dave Wondrich found an article from 1903 referencing the drink with the statement "pink slings for pale people" – perhaps this was Boon's original version being discussed before he tailored it for the hotel in later years.

Noting the "dry cherry brandy" is important, most would assume that this would mean kirschwasser rather than a red liqueur like Cherry Heering. However, the only cherry brandy that appear in local advertisements are red Bols cherry brandy or Cherry Heering (Bols did have a dry version of their flagship cherry brandy, which was the standard version blended with Cognac). To summarise, the cocktail was always red.

Vermeire's book isn't the only time this cocktail makes an appearance, not even close. Several texts list the cocktail, and all under different names. Harry Craddock's *The Savoy Cocktail Book* (1930) lists both a Singapore and Straits Sling:

"SINGAPORE SLING
The Juice of ¼ Lemon. ¼ Dry Gin. ½ Cherry Brandy.
Fill with soda water."

Craddock's sling is more simplified than his 'Straits Sling', which is identical to Vermeire's recipe.

The cocktail was so popular that it even found its way to Havana, Cuba, notably Sloppy Joes Bar and Restaurant. Their *Cocktails Manual Season 32/33* (1932) lists a similar cocktail but has the addition of Benedictine (which was optional at the time). And lists it as:

"1 Peel of a Lemon.
⅓ of Cherry Brandy.
⅓ of Benedictine.
⅓ of Gordon Gin."

As part of Charles H. Baker's travels, he crossed through these colonies and stopped at Raffles Hotel, in the Long Bar. He writes of this experience in his *The Gentleman's Companion* (1939) where he notes "the Raffles drink is the best" and calls it:

"SINGAPORE GIN SLING
The original formula is 1/3 each of dry gin, cherry brandy
and Benedictine... fill up to individual taste with chilled
club soda. Garnish with the spiral peel of 1 green lime."

He speaks of other parts of Asia where the drink is filled with ginger ale or ginger beer in place of soda water, which would make for an interesting cocktail if nothing else.

Finally, David Embury talks of the Singapore Sling in his *The Fine Art of Mixing Drinks* (1948) as a gin sling with cherry brandy and the optional inclusion of Benedictine. Embury notes that he has never seen two recipes for this cocktail that are the same, and to be fair I can attest to this.

Sadly, no record of Boon's original recipe exists as it was lost throughout time and the hotel was occupied by Japanese in 1942 and then Allied Forces used it as a camp for prisoners of war in 1945. The recipe was rumoured to be written on a bar napkin for a guest who requested it in 1936, however whether there is truth in this or not is another question.

Each of these cocktails look similar to the Singapore Sling we know today, however there is certainly a tiki-twist to the modern recipe. There is scepticism surrounding this as when the hotel was being relaunched in the 1970s there was a huge marketing campaign involving the cocktail. Roberto Pregarz took over as general manager of the hotel and launched the hotel's new recipe that included pineapple juice and grenadine, leading people to believe he was jumping on the hype of tiki, which was incredibly popular at the time:

"RAFFLES ORIGINAL SINGAPORE SLING RECIPE (1970S)
30ml Gin
15ml Cherry Heering
7.5ml Cointreau
7.5ml Benedictine
15ml Lime juice
120ml Pineapple juice
10ml Grenadine
One dash Angostura bitters."

There is a popular tale that states Boon created the cocktail to allow for women to consume alcohol in public, as this wasn't socially accepted at the time due to English custom. He guised it as juice, giving those guests the same social pleasure as men. David Wondrich found references to this story in several newspapers dating back to 1897 and found this to be just that, a story.

NOTES
• Most Singapore and Strait Sling recipes used Benedictine liqueur, this is in reference to Benedictine D.O.M not Benedictine and Brandy (B and B) which was not launched until 1938.
• Pineapples grown in Singapore so it is possible that the addition of pineapple juice was used to bolster profits for the hotel.
• A soda called Holy Joe's Singapore sling was being sold in the America around 1936.

SIDECAR

40ml Cognac
25ml Lemon Juice
15ml Cointreau
5ml Simple Syrup

METHOD
• Shaken and strained into a sugar rimmed coupe

If your glass is chilled your sugar will stick naturally, if not then use a lemon wedge around half the rim of glass.

The 'Sidecar' is the successor of the 'Brandy Crusta', a classic cognac cocktail, one which David Embury says is one of the 'Six Basic Cocktails' in his *The Fine Art of Mixing Drinks* (1948). This book is most certainly worth the read if you wish to know more.

Like many cocktails the history is multiple, and the origins are highly disputed. Successive bartenders took it and made it their own, playing with balance, ingredients and presentations. One thing that is not disputed is that it first appears in print in 1922, by both Harry MacElhone and Robert Virmiere. They both say that it was created by a man called Pat McGarry at the Buck's Club in London.

Embury states that the cocktail was created at Harry's Bar, Paris by a friend of his, as it was requested by an army captain who rode up to the bar in a sidecar of a motorcycle. The cocktail was popular in London at the time however it is likely to have spread quickly, and by the end of World War I the two Paris-based bartenders laid claim to the cocktail.

Dale DeGroff suggests in his *The Essential Cocktail* (2008) that the name stems from a different origin:

> *"The word sidecar means something totally different in the world of cocktail: if the bartender misses the mark on ingredient quantities so when he strains the drink into the serving glass there's a bit left over in the shaker, he pours out that little extra into a shot glass on the side – that little glass is called a sidecar."*

I imagine the truth behind this is similar to not using terminology alluding to saying that you made a mistake in front of guests, and so dressing up the name.

The drink evolved, being a Prohibition favourite and never really wavering in popularity. The brandy eventually disappeared and was replaced with Cognac. The Sidecar started to establish itself as a cocktail of some repute, and the components improved. Curacao was hard to find. It was made from oils pressed out of the peels of biter, inedible oranges from the isle of curacao, owned by Spain. It was subbed for the emerging Cointreau, an orange liqueur with much better pedigree.

There are two schools of thought regarding the Sidecar – the French and the English.

The French school consists of the cocktail being made of equal parts of the ingredients as suggested by MacElhone and Vermiere, and the English school follows Harry Craddock's 2:1:1 ratio (built like a traditional sour). I would say modern palates have changed drastically and so I have provided a suitable recipe.

NOTES
- Add a dash of angostura bitters to get yourself a Chevalier cocktail.
- Swap Cognac for Scotch whiskey and you have the Prosperity cocktail.
- A Commando cocktail is a bourbon Sidecar with a dash of absinthe.
- A gin-based Sidecar is known as a Chelsea Sidecar, and adding a dash of angostura bitters gives you a Fine and Dandy.
- Add a dash of absinthe to a Chelsea Sidecar and it morphs into a Queen Elizabeth.

SCOFFLAW

45ml Rye Whiskey
20ml Dry Vermouth
20ml Lemon Juice
10ml Grenadine
Two dash Orange Bitters

METHOD
- Shaken and strained into a coupe

The cocktail first appears in Harry MacElhone's *Barflies and Cocktails* (1927) and was created by a bartender he trained named Jock.

In 1924, during the height of Prohibition, a competition was run to coin a term that would demonise the act of acting and those who would partake in such an act. *The Boston Herald* wanted a word to fit the description put forward to them:

"A lawless drink of illegally made or obtained liquor."

The competition was put forward, and funded, by Delcevare King who was a champion of unpopular cause such as the 18th Amendment.

Out of the 25,000 entries submitted for the competition 'Scofflaw' was selected on January 15th 1924 and the prize was split between two people -Kate Butler and Henry Irving – who received the prize of $200 in gold, not cash.

The word caught on and was so popular that a cocktail, created at Harry's New York Bar, Paris, was created shortly after the competition ended. Much to Mr. King's dismay, he may have encouraged the act that he was trying to prevent.

SILVER BULLET

45ml Tanqueray
20ml Kummel
20ml Lemon juice

METHOD
* Shaken and strained into a coupe
* Garnished with a lemon peel then discarded

A cocktail with a cult following, the definition of you either like it or you don't drinks.

Originating in the 1920s, this cocktail first appears in *The Savoy Cocktail Book* (1930) by Harry Craddock. It includes Kummel liqueur, made of such potent flavours as cumin, caraway seed and fennel.

Traditional serving of this cocktail calls for a coupe however if you are trying it for the first time or want to dilute the flavours further, try serving it as an old fashioned.

SATAN'S WHISKERS

25ml Gin
15ml Dry Vermouth
10ml Grand Marnier
10ml Sweet Vermouth
25ml Orange Juice
10ml Lemon Juice
10ml Simple Syrup
One dash Orange Bitters

METHOD
* Shaken and strained into a coupe
* Garnished with an orange peel

There is no indication as to where the name stems from, however it makes for a great name as can be seen from the East London neighbourhood bar of the same name.

One of the most complicated cocktails to balance with the inclusion of orange juice, the Satan's Whiskers is a close relative of the *'Bronx'* cocktail with the addition of Grand Marnier.

The cocktail first appears in Harry Craddock's *The Savoy Cocktail Book* (1930) with both a 'straight' and a 'curled' variation:

"SATAN'S WHISKERS COCKTAIL (STRAIGHT)
Of Italian Vermouth, French Vermouth, Gin
and Orange Juice, two parts of each: of Grand
Marnier one part: Orange Bitters, a dash.

SATAN'S WHISKERS COCKTAIL (CURLED)
For the Grand Marnier in the foregoing Cocktail,
substitute the same quantity of Orange Curacao."

There is a rumour that the curled version be consumed before dark, and the straight cocktail after hours. Although the real reason is likely that Craddock was working within particular price points.

TORONTO (BEWARE UNDER-DILUTION OF THIS DRINK)

50ml Rittenhouse Rye
10ml Fernet Branca
10ml Simple Syrup
Two dashes Angostura Bitters

METHOD

- Stirred and strained into a coupe
- Garnished with an orange peel

The first appearance of this cocktail is in Robert Vermeire's *Cocktails and How to Mix Them* (1922) and appears under the name 'Fernet Cocktail':

> *"One dash of Angostura Bittters.*
> *two dashes of plain Sugar or Gum Syrup.*
> *¼ gill of Fernet Branca.*
> *¼ gill of Cognac Brandy, or Rye Whiskey to taste.*
>
> *Stir up well with a spoon, strain into a cocktail-glass, and squeeze lemon-peel on top.*
> *This cocktail is much appreciated by the Canadians of Toronto."*

I'm not entirely sure on the final sentiment that Vermeire leaves the reader with, but it is most certainly classic by modern standards.

Later the cocktail would be published by its correct name in David Embury's *Fine Art of Mixing Drinks* (1948). Embury's version reads as:

> *"A modified Old-Fashioned is made with Fernet-Branca, a bitters particularly well-loved by Italians, and is called*
>
> TORONTO
> *1 part Sugar Syrup*
> *2 parts Fernet-Branca*
> *6 parts Canadian Whiskey*
> *one dash Angostura to each drink (optional)*
> *decorate with a twist of orange peel."*

There is quite a large gap (26 years) between both of these printings and there is no definitive answer as to if it was created in Canada, as there could have been plenty of time for the drink to spread. During the 1910s to 1930s there was a large influx of Italians into Toronto, who eventually headed south to New York City.

NOTES
- Fernet Branca was actually being made in New York City from the early 1930s, and being distributed by L. Gandolfi and Co.
- This classic was brought back to the spotlight by Jamie Boudreau in his Seattle bar, Canon.

VIEUX CARRÉ

30ml Rye
20ml Cognac
20ml Sweet vermouth
7.5ml Benedictine
Two dashes Angostura Bitters
One dash Peychaud's Bitters

METHOD
- Stirred and strained into a rocks glass over block of ice.
- Garnished with a cherry and lemon peel.

The drink was coined by Walter Bergeron, the head bartender at the Monteleone Hotel, New Orleans during the 1930s. The hotel was happily nestled in French Quarter on Royal Street and still belongs to the Monteleone's family five-generations in since they purchased it in 1886.

The recipe is first published in *Famous New Orleans Drinks and How to Mix 'Em* (1937) by Stanley Clisby Arthur, but other sources claim the drink wasn't invented until the end of 1938. Clisby lists it as:

"½ teaspoon Benedictine
one dash Peychaud bitter
one dash Angostura bitters
⅓ jigger rye whiskey
⅓ jigger cognac brandy
⅓ jigger Italian vermouth."

Now, the name translates as 'Old Square' or 'Old Quarter', referencing the original name for the New Orleans French Quarter. Even though the name takes from French inspiration, the pronunciation is not: it is pronounced 'Voo Car-ray'.

The hotel boasts a grand and unique bar design, as in 1949 the Carousel Bar and Lounge has had an actual revolving carousel in which guests can sit and watch the world go by, whilst sipping delicious beverages.

NOTES
- The carousel makes a full rotation once every 15 minutes.
- Some will state that the drink is actual equal parts, aside from the Benedictine and bitters, however that yields an unbalanced cocktail in the end.

WHITE LADY

50ml Gin
20ml Triple sec
25ml Lemon Juice
5ml Simple Syrup
20ml Egg white

METHOD
- Wet and dry shaken and strained into a coupe
- Garnished with a lemon peel then discarded

Many triple secs got much drier post 2000

Another famous cocktail with two conflicting tales, however both involve characters called Harry.

The famed Harry Craddock is said to have concocted this cocktail whilst working at The Savoy Hotel, rumour is that F. Scott. Fitzgerald's wife, Zelda, was at the bar and Craddock named it for her and her appearance that evening.

This story behind the name may not hold true, but the cocktail certainly does appear in Craddock's *The Savoy Cocktail Book* (1930) as:

"¼ Lemon Juice.
¼ Cointreau.
½ Dry Gin."

Much like the 'White Lady' we all know today, excluding egg white and sugar. The White Lady is still synonymous with Craddock, and the Savoy, to this day, and when the bar underwent reconstruction in 1927 he actually placed his personal three-piece shaker containing the ingredients for the cocktail within the very walls of the bar.

Harry MacElhone, legendary bartender of the time, first created a cocktail called the White Lady whilst working at Ciro's club, London in 1919, however this cocktail is not like the White Lady we would expect if we ordered one today. It consisted of equal measures of white crème de menthe, Cointreau and lemon juice. In his *ABC of Mixing Cocktails* (1922) MacElhone does omit lemon juice for brandy, moving in a different direction but still not what we see as the cocktail today.

Later, when he purchased Harry's New York Bar in Paris (1923) and released the 1930 edition of his book, the recipe still read as brandy, crème de menthe and Cointreau, but reports say that he was serving the traditional White Lady of gin, Cointreau and lemon juice.

NOTES
- Early adaptions of the cocktail, and both of these bartender's own texts, make no mention of the use of egg white in their cocktails.
- It was Peter Dorelli, former bar manager of the American Bar who suggested a dash of egg white to bind and soften the cocktail. A man of true elegance.

XERES

90ml Fino Sherry
Two dashes Orange Bitters
Two dashes Peach Bitters

METHOD
- Stirred and strained into a coupe.
- Garnished with an orange peel then discard

Jerez-Xeres-Sherry is one of Spain's most historic wine regions. This region has been mentioned in writings from as early as 1100 BC as a wine producing area, but it did not start seeing commercial success until the latter half of the 14th century when it started exporting to the UK.

The English began naming it 'Sherris Sack'. 'Sack' was a generic term for fortified wines from different origins, and *Sherris* was the Arabic name for the city of Jerez (later becoming Sherry).

The Xeres cocktail was first printed in *The Savoy Cocktail Book* (1930) paying tribute to the wine and produce that came from the area, only enhancing the sherry with two different types of bitters. The drink would later resurface in *A Spot at the Bar* (2016) from the acclaimed team at The Eveleigh.

NOTES
- Since 1933, Jerez-Xeres-Sherry is an official Denominacion de Origen (D.O) and was the first of its kind in Spain.

XYZ

40ml Aged Rum
25ml Cointreau
15ml Lemon Juice
5ml Simple Syrup

METHOD
* Shaken and strained into a coupe
* Garnished with lemon peel.

Built in the same structure as a sour, and a riff on a 'Sidecar' using rum in place of brandy.

First appearing in *The Savoy Cocktail Book* (1930) by Harry Craddock, the original recipe called for *Bacardi Rum,* typically meaning white rum. However modern recipes have started using aged rum to manipulate flavour.

I have added a touch of sugar syrup to balance the cocktail as it comes across as tart if sticking to the Savoy's printed recipe.

POST-PROHIBITION
AND
THE TIKI
MOVEMENT
(1935 –1970)

When Prohibition ended in 1933, the cocktail movement sprang back to life and moved forward like never before. Advancements in entertainment and a distribution of wealth allowed cocktails to be more well-known than ever, films would show cocktails on screen and novels like James Bond would highlight drinks as a sign of sophistication. In a world shrouded with a cloud after the Great Depression and World War One, nightlife entertainment became coupled with a better life on the horizon.

However it wasn't all as positive as it seems, some of the lingering impacts of Prohibition laws saw a degradation of service and drinks meaning that many of the less grand venues struggled to recoup from the previous decade of the nation being dry. Many would agree that this fact, paired with the mass exodus of bartending talent from the United States during Prohibition, led to the American bar scene not fully recovering.

The American public began to a have a love affair with South Islands of the Pacific during the 1920s as it was an escape from Prohibition. This escapism and idealism of drinking and adventure led to the rise of tiki culture throughout the United States. The two men who spearheaded this movement were Ernest Raymond Beaumont Gantt, aka Donn the Beachcomber, and Victor 'Trader Vic' Bergeron. What this meant is that they translated a Polynesian way of life to the United States and made it extremely popular with the people. Tiki venues peaked in the 1950s and 60s, a time when escapism from constant bad world news would ever-increasing and this would bring with it the creation of the Zombie, Mai-Tai and many other rum-fuelled tropical concoctions.

This movement of tiki would spawn one of the greatest rivalries of hospitality, the one between Trader Vic and Don Beachcomber. There were many recipes kept secret from one another, employees couldn't go and work for the other's company and most well-known, the debate as to who created the original Mai-Tai cocktail.

Even during the rise of rum and tiki, vodka would undergo its own rise to fame from the shadow of obscurity. This is due mainly the spirit itself as Americans discovered that it mixed with almost anything, lacked that particular heavy alcohol smell and it looked clean and pure. Due to this a plethora of cocktails came to the forefront of the public's mind once created, namely the Screwdriver, Moscow Mule and Vodka Martini.

3 DOTS AND A DASH

40ml Rhum Agricole
20ml Blended Aged Rum
10ml Allspice Dram
12.5ml Velvet Falernum
15ml Honey Syrup
20ml Lime Juice
15ml Orange juice

METHOD
- Blended with a small amount of crushed ice
- Poured into a highball
- Three cherries and a pineapple leaf – representing the Morse code three dots and a dash

Named after the Morse code for 'Victory', three dots and a dash was created during WW2 by Donn the Beachcomber.

This recipe was discovered by Jeff 'Beachbum' Berry and retold in his book *Sippin' Safari* (2007).

TWENTIETH CENTURY

35ml Gin
20ml Crème de Cacao Blanc
15ml Lillet Blanc
15ml Lemon Juice
5ml Simple Syrup

METHOD
- Shaken and strained into a coupe
- Garnished with a lemon peel

First appearing in W.J. Tarling's *Café Royal Cocktail Book* (1937) as:

"⅖ Booth's Dry Gin.
⅕ Crème de Cacao.
⅕ Lillet.
⅕ Lemon Juice."

Created by British bartender C. A. Tuck in the 1930s as a celebration of the twentieth century limited railway company that ran from Chicago to New York, only taking 16 hours. The railway operated from 1902 until 1967 and was one of the most famous and luxurious railway lines in the world. Luxurious art deco, and complete with a red carpet that was rolled out at the station for guests to disembark. In fact, the term 'red carpet treatment' actually comes from the practise used by the train company.

Tuck was head bartender at London's Piccadilly Hotel for almost two decades and actually release his own book in 1967 – *Cocktails and Mixed Drinks*.

NOTES
• This drinks needs to be made perfectly every time or else it is rather sub-par.

AIR MAIL

40ml Aged Rum
15ml Lime Juice
15ml Honey Syrup
Prosecco top

METHOD
• Shaken and strained into a highball over ice
• Lime wedge and orange peel discard

People think it was originally served in a flute, but it was actually a highball.

The Air Mail (two words) most noticeably appears in W. C. Whitfield's 1941 wooden covered book *Here's How* accompanied by the note:

"It ought to make you fly high."

The history of the 'Air Mail' has been rewritten over the past several years.

In 2007, Dave Wondrich – one of the world's premier cocktail historians – wrote that this was published in the *Esquire Handbook for Hosts* (1949). He also *"it'll get you from Point A to Point B in a hurry."*

He added a few notes in regards to the clever name, which referenced the airmail system that was popular and futuristic at the time.

Fast forward to 2015, when Douglas Ford wrote a piece on the drink, claiming it actually came from a 1930s Bacardi promotional pamphlet in Cuba. He added the date and time rationally explain the cocktail's name, since Cuba had just added an airmail system in 1930. Until then it was considered a 50s drink from the U.S.

After searching high and low, through vintage cocktail books and online it was ultimately a friend that directed me to a 2011 interview with Cocktail Kingdom founder and avid Cuban pamphlet hoarder, Greg Boehm.

*"The Air mail (2 words) cocktail is originally from a
Bacardi Booklet. With the Air Mail a lot of people are like
'Oh it came from here, it came from there,' but by fat
the oldest I've gotten it back is in a Bacardi booklet.*

Now I've never come across any literature from the liquor companies saying outright, 'we created this' or claiming direct authorship of these cocktails, but certainly their first printed appearance is in the booklets. Of course, you never really know who wrote these books, and therein lies the frustration."

A second interview in 2012 for Umami Mart reinforces this claim, along with the 1930s timestamp.

The time makes sense as it is scarily similar to the French 75, also created around that time.

ARNAUD'S SPECIAL

50ml Scotch
25ml Dubonnet
One dash Orange Bitters

METHOD
* Stirred and strained into a coupe
* Garnished with lemon peel

The recipe first appears in Ted Saucier's *Bottom's Up!* (1951) as:

> *"⅔ Scotch, ⅓ Dubonnet, Dash orange bitters. Shaken*
> *and served in a cocktail glass with a lemon peel."*

This cocktail was named for the Famous Arnaud's *Restaurant,* New Orleans which was opened in 1918 by Arnaud Cazenave (a local French wine specialist).

This cocktail was a huge success for the restaurant and would be their signature drink throughout the 1940s and 50s. As with most areas and people times change and this would bring with it a new signature serve – the Arnaud's French 75 – a Cognac-laced variant of the cocktail that has a Cognac base rather than a gin-based serve, which has become unanimous with the restaurant's *French 75 Bar.*

NOTES
• Like most cocktails of its type at the time, it was shaken, where modern preferences would stir the cocktail.

AVENUE

30ml Bourbon
30ml Calvados
7.5ml Grenadine
5ml Simple Syrup
Two dashes Orange Blossom Water
Pulp of one Passionfruit

METHOD
• Shaken and strained into a coupe

This cocktail originally appeared in the *Café Royal Cocktail Book* (1937) by W.J. Tarling where he credits another bartender who allowed him to include it in his recipe manual. It was created by W. G. Crompton and is listed as:

> *"⅓ Seagram's Bourbon Whisky.*
> *⅓ Calvados Cusenier.*
> *⅓ Passion Fruit Juice.*
> *Dash Grenadine.*

Dash Fleur d'Orange.
Shake."

How the ambiguity arises from what is meant by passionfruit juice at the time, whether it be the fresh pulp of the fruit or a cartooned juice (if that would have even been accessible at the time).

For consistency purposes, the use of the pulp of an actual passionfruit makes for a delicious version of this cocktail.

BELLINI

10ml Crème de Peche
15ml Peache Puree
5ml Simple Syrup
Prosecco Top

METHOD
* Build in a small highball and give a short stir

Harry's Bar, Venice, takes its name from a gentleman named Harry Pickering. Pickering was an American who befriended Giuseppe Cipriani, who looked after the bar at Hotel Europa whilst living in Venice.

There is an interesting story behind the cocktail and the relation these two men shared. Pickering borrowed 10,000 lire from Cipriani and then left Venice. He would later return to repay the debt fivefold and thus Cipriani could open his own bar, which opened in 1931. The bar would play host to many who shared a seat at the Algonquin Round Table such as F. Scott Fitzgerald and Ernest Hemingway.

The cocktail was primarily made with white peaches that were available throughout the summer months in Italy, and as such the cocktail was only available during this time. Due to updates in technology, the fruit can be prepared and stored much more easily.

NOTES
* Named after the Renaissance painter Giovanni Bellini (1430-1516)

BIRDS OF PARADISE FIZZ

50ml Gin
25ml Simple Syrup
12.5ml Lime Juice
12.5ml Lemon Juice
25ml Double Cream
Three dashes Orange Blossom Water
Two Raspberries
20ml Egg White
Soda Water

METHOD

* Add soda to a highball
* Shake with one large block ice and two small cubes
* Strain into highball primed with fresh soda water
* Rest drink in freezer for 1 minute
* Add more soda to the tin, then strain into glass and let head rise
* Straw should sit directly in the middle of drink

This drink is a bit of an outlier. It showcases gin, and it hails from Panama, which is part of the Caribbean region, but not one of the islands. Still, it's delicious and a perfect example of what a Caribbean cocktail can be.

This pretty pink sipper makes an appearance in *The Gentleman's Companion: Around the World with Jigger, Beaker and Flask* (1939) written by Charles H. Baker. The drink originated at the Strangers Club in Colón, once a popular watering hole for weary travellers who sought passage through the Panama Canal Zone:

> *"We always have found welcome there during the [12 or so times] we have been in the 'Zone' going west to east, or vice versa," wrote Baker, where this vibrantly hued drink provided "a colourful, eye-filling experience."*

This was discovered by Beachbum Berry in his book *Potions of the Caribbean* (2013) so we have him to thank for this wonderful insight.

DAISY DE SANTIAGO

50ml White Rum
15ml Yellow Chartreuse
25ml Lime Juice
15ml Simple Syrup
Soda Water

METHOD
* Shaken and strained into a sling over crushed ice
* Garnished with a mint sprig, lemon wedge and Chartreuse float

Charles. H. Baker Jr. published this drink in his *The Gentleman's Companion* (1946) and is simply a modified Daiquiri. Daisies are essentially sours topped with soda and are also enhanced with some flavoured liqueur.

Baker himself thought of the cocktail as a tribute to the founder of the Bacardi group, Facundo Bacardi, and also indirectly credited him with the authorship of the cocktail (although this is doubted by some), Mr. Baker said about the Daisy De Santiago:

> *"A lovely thing introduced to us through Gracious Offices of the late Facundo Bacardi, of lamented memory. To our mind, along with the immortal Daiquiri this is the best Bacardi drink on record."*

Mr. Baker was primarily based in Florida, where Ernest Hemingway would spend quite a lot of time. Baker travelled extensively and picked up this cocktail whilst in Cuba, during its 'Golden Era' of mixed drinks. Mr. Baker actually credits the founder of the Bacardi Group with the creation of this cocktail, but this is highly unlikely.

The garnish on this drink is exceptionally important, adding depth and flavour through the sense of smell.

DIAMONDBACK LOUNGE

40ml Rye
20ml Applejack
20ml Yellow Chartreuse

METHOD
- Stirred and stained into a rocks glass over block ice
- Garnished with an orange peel

First appearing in Ted Saucier's *Bottom's Up!* (1951) the Diamondback Lounge was a staple at the Diamond Cocktail Lounge, located at the Lord Baltimore hotel, Maryland. Locally a diamondback was not in reference to a dangerous rattlesnake species, but the turtle that was the universities mascot.

The split base of rye and apple brandy is particularly north-western for the time, however it is very difficult to pin this drink's creation to any one particular person. The interesting component is the Chartreuse where you would assume vermouth. This is typically characteristic of the way stirred drinks were evolving during the mid-century.

The originally recipe calls for yellow Chartreuse however the addition of green Chartreuse makes for an extremely interesting cocktail.

EL DIABLO

45ml Blanco Tequila
10ml Crème de Cassis (poured at the end)
15ml Lime Juice
10ml Ginger Syrup
5ml Simple Syrup
Top with Ginger Ale

METHOD
- Shaken and strained into a highball over ice
- Garnished with a lime wedge and drizzled crème de cassis

This cocktail's name translates to 'the Devil' in Spanish. This drink falls into a small category of tequila drinks that are served long, such as the Paloma, Tequila Tickler, or Zebra (a Tequila Rickey with Campari in *A Spot at the Bar*, 2015).

The drink is mentioned in a Ronrico rum pamphlet from the 1930s, discovered by Greg Boehm, an acclaimed drinks writer. After searching, the next references to the original cocktail come from Trader Vic's book from 1946 and 1947, however whether or not it was an original of his is another matter. It is in the Trader Vic *Book of Food and Drink* (1946) and is called a 'Mexican El Diablo', labelled as an original cocktail. Again it appears in Trader Vic's *Bartender's Guide* as the 'Mexican El Diablo'.

Later in 1968, Trader Vic's *Pacific Island Cookbook* lists it as an 'El Diablo', a small but significant change. Finally in 1972, *Trader Vic's – Bartender Guide Revised* calls it an 'El Diablo', but does not claim it to be his own drink. This edition separates original drinks from those that aren't.

NOTES
• The original recipe calls for Blanco Tequila, and so we have stayed true to this tradition.

FOG CUTTER

35ml White Rum
20ml Cognac
10ml Gin
7.5ml Manzanilla Sherry (float)
30ml Orange Juice
20ml Lemon Juice
12.5ml Simple Syrup
7.5ml Orgeat

METHOD
• Shaken and strained into a highball
• Garnished with a mint bouquet

This is an original drink by Trader Vic, and falls alongside other great drinks of a similar nature including the 'Mai-Tai' and the 'Scorpion'.

In Trader Vic's *Bartender Guide* (1947), this is a shaken drink served long. It's listed as:

"2oz Puerto Rican Rum
1oz Brandy
½ oz Gin
2oz Lemon juice
1oz Orange juice
½oz Orgeat, with a sherry float."

As seen with this recipe, it is incredibly potent and Vic himself said in a later book *"After two of these, you won't even see the stuff."*

Several years later Vic edited this drink to create the 'Samoan Fog Cutter', a weaker version of the original and featured in his *Bartender's Guide* (1972). This was blended and the garnished was changed to mint.

A bartender from Donn the Beachcomber's Bar, Tony Ramos, states that the Fog Cutter actually came from a Hollywood bar called Edna Earl's Fog Cutter Restaurant. Edna Earl was a former actress who bought and rebranded the restaurant in 1950. However, the Fog Cutter was already on Vic's menu in 1941 which predates Earl's bar.

NOTES
- A fog cutter is the name of a diving knife.
- This drink had its own mug created for it in order to hold the sheer volume of liquid.
- Listed in the original spec was a sherry float. Some call for sweet sherry and others for dry. The choice is your own, but with the addition of sugar, a dry sherry may be optimal.

GOLDEN CADILLAC

20ml Galliano Vanilla
20ml White Crème de Cacao
20ml Orange Juice
20ml Half and Half

METHOD
- Shaken and strained into a coupe
- Garnished with grated nutmeg

This odd-looking cocktail was spawned in 1952 and created at Poor Red's Bar-B-Q located in a small town of El Dorado, California. Perhaps it took inspiration from the 'Alexander' cocktail from the early twentieth century.

El Dorado was a Gold Rush town, and the bar building was actually constructed to be a weigh-house for Wells Fargo. It operated as Kelly's Bar between 1927–1945. Poor Red won the bar in a game, and ran the operation with his wife.

A newly engaged couple come through to celebrate and wanted to commemorate the occasion with a special cocktail just for them. The couple wanted the drink to match their newly purchased, you guessed it, golden Cadillac. Frank Cline, bartender at the time, made a few variations until he landed on one that was just how he wanted it. There was so much made that Frank decided to serve the extra in a highball, so the couple could top their drinks as they went on.

Galliano would run an advertising campaign for three years (1964–67) using this drink as the forerunner, and made *Poor Red's Bar* the largest consumer of Galliano in North America (and now, in the world). For this momentous title, the drinks group even gave the venue a Golden Cadillac to display outside the building.

NOTES
- The original Golden Cadillac was served frozen/blended.
- Originally the white crème de cacao was Bols brand.

There is a drink of a similar nature called a *'Golden Dream'* that substitutes white cacao for triple sec and was created by Raimundo Alvarez at the Old King Bar, Miami. It is said to be dedicated to actress Joan Crawford, and the drink saw much success before falling to the wayside of classic drinks.

HOTEL GEORGIA

60ml Gin
25ml Orgeat
15ml Lemon Juice
Three dashes Orange Blossom Water
20ml Egg white

METHOD
- Wet and dry shaken then strained into a coupe

At first glance this cocktail doesn't look like it should work. Heavy sweetener, less citrus and orange blossom water blend to make a delicious beverage, not dissimilar to a Ramos Gin Fizz.

The historic Hotel Georgia opened in Vancouver in 1927, and this cocktail was created in 1945. The building went through massive reconstruction in 2006, and when it reopened in 2011 as the Rosewood Hotel Georgia, bar manager Brad Stanton was diving through several books and stumbled across this recipe in Ted Saucier's *Bottoms Up* (1951). After some tweaking and updating this drink ended up winning 'Cocktail of the Year' in *enRoute* Magazine's Best Hotel Bars edition.

The original recipe from Saucier's book was likely much too perfumed, earthy and unbalanced:

"2 parts gin
1 part orgeat syrup
½ part lemon juice
10 Drops orange flower water
1 egg white"

HEMINGWAY DAIQUIRI

50ml Light Rum
5ml Maraschino
20ml Pink Grapefruit Juice
10ml Lime Juice
5ml Simple Syrup

METHOD

• Long shake with block ice then strain into a coupe

Hemingway used to ask for the 'Daiquiri No. 3', however he asked for twice the lime juice and three times the grapefruit. This is the version that became known as the famous 'Papa Doble'. First appearing in *Bar La Florida* (1934), and then updated in 1939 by Constante Ribalaigua Vert, listing it as:

"E. HENMIWAY" SPECIAL
2 Ounces Bacardi.
1 Teaspoon Grape Fruit Juice.
1 Teaspoonful Maraschino.
The juice of ½ lemon.
Frappe Ice."

A journalist named A.E. Hotchner, wrote a piece on Hemingway called *Papa Hemingway* (a nod to the 'Papa Doble' cocktail) after a visit to the bar in 1948 to drink with him. Hemingway disclosed a secret, the 'Papa Doble' that he gets made for him is different to that served to guests at the bar (and that printed in the 1939 version of the bar's book).

It was as follows:

> *"Two and a half jiggers of Bacardi White label Rum, the juice of two limes, half a grapefruit, and six drops of maraschino."*

Blended, I may add.

NOTES
- Hemingway has a disease called hemochromatosis, which can lead to the onset of diabetes, this is why he chose to omit sugar.
- There is a known rumour that Hemingway once consumed 15 Papa Dobles in one sitting, between 10:30am and 7pm.
- Bumping up the Maraschino liqueur and trading rum for tequila will yield a 'Dovetail' cocktail.

HOTEL NACIONAL

30ml White Rum
30ml Aged Rum
15ml Apricot Liqueur
30ml Pineapple Juice
20ml Lime Juice
5ml Simple Syrup

METHOD
- Shaken and strained into a coupe

During the 1930s when this drink was created, the Hotel Nacional de Cuba was one of the world's finest, it played host to politicians, celebrities and even gangsters. All the news of this travel destination and its opulence made it a hotspot for Prohibition-bound Americans.

The hotel also played part to the infamous 1946 Havana Conference, the gangster meeting as retold in the second *Godfather* film.

What is known for sure is that three well-established bartenders worked at the hotel in some capacity, and have at one point or another being credited with the creation of the flagship cocktail. Whether it was one, or all three, they would have all played a hand in its inception. These three men were Will Taylor, Fred Kaufman (also credited with the 'Mary Pickford'), and Eddie Woelke – however Eddie worked in the Casino Nacional, not the hotel.

One of the earliest written references regarding this cocktail comes from Charles H. Baker's *The Gentleman's Companion* (1939), in which Will Taylor in given credit:

> *"Wil P. Taylor's Nacional Special, which along with the Tropical Daiquiri and the Santiago De Cuba Mint julep is one of the three finest Bacardi drinks known to science.*
>
> *Carta de Oro Bacardi, I jigger*
> *Fresh Pineapple juice, I jigger*
> *Lime, juice ½*
> *Dry apricot brandy, I tsp."*

Oddly enough this drink is listed in *Bar La Florida* (1934), but it is listed without lime juice in the recipe. And the updated 1939 recipe is as follows:

> *"1 jigger Bacardi Gold, 1 jigger pineapple juice, Juice of ½ lime, 1 tsp dry apricot brandy, Shaken."*

One of the few issues surrounding a direct replication of this cocktail is that actual apricot brandy is neigh impossible to come across these days, without tasting overly sweet or artificial.

NOTES
* This cocktail is sometimes referred to as a *"Nacional"*, *"Hotel Nacional de Cuba"*, or *"Hotel Nacional Special"*.

HARVEY WALLBANGER

45ml Vodka
15ml Galliano
Top with Orange Juice

METHOD
* Built in a highball and given a short stir
* Garnished with an orange wedge

There's a widely circulated story regarding this 1970s drink – made with vodka, orange juice, and Galliano – was created by Donato 'Duke' Antone at his L.A bar, the Blackwatch (a bar that had no menu), for a surfer named Tom Harvey. He apparently got so drunk he started running into walls, giving the drink its name. According to folklore, Donato 'Duke' Antone invented the Harvey Wallbanger in 1952, however Antone lived in Connecticut during this relevant time period, not in Los Angeles.

This wasn't 'Duke's' only cocktail involving Galliano, there were others such as the 'Italian Fascination' – Galliano, triple sec, Kahlua, and sweet cream. Soon after Smirnoff and Galliano approached him to come onboard as a corporate bartending consultant.

In an interview held with 'Duke's' grandson, there was a drink developed at the Blackwatch bar called 'Duke's Screwdriver', which was made the same way as a Harvey Wallbanger.

In 1969 George Bednar, the now former marketing director of McKesson Imports, which imported Galliano, introduced a cartoony-like surfer character named Harvey Wallbanger to help market the drink featuring a simple catchphrase:

"My name is Harvey, and I can be made."

Harvey even became a write-in candidate for the presidential election in 1972, and due to this campaigning, Galliano's sales tripled and the drink became a disco staple.

Therefore, the drink could simply be a corporate collaboration of an already existing drink, done under a new marketing ploy.

HURRICANE

30ml Aged Barbados Rum
30ml Light Rum
25ml Lime Juice

35ml Orange Juice
15ml Passionfruit Syrup
10ml Simple Syrup
2.5ml Grenadine
Two dashes Angostura Bitters

METHOD
- Shaken and strained into a Hurricane glass
- Garnished with an orange wedge and cherry

The history if the Hurricane is an interesting story of supply and demand which would lead to the creation of this legendary cocktail. The initial concept is said to have been created at the New York Fair, Queens in 1939, at the aptly named Hurricane Bar, which is also the venue that made the 'Zombie' famous. There isn't much detail stemming from this drink at the venue, aside from it contained rum and the glass in which it was served.

Another favourite theory of the creation is one that is linked to Pat O'Brien's, New Orleans. In the mid-1940s, shortly after the second World War, bourbon and scotch whisky were in short supply, whilst rum was plentiful on the market. It would arrive at the New Orleans port from cargo ships after trips to the Caribbean to carry out trade, and this volume of spirit led distributors to get creative. There was a popular whiskey cocktail at the time, so in order for venues to get a whiskey allocation they also needed to purchase multiple cases of rum.

The story shapes up that Pat O'Brien along with his partner Charlie Cantrell, decided to develop a cocktail to help alleviate the abundance of rum in their stockroom. However, other sources suggest it was actually their head bartender Louis Calligan who coined the cocktail's creation. Regardless of who it was, Culligan would go on to publish the original recipe for the cocktail in the now fossilised *Cabaret* magazine (1956).

NOTES
- There are several variations of this drink that appearance throughout a variety of renowned texts.
- Gary Regan's *Joy of Mixology* (2003) showcases one Chuck Taggart's variant that was on his website.

- Dale DeGroff's *The Essential Cocktail* (2008) highlights a recipe with Galliano and pineapple juice, which gained a fair bit of traction.
- The name stems from the glass in which the cocktail is served, which comes from the style of lamp also called a hurricane.

IRISH COFFEE

100ml Sweetened Demerara-infused Coffee
45ml Irish whiskey
Whipped Double Cream Float

METHOD

- Preheat an Irish coffee glass with boiling water
- Add whiskey and sweetened coffee
- Float cream on top
- Garnished with grated nutmeg (essential)

OR
- Just go to Bar Swift

To anyone reading this that knows me well, Bar Swift is one of my all-time favourite spots, and this is primarily because their Irish coffee is the world's best.

Created by Chef Joe Sheridan at Foynes airport, Ireland. The airport was an airbase near Limerick, the main airport for fly boats between America and Europe, and by the 1940s it was handling mainly high-end passengers.

The West coast of Ireland can have notoriously poor weather and the airport was only meant to be a stopover. In 1942 a new restaurant opened tasked with providing guests with a positive image of Ireland during their layovers. One night a Pan Am flight returned to Foynes due to bad weather so young Joe Sheridan prepared food and drink for the passengers. He was asked If his concoction was 'Brazilian Coffee' and he replied with "*No, it's Irish Coffee.*"

Joe offered this recipe as a how to make a true Irish Coffee:

"Cream – Rich as an Irish Brogue
Coffee – Strong as a Friendly Hand
Sugar – Sweet as the tongue of a Rogue
Whiskey – Smooth as the Wit of the Land."

The drink may not have become the international success it did had it not been for travel writer, Stanton Delaplane, bringing the recipe to his close friend Jack Koeppler, the owner/operator (and bartender in his own right) at Bueno Vista cafe, San Francisco.

They spent months trying to recreate the drink and attempting to get the cream to float, I'm sure this was would have been a delicious, yet laborious process. After many attempts, they decided to enlist the help of San Francisco's mayor, George Christopher, who happened to be a dairy owner/farmer. He claimed that the cream should be aged for at least 48 hours, and this should solve their problem.

The Buena Vista used a Tullamore Dew private blend from the Cooley distillery, Dublin in their Irish coffees, which they have been serving from November 10th 1952.

NOTES
- Chef Joe Sheridan is pictured serving an Irish coffee to Marilyn Monroe.

KIR AND KIR ROYALE

Kir – White Wine and 10ml Cassis

Kir Royale – Champagne and 10ml Cassis

Add cassis to flute and top with either wine or champagne

Kirs, or Kir Royales, are cocktails that use a
table or sparkling wine as the base and pair it
simply with a sweetener, usually a liqueur.

Kir is another such branch of the cocktail family tree, and I'm sure one we are all family with, the delicious combination of liqueur and wine is quite the match.

But where does it come from and how did it get such a name?

Conceptionally called the Cassis Blanc, it was made famous by a man named Canon Felix Kir, who was the Major of Dijon. Such an advocate of local products of the region, Kir decided to promote and popularise the Cassis, so much so that the eventual recipe would be named in his honour.

The first Kir created was with another local product, a white wine name named Bourgogne Aligoté (which is named with primarily Aligoté grapes, however around 15% Chardonnay is permitted) and *Lejay Cassis*.

Felix Kir was a Catholic Priest, and decorated member of the French resistance during the second World War. As German soldiers marched into Burgundy in 1940, many locals and officials fled, however Kir stayed and aided in the escape of more than 4000 prisoners of war.

As far as rumours go, Kir wanted to imitate the famous Burgundy red wines as they had been confiscated from the local population, in an act of defiance against those invading his home. So by taking local, dry white wine (Aligoté) and Cassis he mimicked the colour of the class reds.

NOTES

- *Lejay Cassis* were the original inventors of crème de cassis and they started making it in 1841.
- The cassis buds from the fruit are also found in the blend of Chanel no. 5 perfume.
- The Aligoté grape is much less known than the famous Chardonnay grape of Burgundy.

MEXICAN FIRING SQUAD

60ml Tequila
25ml Lime Juice
10ml Grenadine
10ml Simple Syrup
Four dashes Angostura Bitters on top
Soda Water top

METHOD
* Shaken and strained into a highball with cubed ice
* Top with soda, float bitters on top.
* Garnish with lime wedge and cherry.

This cocktail is brought to light in Charles Baker's *Gentleman's Companion, Around the World with Jigger, Beaker and Flask* (1946). The cocktail was discovered at La Cucaracha Bar, Mexico City, 1937 and was noted in his book as:

"Is a creation we almost became wrecked upon in – of
all spots- La Cucaracha Bar, in Mexico City, 1937.
Now and again we found ourselves just a little fed up with rather
casual Mexican mixes, and the guidance of 2 young Mexican caballeros
whose parents mattered in official circles in that city of Mexico.
This drink is based on tequila, top-flight distillation of the maguey
plant. Use a tall Collins glass and snap fingers at the consequences.
Take 2 jiggers of tequila, being sure to purchase a good brand, for
there are many raw distillations. Add the juice of 2 small limes,
1 ½ to 2 tsp of grenadine. Add two dashes of Angostura bitters...
garnish with slice of orange, 1 of pineapple and a red cherry."

This is built like a sour but also has the inclusion of bitters and soda water. The Angostura bitters play a crucial factor into flavour balancing, however I would opt for a rocks style glass as to step away from the feeling of a highball if you so desire.

NOTES
* Splitting the grenadine with simple syrup can also lead to a more harmonious balance of flavour.

MISSIONARY'S DOWNFALL

40ml Cuban White Rum
10ml Demerara Overproof Rum
10ml Crème de Peche
30ml Pineapple Juice
15ml Lime Juice
15ml Simple Syrup
Five Mint Leaves

METHOD

- Shaken and fine strained into a highball over crushed ice
- Float the overproof rum
- Garnished with a mint sprig and pineapple wedge

A thing to note for this particular tiki cocktail, is that it is rather low in alcoholic content in comparison to its counterparts of the time.

The Missionary's Downfall was created in the 1930s during the beginning of the tiki movement in America. The original recipe called for the use of the popular peach brandy (made from fermented peaches) instead of peach liqueur and was traditionally blended rather than shaken. The cocktail also used fresh herbs in the mix, and this was seen as forward thinking at the time, and wouldn't catch on for also 60 years after.

During the World War II, numerous active missionaries in Asia and Africa in French and British colonies were expelled or detained for the duration of the war (if their nation was at war with the colonial authority – a case of 'wrong place at the wrong time'). Don Beach was in the military prior to opening his tiki-themed restaurants, and this likely had an influence on his drinks.

During my first week in New Zealand several years ago two of my close friends, Ryan and Tom, and myself set out to find the most delicious interpterion of this cocktail. To this day we're still in the game and so this is dedicated to you both.

MARGARITA

50ml Tequila Blanco
12.5ml Cointreau
12.5ml Combier
25ml Lime Juice
10m Simple Syrup

METHOD

* Shaken and strained into a coupe or rocks glass with a half-salt rim.
* If your glass is chilled your salt will stick naturally, if not then use a lime wedge around half the rim of glass.

I think it's safe to say that the Margarita is well and firmly in the classic cocktail's library, however it has undergone a resurgence of popularity in the past two decades particularly in the United States. The rise in the consumption of agave spirits has led to a coupled rise for requests for this cocktail, so let's find out where it came from.

The name translates to 'Daisy' in English which is probably because it is essentially a tequila daisy. A daisy is a style of drink compromised of spirit, citrus and a Mediterranean fruit-style sweeter (most notably orange liqueur or grenadine).

This category of drink was popular in the early twentieth century with the nineteenth July 1939 edition of the *Albuquerque Journal* describing the daisy as *"ubiquitous to American Drinking."* There is a simple theory that the Margarita is an evolution on the 'Daisy Cocktail', this backed by an Irishman, Henry Madden, who gave an interview in *Moville Mail* on July 23rd 1936, in which Henry Madden recalls this story.

Whilst working in Turf Bar, Tijuana he made a gin daisy that was requested by an American guest escaping Prohibition. Henry accidentally used tequila in place of gin, yet the guest asked for the recipe and kept drinking them.

In *Cafe Royale Cocktail Book* (1937) book there was a drink called a Picador (Tequila, Cointreau , lime or lemon juice) which predates the margarita by 16 years in UK print, but doesn't have the inclusion of salt rim.

However, the first time it appears listed as a 'Margarita Cocktail' comes from an issue of *Esquire* magazine in 1953 – here it was the cocktail of the month for December:

"1 oz tequila, a dash of triple sec and the
juice of half a lemon or lime.
She's from Mexico, Senores, and her
name is the Margarita Cocktail."

There are a number of theories relating to the origins of the Margarita, so let's distil them. Carlos 'Danny' Herrera is said to have created the cocktail in either 1947 or 1948 at his Rancho la Gloria Bar, Mexico, for actress Marjorie King who was apparently allergic to all spirits except tequila, but didn't enjoy it raw.

He added Cointreau and lime with a salt rim to grab people's attention. The drink was named Margarita, the closest Spanish name to Marjorie.

The next story is said to credit a man called Danny Negrete. He and his brother opened a bar at the Garci Crispo Hotel in Puebla, Mexico and made it for his brother's wedding in 1936 and named it after his new sister-in-law, Margarita. Soon after this, in the 1940s, he moved to the famed Agua Caliente Racetrack. Rita Hayworth performed here in her teenage years and it is possible that the cocktail was named after her (her real name is Margarita Cansino).

There is also a story of an American socialite named Margaret Sames, who claims to have mixed the cocktail at her annual Christmas party at her house in Acapulco, 1948. Tommy Hilton was at the party and took the cocktail with him to his Hilton Hotels to be put on the menu.

Tail o' the Cock, a Los Angeles restaurant where John Durlesser claims to have created it in 1936 when the flow of tequila first became available to L.A.

Enter Vernon Underwood In the 1950s, he started distributing Jose Cuervo tequila in America at this point and began to realise that this single account was using massive amounts of the product. Durlesser pinpointed the success to the Margarita cocktail, named after his wife, and Underwood decided to market the cocktail with the tagline *"Margarita, more than a girl's name."*

Another lady thrown into the mix is Peggy Lee, her actual name is Norma Egstrom. A traditional nickname of Margaret is Peggy, hence Margarita. The correlation is that she was recording at a studio in Galveston, Texas.

Santos Cruz, head bartender at The Balinese Room, made her a Sidecar with tequila in place of brandy. Her husband, guitarist in the group, made the correlation of the name and thus the cocktail was born.

MOSCOW MULE

60ml Vodka
20ml Lime Juice
10ml Ginger Syrup
5ml Simple Syrup
Top with Ginger Beer

METHOD
* Shaken briefly and strained into a highball over ice
* Garnished with a lime wedge and mint sprig

This cocktail first appears in *The Stork Club Bar Book* (1946) by Lucius Beebe where he lists it as:

"2oz. vodka
1 split ginger beer
Crushed ice
Serve in mug and decorate with sprigs of mint."

What about the cocktail, where did it come from?

This also has two competing, but similar stories that occur in 1941. It involves three men: Jack Morgan who owned the Cock 'n' Bull pub in Hollywood, John Martin who was head of Heublein and Brothers that had recently purchased the rights for Smirnoff in 1939, and Rudolph Kunett who was head of the vodka division for Heublein and Brothers. They are sat in the Chatman Hotel, New York brainstorming how to sell their surplus of products on hand. The Cock 'n' Bull had a ginger beer that was not selling well and Smirnoff vodka was in the same position (Americans were too involved with beer and whiskey at this point to pay vodka any heed). During this time they decided to add lemon juice to the mix and dubbed it the Little Moscow in 1941. This story is credited by George Sinclair, a bartender turned journalist, speaks about 1948 in the *New York Herald Tribune* (2007) stating that John Martin, John Morgan and Rudolph Kunett pooled their resources of Cock 'n' Bull ginger beer, Smirnoff vodka and copper mugs to create a drink, *"four or five days later the mixture was christened the Moscow mule."*

The other story involves three men but a different setting, they are sat in the Cock 'n' Bull pub , however it is Wes Price, head bartender at the time, present instead of Kunett. The two men are brainstorming how to shift their products whilst Wes is clearing out the cellar of dead stock and mixes the two together. The pub was a regular of movie stars at the time and Wes states he served one to Broderick Crawford and *"it caught on like wildfire."* This story is backed up by Eric Felton's article in *The Wall Street Journal* (2007):

> *"I just wanted to clean out the basement. I was trying to get rid of dead stock. It caught on like wildfire."*

When you think of the Moscow Mule, a copper mug comes to mind but how and why?

The story of the copper mug was uncovered by Ted Haigh in his *Vintage Spirits and Forgotten Cocktails* (2004). Jack Morgan had a girlfriend, Osalene Schmitt who had inherited a copper company that produced mugs. These mugs were previously rather poor selling items until Jack decided to market his kick in them with the engraved image of a kicking mule.

This was brought one step further with the invention of the Polaroid camera in 1947. John Martin bought one of the cameras and would bars, taking pictures of bartenders holding the copper 'mule' mug and a bottle Smirnoff. He would give one picture to the bartender to display, and then bring that picture to the next bar to show the venue what they were missing out on. It was an early form of viral marketing, and a stroke of pure genius.

MAI TAI

30ml Appleton Estate VX
25ml Smith and Cross
25ml Lime Juice
20ml Pierre Ferrand Curacao
12.5ml Orgeat
One dash Angostura Bitters

METHOD
- Shaken and strained into a large rocks glass over ice
- Garnished with mint sprig, orange wedge and cherry

DONN'S MAI TAI

40ml Aged Jamaican Rum
15ml Dry Curacao
10ml Falernum
20ml Pink Grapefruit Juice
15ml Lime Juice
5ml Simple Syrup
Two dashes Absinthe
Two dashes Angostura Bitters

METHOD
- Shaken and strained into a rocks glass over ice
- Garnished with a mint sprig, orange wedge and cherry

There is no cocktail that suffers greater misinterpretation than the Mai Tai.

As with many famous cocktails there are generally conflicting stories of great contention, and that of the Mai Tai is no different. The two main characters in these tales are Victor 'Trader Vic' Bergeron and Ernest Raymond Beaumont Grant aka Donn the Beachcomber. Lucky for us Jeff Berry and Martin Crate, authors of *Beachbum Berry Remixed* (2009) and *Smuggler's Cove* (2016) respectively, have devolved deep into this topic and uncovered many truths.

I believe Donn Beach gets overlooked in this story so I will begin with him. Donn started the Tiki craze that swept America in the early

1940s, and it was a visit to one of his restaurants in 1937 that led Trader Vic to open his own Polynesian venue.

According to Donn's widow, Phoebe Beach, in her book *Hawaii Tropical Rum Drinks and Cuisine by Donn The Beachcomber* (2001) he had created a cocktail named the 'Mai Tai Swizzle' in 1933 which consisted of:

"1 ½ oz Myer's Plantation rum, 1 oz Cuban rum, ½ oz Cointreau, ¼ oz Falernum, 1 oz grapefruit juice, ¾ oz lime juice, 6 drops Pernod, Dash Angostura bitters, Garnished with 4 mint sprigs."

This predates Trader Vic's claim of making it in 1944 by 11 years, however Jeff Berry obtained a bar book from Dick Santiago who worked for Donn Beach. This book contains no recipe for a Mai Tai or Mai Tai Swizzle which means that Trader Vic could not have stolen said recipe, like many claim.

Adding to this tale Edward 'Mick' Brownlee, a gentleman who worked with Donn Beach for over a decade, states that Donn never said that Trader Vic stole his Mai Tai recipe – but that it was a riff on his '*Q.B. Cooler'* cocktail instead. The Q.B. Cooler is laid out in Berry's book as:

"1 oz gold Jamaican rum, 1 ox light Puerto Rican rum,
½ oz Demerara rum, ½ oz honey mix (1:1), ½ oz falernum,
1 oz orange juice, ½ oz lime juice, ½ teaspoon ginger
syrup, two dashes Angostura bitters, 1 oz soda water."

This drink shares more similarities with Vic's Mai Tai than Donn's 'Mai Tai Swizzle' does but there is still no cut and clear evidence that it was stole, many cocktails at this time were influenced from one another particularly between competing businesses.

Now for Trader Vic who claimed that he invented the Mai Tai in 1944 at his Oakland restaurant when two of his friends, Carrie and Eastham Guild were visiting from Tahiti. They asked for a cocktail and Vic presented them with something that he had been working on: a mix of Wray and Nephew 17-year-old rum, orange curacao (a rarity at this time imported from Holland), orgeat (Vic's parent were French Canadian so he had grown up around such flavours), lime juice and his own rock candy syrup (a concentrated sugar syrup). Carie took one sip and uttered *"Maita'i ~ roa Ae!"* which means *"out of this world – the best!"*. Following this he named the concoction the 'Mai Tai' and his original recipe was.

"2 oz Wray and Nephew 17yr, ½ oz Holland DeKuyper orange curacao, ½ oz French Garnier orgeat syrup, ¼ oz Trader Vic's rock candy syrup, Juice of one fresh lime."

I don't believe Trader Vic expected the cocktail to become such an instant hit, the drink spread so fast that the world's supply (this is not an exaggeration) of Wray and Nephew 17 year became so scarce to the point of running out. The next logical step was to use the 15-year rum in its place, however this also started to dwindle – so Vic had to alter his drink twice due to popularity and access to products. To combat the second shortage Trader Vic began blending his spirit base to extend his supply of Wray and Nephew 15-year by adding one part Red Heart and Coruba to one part of the 15-year-old rum. This only lasted so long as the 15-year-old Wray and Nephew suffered the same fate as its predecessor and ran dry, so Vic decided to bottle his own private reserves under his own brand. With these private reserves he mixed in Martinique rum in order to replicate the flavour of the original spirit used in the cocktail (your palate would need to be sensational for this to occur).

The rum that was used was described as a more molasses based 'Rhum Traditionnel' rather than the Agricole style we may normally assume of Martinique. Martin Cate states this in his *Smuggler's Cove* (2016) book and points out the description of the Agricole that was being used by both Donn Beach and Trader Vic – *"nutty and snappy"* rather than the usual 'grassy and smoked' notes you would associate with the style.

In the 1960s Vic had bottled a Mai Tai rum blend, consisting of his more up to date spirit base for his cocktail.

The Mai Tai's decline started in the 1950s when the post-war period saw increased travel to island destinations, notably Hawaii. The A shipping company – which was known for popularising trips to Hawaiian islands – hired Trader Vic to oversee and create their cocktail menus in their hotels. In 1954, pineapple and orange juice would enter the scene in order to make the cocktail more approachable and tourist-friendly. Vic's originally garnish of a spent lime shell and a mint spring to mimic the look of an island was a huge hit with the masses consuming the beverage.

The Mai Tai was listed officially in Trader Vic's *Bartender's Guide* (1972) as:

> *"1 lime, ½ ounce orange curacao, ¼ ounce rock candy
> syrup, 2 ounces Trader Vic Mai Tai rum or 1 ounce
> dark Jamaica um and 1 ounce Martinique rum."*

Also within this book, Trader Vic details the origins of the Mai Tai, its rapid spread, and famed quote *"Anybody who says I didn't create tis drink is a dirty stinker."*

I believe it is fair to say that both characters play a role in the cocktail's story however the version we associate with today is Trader Vic's created in 1944.

NOTES
• Q.B in the 'Q.B. Cooler' stand for 'Quiet Birdmen' – an all-male fraternity made up of World War I air pilots in 1921.

PAINKILLER (AKA SOGGY DOLLAR COCKTAIL)

60ml Pusser's Rum
60ml Pineapple Juice
25ml Orange Juice
25ml Coco Lopez

METHOD
• Long shake and strained into large rocks glass over crushed ice
• Garnished with grated nutmeg and orange slice

This is a personal favourite, my first experience of this cocktail was at Black Pearl, Melbourne in 2016. I had just finished work and had been introduced to a group of new friends whom were headed there. I'm pretty sure there was a collaboration with Pusser's Rum happening at the time. Anyway, I tasted it and I'm quite sure I had another three after that.

This cocktail originated in a bar called the Soggy Dollar, it had six seats and no dock for boats. The only way to get to it was to swim, so your money got wet, hence the name. Genius if you ask me.

It was the brainchild of one by Daphne Henderson, a British bartender who served it at the Soggy Dollar in the 1970s, and Charles Tobias (founder of Pusser's Rum) caught wind of the attention it received. Despite their friendship, Daphne refused to share the secret and it wasn't for another two years until Charles brought one back to his boat and uncovered it for himself. He reached the conclusion of a 4:1:1:1 recipe and the public preferred his as it was slightly less sweet.

Tobias returned to the Soggy Dollar Bar for another afternoon of West Indian food and Painkillers the following Sunday. Shaking the water off after his swim ashore to the bar, Tobias declared that he had finally broken Daphne's secret, *"At last, Daphne, I have the Painkiller recipe which I promise to not divulge to anyone if you tell me that I'm right,"* he said.

Daphne was unconcerned at the fact and Tobias decided to make a Painkiller himself to evidence his claim. He laid his aside one of hers and noticed a slight difference, but rated his as a better version. Daphne, unsurprisingly, disagreed and the two settled on a $100 bet to decide which recipe was preferred.

Rumoured is that there were ten patrons at the bar that day. Tobias thought it best to order two rounds of ten drinks: one made by Daphne and her recipe, and the others would be Tobias' recipe. They marked Pusser's Rum metal mugs and the taste test began. An astonishing ten out of ten sweep came from Tobias' recipe and Daphne claimed he must have paid everyone off. Tobias thought it best to take his payment in the guise of 40 Painkiller cocktails, what a day that must have been in the Soggy Dollar bar.

NOTES

- The Soggy Dollar cocktail bar actually has a consistent webcam showing the beach front and the entrance leading up to the bar, pretty amazing feature for those who would find it difficult to reach the remote destination.

PAN AMERICAN CLIPPER

50ml Applejack
20ml Lime Juice
12.5ml Grenadine
Absinthe Rinse

METHOD
* Shaken and strained into a coupe
* No garnish

First appearing in *The Gentleman's companion, or Around the World with Jigger, Beaker and Flask* (1939) by Charles H. Baker, this guide connected the two separate worlds of cocktail books and travelogues. This text would put less distance between tropical drinks such as 'The Mexican Firing Squad' to cocktail enthusiasts the world over.

What is a 'clipper' and why did this drink get named after one?

A clipper was a nineteenth-century merchant ship, specifically designed for speed, and eventually transoceanic voyages. These voyages generally were between the UK and China, UK and New York, and it eased trade routes for the Dutch tea trade.

Pan Am is reference to 'Pan American Airways', as it was seen as the unofficial flag carrier of the United States in the aviation industry from 1927 until 1991. The airline would use the word 'clipper' to name its planes, particularly when it started its South-American flight routes, nicknames like American Clipper and Caribbean Clipper became iconic to the airline.

This cocktail isn't the only one of its kind to exist: it is one of few that were at times served on the aircrafts. According *to Pan-Am clippers: The Golden Age of Flying Boats* (2007) by James Trautman, there was in fact a proprietary clipper cocktail recipe on hand consisting of *"Golden Rum, dry vermouth, a dash of grenadine – similar to an El Presidente."* Other routes took a different approach, in order to showcase a point of difference between flight routes. The South Sea Clipper would serve a concoction of gin, curacao and orange juice.

Baker's book leaves us a note to show where the drink came from, but not from whom:

*"From the notebook of one of our pilot friends,
who-when off Duty may seek one."*

Pilots used to be thought off as daredevils and adventurous. When Charles Baker retired from his travels and career, he settled down in Coconut Grove, Florida, this was extremely close to where Pan Am had opened the first international airport. Perhaps this is why it is included in the cocktail's name.

PINA COLADA

45ml White Rum
20ml Coconut Rum
5ml Aged Overproof Rum
40ml Pineapple Juice
25ml Coco Lopez
15ml Half and Half
Two Fresh Pineapple Wedges

METHOD
- Blend with half ice scoop of crushed ice, pour into Hurricane glass/tiki vessel
- Garnished with a straw, mint spring and pineapple wedge

Claimed to have been made by Don Ramon 'Moncito' Marrero in 1963 using the newly created Coco Lopez from 1954, and the name of this cocktail literally translates to *"strained pineapple."*

This cocktail was born in Puerto Rico, created specifically at The Caribe Hilton in San Juan, one of the luxury resorts in the area in 1954. Some 20 years later, in 1978, the Pina Colada was declared the Puerto Rico's national drink, which was aided immensely by the popularity of Trader Vic, Donn the Beachcomber, and electric blenders I imagine.

The tale of this cocktail is disputed as three bartenders claimed to have concocted this delight: Don Ramon 'Moncito' Marrero, Ricardo Gracia and Ramon Mingot. The following is what I uncovered about each of the stories.

Hotel management tasked Ramon Marrero to create a signature cocktail for the bar, inspired by the island and its flavours. Embracing this, he took several months before landing on rum, cream of coconut and pineapple juice. He is reported to have served many of these until his retirement in 1989. Joan Crawford is said to have drank one, served by Marrero and said it was *"better than slapping Bette Davis in the face."*

Ricardo Gracia also worked at the hotel along with Marrero and his claim is not to be discredited. As told in a 2005 interview, Gracia said there was a coconut-cutters strike which made sourcing coconut very difficult. The hotel had a popular drink of rum, cream of coconut and crushed ice served in a half coconut, without access to this he improvised and used a half pineapple instead. When the pineapple flavour was popularised, he added freshly strained pineapple juice to create the Pina Colada.

Whether they worked on the cocktail together, or he was simply in the wrong place at the wrong time, the hotel tends to lean in Marrero's favour.

In the Old City, a few miles West of the hotel, another San Juan hotspot stakes a claim as the birthplace of the cocktail. Restaurant Barrachina opened in the 1950s and quickly gained renown for its paella dish. On a trip to South America, Pepe Barrachina, a Spanish chef, convinced Ramon Mingot, a Spaniard who wrote cocktail books and worked in what were some of the best venues in Buenos Aires, to leave Argentina and become head bartender at his Puerto Rican restaurant. There is a marble plaque at the entrance of the restaurant dedicated to Mingot stating he created the first Pina Colada there in 1963, however I find this unlikely as the cocktail had started to see fame and favour prior to this time.

This cocktail would not be what it is today without the creation of Coco Lopez, a delicious cream of coconut mixed with cane sugar that comes in a can for ease of use. Don Ramon Lopez Irizarry wanted to minimise the effort in obtaining cream of coconut, as it was a popular ingredient in island desserts. So he released his product in 1954, and from there it only gained more fame and success.

If you finish reading the history on this cocktail and haven't once thought of the Pina Colada song 'Escape' by Rupert Holmes, then you certainly will now.

NOTES
- Coco Lopez is crucial in making an authentic Pina Colada

PERFECT LADY

50ml Gin
15ml Crème de Peche
20ml Lemon Juice
10ml Simple Syrup
20ml Egg white

METHOD
• Wet and dry shaken, then strained into a coupe

A lighter and more fruit-centric cousin to the 'White Lady' as triple sec is swapped out for peach liqueur.

This cocktail was created by one Sidney Cox for 'The British Empire Cocktail Competition' in which he was awarded 1st place, and it appears in *The Café Royale Cocktail Book* (1937) by W.J. Tarling the following year:

> *"½ Seager's Gin.*
> *¼ Peach Brandy (Garnier).*
> *¼ Fresh Lemon Juice.*
> *Dash of White of Egg.*
>
> *Invented by S. Cox 1st Prize, cocktail*
> *Competition, London, 1936."*

The naming of the drink is interesting, it is inspired by a drama at the time involving King Edward VIII's abdication so he could marry his 'perfect lady', Ms. Wallis Simpson who was a twice divorced American. Despite opposition on many fronts, Edward married Wallis and they remained that way until his death some 35 years later.

ROYAL HAWAIIAN

50ml Gin
25ml Pineapple Juice
15ml Lemon Juice
15ml Orgeat
One dash Orange Bitters
One dash Angostura Bitters

• Shaken and strained into a coupe

Originally this was known as the 'Princess Kaiulani' cocktail.

This was the signature serve of the Princess Kaiulani Hotel, but when the name of the hotel changed to the Royal Hawaiian in the 1950s they changed the name of the cocktail also, or so says Dale DeGroff in *The Essential Cocktail* (2008).

Victoria Ka'iulani was Crown Princess and heir to the throne of Hawaii, however the royal family was overthrown in 1893 and so she lost her royal authority.

The cocktail first appears in Ted Saucier's *Bottom's Up!* (1951) as:

*"1 jigger gin, 1 jigger pineapple juice, ⅓ jigger lemon juice,
1 teaspoon orgeat, shaken, and served in a champagne glass."*

Jeff 'Beachbum' Berry confirms this and states that it was served as early as 1948 at both the Royal Hawaiian and Moana Hotels, Honolulu (Saucier only credits the latter even though the Moana Hotel was built in 1901).

NOTES
• The addition of bitters in this version is to aid in balancing the cocktail, particularly the orgeat. Too much or too little can throw the drink off completely.
• Today, the Mai Tai has become the hotel's signature serve.

SPANISH MONK

40ml Gin
15ml Green Chartreuse
20ml Lemon Juice
15ml Simple Syrup
15ml Egg White

METHOD
• Wet and dry shaken, then strained into a coupe.

This cocktail appears in Charles H. Baker's *The Southern Gentleman's Companion* (1951) in which he speaks of mixing a cocktail with gin and Chartreuse and lengthening the herbaceous flavours with egg white. A herbaceous gin sour if you wanted to try something a little different.

SALTY DOG

40ml Vodka
Top with Pink Grapefruit Juice

METHOD
* Build in a highball
* Garnished with salt rim and grapefruit wedge

The Salty Dog is an evolution of the Greyhound cocktail, with the addition of a salt rim on the glass.

The Greyhound dates back to Harry Craddock's *Savoy Cocktail Book* (1930) in which it was the combination of gin and grapefruit juice, so it is likely he is the creator. Craddock spent a lot of time in the United States before starting at the Savoy Hotel, and he returned when Prohibition was in full swing.

It was the public's precognition to sub gin for vodka just like with the Martini and Gimlet.

The Salty Dog came about in the 1950s and likely a creation by George Jessel, or so it is claimed, as a way to make the tart grapefruit juice more palatable to consumers.
Seeing as it is a two-ingredient drink, it is crucial to use a quality base spirit.

SATURN

40ml Gin
10ml Velvet Falernum
20ml Lemon Juice
10ml Orgeat
10ml Passionfruit Syrup
Two dashes Orange Bitters

METHOD

- Blended with small cup of crushed ice and poured into a Hurricane glass
- Garnished with a lime wheel and cherry

Created in 1967 by J. 'Popo' Galsini, recorded to be one of the best tiki bartenders of the 1950s and 60s. He held mantle at Kona Kai, Huntington Beach, California according to Jeff Berry's *Beachbum Berry Remixed* (2009) which was also a favourite watering den of Douglas Aircraft engineers who designed rockets and planes.

The cocktail was originally named the X-15, which was the name of a rocket that the USA attempted to fly to the edge of space and back. However in October 1967, shortly after the cocktail was created, one of the X-15s crashed killing the pilot. Galsini decided to abandon the X-15 and renamed it the Saturn Cocktail instead, and with this drink he won the International Bartender's Association World Cocktail Championship in that same year.

I believe that Galsini chose 'Saturn' in order to keep in theme with the space-race, and it was a nod to the Saturn V rocket that propelled the first manned Apollo flight.

SCREWDRIVER

One part Vodka
Three parts Orange Juice

METHOD

- Built in a highball and given a short stir
- Garnished with an orange wedge

One story is attributed to the marines in WW2 who would dose their orange juice with vodka – I would imagine not a regular occurrence, nor does this have any substantive evidence.

There is a reference to this cocktail in a 1949 edition of *Time* magazine stating that *"in the dimly lighted bar of the sleek Park Hotel... the latest Yankee concoction of vodka and orange juice, called a 'screwdriver'."*

Not implying that the drink was made there, but it was certainly made popular by them. The timing matches that of the same time when vodka was becoming the popular spirit of choice in the States.

Another story is attributed to oil workers in the Persian Gulf. With minimal tools at their disposal, and not a high access to liquor, they mixed vodka into their orange juice and stirred it with... a screwdriver.

Perhaps it was the facial expression of someone drinking the vile tasting homemade vodka, during the Prohibition-era, that prompted the idea. Mixed with the need to disguise any talk of alcohol, the code word, screwdriver, was put into use to mislead authorities. So that takes us to the 1920s and 30s before WWII and certainly before mid-century!

But, hey, what about this quote from *Journalism* quarterly, Volume 44 in 1938....

> *"And answered it 'The famous Smirnoff Screwdriver',*
> *Just pour a jigger of Smirnoff vodka over ice cubes,*
> *fill glass with orange juice and serve."*

This meant the cocktail was have certainly been popular by this time but as to who created it, that remains a mystery.

NOTES
• Vodka, Galliano and orange juice gives you a 'Harvey Wallbanger'.

TOREADOR

50ml Reposado Tequila
25ml Lime Juice
15ml Crème de Apricot
10ml Simple Syrup

METHOD
• Shaken and strained into a coupe
• No Garnish

This cocktail first shows face in *Café Royal Cocktail Book* (1937) by W.J. Tarling, it contains around 15 tequila-based cocktails and was printed 16 years prior to the first written Margarita recipe. The recipe is listed as:

"½ Tequila.
¼ Apricot Brandy.
¼ Fresh Lime or Lemon juice."

Alongside this cocktail is the 'Picador' which is the true precursor to the Margarita, as it is identical only it omits salt. There is evidence of tequila arriving in the UK in the mid-1930s, and then being distributed to top bars at the time. With access to a new spirit, bartender attempted to concoct new mixes to tantalise their guests, and the Café Royal book showcases this. Although this is simply speculation, the names are derived from Mexican bullfighting traditions, though this is not confirmed by Tarling.

In the glossary of the *Café Royal Cocktail Book* (1937) Tarling thoughtfully provides an entry for those who had never come across tequila before. He describes tequila as:

"A pale yellow spirit distilled from the Mexican cactus.
It has a distinctive flavour, and in Mexico is drunk as
an aperitif. It is used with success in cocktails."

There is a debate as to whether lime or lemon juice is better suited to this cocktail, and for balance I would have to suggest lime.

NOTES
* A Matador is a bullfighter whose task is to kill the bull.
* A Picador is someone on horseback during bullfighting who prods the bull with a lance.
* A toreador is simply a bullfighter.

VESPER (LYND)

60ml Gin
20ml Vodka
10ml Lillet Blanc

METHOD
* Shaken and strained into a coupe.
* This cocktail can also be stirred for a different texture – however it is not classically how it is served.
* Garnished with a lemon peel.

This is the epitome of Harry Craddock's famous phrase of *"Drink it while it's laughing at you."*

This falls into the category of cocktails whose history is rather well-known, however the recipe has been adapted over time due to availability and changing of products.

The Vesper, or Vesper Martini as it may be before known as, actually comes from the Ian Fleming novel *Casino Royale* (1953) starring James Bond. The excerpt reads:

> *"A dry Martini. One. In a deep champagne goblet...*
>
> *Just a moment. Three measures of Gordon's, one of vodka, half a measure of Kina Lillet. Shake it very well until it's ice-cold, then add a large thin slice of lemon peel."*

The name of the cocktail comes from the double agent know as Vesper Lynd, possibly a reference to occupation in West Berlin (same them together and they sound sensationally similar).

And thus the craze of the Vesper was born. The fact the cocktail is shaken is rather odd, as being a spirit only drink these are normally stirred for texture and dilution. So for historical accuracy it is shaken, but for balance and texture, it should be stirred.

The cocktail is almost impossible to replicate as Kina Lillet was discontinued in 1986, along with new recipes adjusted to contain less quinine, and the ABV of Gordon's was reduced in 1974. However I'm sure some antique bottling collector somewhere in the world could make an extra replica if they so desired. A reasonable substitute would be Cocchi Americano or Lillet Blanc.

Fleming would write the cocktail into his novel the year after Ted Saucier's *Bottom's Up!* (1951) cocktail book was released, which bears first mention of a vodka Martini. Whether this has any influence on the Vesper, or the amount of time Fleming spent at Duke's Bar, London remains a mystery, however they likely all played a factor.

Another theory as to who truly created the Vesper is that it was Fleming's close friend Ivar Bryce. It is said that the version that appears in the novel was actually coined by Ivar, and in the copy of *Casino Royale* that was gifted to him Fleming wrote:

"For Ivar, who mixed the first Vesper and said the good word."

NOTES
- Fleming had an estate named 'Goldeneye' in Jamaica where he and his friends would vacation. There he would serve a rum cocktail of his own making, which he called a 'Vesper'.
- Gilberto Preti of Duke's Bar is sometimes brought into conversation regarding the creation of the Vesper, however he didn't start at Duke's until 23 years after Fleming passes away.

VANCOUVER

50ml Gin
20ml Punt e Mes
5ml Benedictine
Two dashes Orange Bitters

METHOD
- Stirred and strained into a coupe
- Garnished with a lemon peel

Seeing as I've covered the 'Toronto' cocktail, it seems only apt that the Vancouver makes its way onto the pages also.

Legislation was passed in Vancouver to allow the sale of spirits, beers and wine with food in restaurants in 1952, which spawned the creation of this drink in 1954 at the Sylvia Hotel – the hotel had the city's first legally licensed cocktail bar.

However it seems to have fallen from grace in the 1960s, only to be revived by cocktail historian and bartender Steve Da Cruz, who has added it to his own menus since 2006.

Steve Da Cruz he states his story as to where he got the recipe the for the Vancouver cocktail after discussing it with Josiah Bates in 2006:

"Joe (Josiah) Bates... drinks BandB like he owns stick in the company. I had already been good friends with him and

one day he asked me if I had ever heard of a 'Vancouver Cocktail'. I said 'No,' so he wrote the recipe on the bar napkin for me and claimed that he used to drink them at the Sylvia Hotel when he first arrived in Vancouver in 1955."

NOTES

- The Vancouver was the last cocktail Errol Flynn consumed before her death.
- There are rumours that Errol Flynn jumped to his death from the roof of the Sylvia hotel after drinking two Vancouver Cocktails.
- 'BandB' is actually Benectine and brandy, a drier version of Benedictine created by a bartender at the Twenty-One Club, New York, 1937.

WHITE RUSSIAN

40ml Vodka
30ml Coffee Liqueur
5ml Simple Syrup
Half and Half floated

METHOD

- Build in a rocks glass and give a gentle, quick stir
- Layer the half and half on top of the cocktail

Conceived by Gustave Tops, a Belgian bartender in 1949, at Hotel Metropole to celebrate Perle Mesta, U.S. ambassador and regular guest of his, to Luxemburg.

The drink was popularised in the 1950s, when vodka was beginning its invasion of the Western world. Its progenitor was a drink called a 'Russian', made with gin, vodka and crème de cacao. Cream was added to the mix and it was renamed a 'Barbara', a name later toughed up to a 'Russian Bear'. When the Bear was dropped, there were two types of 'Russians'. The black made with Diet Coke, and the white made with cream.

The traditional cocktail known as a Black Russian, first appeared in 1949, becomes a white Russian with the addition of cream. Neither drink is Russian in origin, but both are so named due to vodka being the primary ingredient.

A reference to the name 'White Russian' in the sense of a cocktail appears in *California's Oakland Tribune* in November 21, 1965, it used one oz of Southern Coffee, a short lived coffee brand by Southern Comfort. It fell off the radar until the 1988 film *The Big Lebowski*.

NOTES

- If you mix a standard White Russian (vodka, coffee liqueur and cream) and top it with Coca-Cola, you have yourself a 'Colorado Bulldog'.
- Milk makes for a thin cocktail, use either cream or a blend of milk and cream.
- A 'White Seal' cocktail is a classic White Russian but uses Goslings rum in place of vodka.
- Swapping vodka for aged dark rum gives you a 'La Dominicana'.
- Perle Mesta is hailed as the person with whom the phrase *"hostess with the mostest"* was created for.

ZOMBIE

40ml Jamaican Rum
40ml Golden Puerto Rican Rum
25ml 151-proof Demerara Rum
15ml Falernum
15ml Donn's mix – two parts Grapefruit Juice to one part Cinnamon Sugar
25ml Lime Juice
One barspoon Grenadine
One dash Angostura Bitters
One dashes Absinthe

METHOD

- Shaken and poured into a hurricane glass or tiki vessel
- Garnished with mint bouquet and flaming lime husk

*The Zombie cocktail reached new heights of
popularity after it appeared on the menu of the
Hurricane bar at the 1939 New York World's Fair.*

Firstly, Jeff 'Beachbum' Berry is to thank for discovering the long-lost recipe for this mysterious cocktail. The Zombie was not the first drink to blend multiple rums into a single cocktail, the 'Rum Runner' did this in the 1950s, but the Zombie did popularise it.

Interestingly, the Zombie is actual a build on another rum drink called a 'Planter's Punch', and was the first big 'Rhum Rhapsody' cocktails that Donn would create.

Ernest Raymond Grant joined the navy at 18 that took him all over the pacific, most importantly, the Polynesian islands. His travels fascinated him and instead of spending his collected money on college, he decided to return to the islands and pick up bric-a-brac and alcohol along the way. When Donn opened his own venue in 1933, he filled it with his personal collection of artefacts.

Realistically it was the first famous tiki drink and it cleared the path for tiki to become the widespread phenomenon that it did, due to the way the media could convey the mysterious liquids from the Caribbean as Donn's marketing involved the famed *"maximum two per customer!"* tagline. Couple this with the fact that Donn's venue was the place to be in Hollywood and you can guarantee a surefire spread on the cocktail.

The nickname Donn the Beachcomber came from film producers he met as a consultant in Asia-Pacific. It was the vision of a new-age of cocktail that thrust the Zombie into the future whilst 'classics' remained museum pieces.

Donn would never give out his recipes, even coding his bottles and mixes like 'Don's Mix' so bartenders and the like would borrow the name and dish out a similar looking rum cocktail as long as it was very strong, thus piggybacking off the trending drink. Donn would readjust the formula several times over the years in order to stop the drink being copied or ruined, and would use code to do so. Donn would finally settle on his final recipe when he moved to Hawaii after losing control of his restaurants to his wife. This 1956 version was served at the Polynesian Village in Waikiki and was dubbed the 'Aku-Aku' cocktail.

One of Donn's most secretive ingredients was 'Don's Mix' which had stumped this drink's recreation. This is where Jeff Berry comes into the mix, in 1995 Jeff came into possession of a recipe book that was previously owned by Dick Santiago who was a bartender at one of Donn's restaurants. After many years this ingredient was discovered to be two parts white grapefruit juice to one part cinnamon syrup. The book even contained the original recipe for the cocktail which is retold in *Sippin' Safari* (2007):

"Zombie Punch 'old'
¾ oz lime juice, ½ oz Don's Mix, ½ oz swizzle or falernum,
1½ oz Lownes Jamaica, 1 ½ oz Puerto Rican Dk.,
1oz Demerara 151, dashes angostura, grenadine and absinthe."

The cocktail was originally served in a simple glass highball and garnished with a mint spring, additions to the cocktail started with Trader Vic putting it in Faux-Polynesian ceramics. Even up to as recent as 2006 the Zombie has been receiving aesthetic treatment. Around 2006 Mahiki, London started putting the flaming lime husk on top and many people were convinced that the cocktail must be garnished this way.

NOTES

• Donn was so secretive, that not even the bartenders in his venue would know the complete recipe of ingredients for his cocktails.

MODERN
COCKTAIL
REVIVAL
(1970 –
PRESENT
DAY)

There was what essentially was a 'gap' between 1970 and the late 1980s when it comes to the bartending world. This is what has been referred to as 'Dark Age of Mixed Drinks' which may come across as rather over the top. Sadly, despite how you try to dress it, this is an apt way to describe what was happening during this time.

Many cocktails of this time were likely the creation of marketing teams or overstretched brand managers working for spirit companies looking to promote new products being released. Along with this the increased usage of premixes, packaged juices and soda guns led to the decline in flavour and balance within cocktails as many businesses focused on profitability rather than product offering. This led to the creation of cocktails like the Harvey Wallbanger, Blue Lagoon and Tequila Sunrise and thus the execution of a well-made cocktail had almost disappeared from expectation.

The cocktail scene was bottom barrel and mixed drinks like the 'Woo Woo' were becoming fan favourites, this was until both Dale DeGroff and Dick Bradsell stepped in. Independently they were working to change the cocktail scene by taking it back to basics – fresh ingredients, effective training and relighting their enthusiasm for the industry – just like bartenders of old.

Between them they coined cocktails like the Russian Spring Punch and Cosmopolitan as well as training a huge number of influential bartenders who would travel with their newly found skills and knowledge to reshape the cocktail scene throughout the world.

One thing that these two men both looked back on was classic cocktails and their impact on the drinking culture at the time. The accessibility, familiarity and strict balance of mixed drinks is something that had been lacking for almost two decades and it was the gap in the industry that needed to be cemented.

Nowadays many other names come to mind when you consider influential names within the cocktail world, and many of these people have created their own classic cocktails to add to the ever-growing encyclopedia: Sam Ross, Audrey Saunders and Sasha Petraske to name a few. Wherever they drew inspiration from, they have certainly contributed to what can confidently be described as the Golden Age of the cocktail.

BRAMBLE

50ml Gin
20ml Lemon Juice
15ml Simple Syrup
10ml Crème de Mure (poured through the middle of the finished cocktail)

METHOD
- Built and muddled over crushed ice in a rocks glass
- Pour Mure through the cocktail
- Garnished with lemon wedge and blackberry

The brainchild of London bartender Dick Bradsell who created the cocktail at Fred's Club, Soho, London whilst he was the bar manager in the 1980s.

Bradsell discusses this cocktail in many interviews and the story behind the idea for the cocktail was that and importer for a brandy of liqueurs called 'Cave de Bissey' brought a bottle of their Crème de Mure into the venue one day. Bradsell was urged to try it, and upon doing so states that it reminded him of picking and tasting blackberries with his uncle on the Isle of Wight.

Often compared to that of Jerry Thomas' Gin Fix, swapping the latter's raspberry syrup for blackberry liqueur. Bradsell followed his own format for 'sour' family cocktails, such as the Russian Spring Punch, but decided to use a short glass rather than a highball.

Bradsell has told conflicting stories about what gin was originally used in the first version of the cocktail, some say it was Bombay Original which was the precursor to Bombay Sapphire and had fewer botanicals. Others, such as Robert Simonson, have said that he has quoted them saying it was Booth's Finest.

The drink gets its name from the native English bush. It was inspired by his work with his uncle on the Ilse of Wight picking blackberries. Dick considered it a sentimental play on the Singapore Sling, using all British products.

Bartender and author Toby Cecchni sums up the drink calling it *"the Riesling of the cocktail world, known by drink weenies wince forever."*

NOTES
• Swapping gin for rum gives you a Rumble.

COBBLE HILL

60ml Rye Whiskey
15ml Dry Vermouth
15ml Amaro Montenegro
Two Muddled Cucumber Slices

METHOD
• Bruise the cucumber slices, stir and fine strain into a coupe.

Created by Sam Ross at Milk and Honey in the early days of the bar at Milk and Honey in 2009. Sasha and Sam were thinking about a light, Manhattan style drink, perfect for summer drinking.

This cocktail encompasses a light and floral flavour aspect to what is typically seen as a spirit-forward cocktail, making it much more approachable.

COSMOPOLITAN

45ml Vodka
20ml Triple Sec
20ml Cranberry Juice
10ml Lime Juice
5ml Simple Syrup
1 Lemon Peel in Tin

METHOD
• Shaken and strained into a coupe
• Garnished with a flamed orange peel

The drink that was originally considered the bartender drink of choice due to dryness, and use of three different styles of citrus – lime, orange, cranberry. The grasp of this cocktail was unlike any other of its time during the twentieth century, and there are few cocktails more recognisable than the Cosmopolitan.

The Cosmopolitan was born during the inception of the Gay Rights Movement, boarding into what would be the new cocktail renaissance and would make itself a new modern classic.

Like many classic cocktails there is a debate as to where it came from and who created it, and this is no different – there are plenty of bartenders who would love to lay claim to this drink.

These people start with John Caine from San Francisco who states that this cocktail actually stems from the vodka gimlet, slightly prior to WWII. Spirits being used at this time were poor, he says, and thus needed flavouring to be palatable. Then post war, the Cointreau brand was popularised and the vodka gimlet became the 'Kamikaze' cocktail – consisting of vodka, lime juice and Cointreau. As the years progressed and flavours changed, bartenders began adding cranberry juice to the mix and renamed the drink.

> Several other people claim to have created the cocktail also including the Global Brand Director of Absolute Elyx during the 1980s and 90s. She claims it was the introduction of the 'Martini glass' that spiked the spread of the cocktail.

I like to believe from the stories I have read that it was Cheryl Cook, a bartender from South Beach, Miami who created the cocktail during the 1980s. She gave an interview in which she was questioned about the drink, during which she replied:

"Absolut Citron, a splash of triple sec, a drop of Rose's Lime Juice and just enough cranberry to make it oh so pretty in pink..."

"It's merely a Kamikaze with Absolut Citron and a splash of cranberry juice."

This seems to fall in line with the timeline of the release and marketing of the newly launched Absolut Citron vodka at the time. From here, the Cosmopolitan made its way to San Francisco where it was an instant hit with the LQBTQ community within the city.

The most prominent and substantiated story in this cocktail's history is that Tony Cecchini created and popularised the cocktail as we know it today. He was working in the TriBeCa area of New York in 1988. He was working on the recipe and was replaced the Rose's lime cordial with lime juice and the grenadine in the cocktail with cranberry juice that was one hand to make the 'Cape Codder'. Cecchini gave it to the team to try and it was a resounding success, so much so that Madonna would come by regularly for one.

It was actually Dale DeGroff who really solidified this cocktail's place in history when working at the Rainbow Rooms, New York. He took the cocktail that was going around New York at the time that he says was "*awful*," added fresh lime juice to it and flamed an orange peel on top – "*that was all.*" A rather humble statement from 'King Cocktail' himself.

Cecchini was the only one of 12 people who claimed to have invented it to be able to maintain a consistent story and dates.

The cocktail makes its first appearance in *Pioneers of Mixing at Elite Bars* (1934) by C.C. Mueller in which it isn't actually too far off what we consider a modern version of the cocktail. The cocktail is listed as:

"Jigger of Gordon's gin, two dashes Cointreau, juice of one lemon, a teaspoon of raspberry juice."

DEATH IN VENICE

15ml Campari
Two dashes Grapefruit Bitters
Prosecco to washline

METHOD
* Built in flute and given a gentle stir
* Garnished with an orange peel

This bitter take on the classic 'Death in the Afternoon' was created in 2010 by Tony Conigliaro at 69 Colebrooke Row, London.

ESPRESSO MARTINI

45ml Vodka
10ml Mr. Black
10ml Kahula
30ml Good Quality Espresso
10ml Simple Syrup

METHOD
* Shaken and strained into a coupe
* Garnished with three espresso beans on the foamy head

Originally called the 'Vodka Espresso' and created in 1983 by Dick Bradsell at the Brasserie, SoHo, London (creator of other such drinks as the Bramble, Russian Spring Punch, Treacle, Carol Channing and the Wibble).

A famous model (many have speculated as to whom this was, however it seems to be a closely guarded secret) asked for a drink that would "wake her up then fuck her up." An espresso machine was right beside where Bradsell made drinks, so it was on his mind, and vodka was all the spirit of choice for that time period in London.

The original recipe called for vodka, sugar syrup, two types of coffee liqueur (Tia Maria and Kahula), and freshly made espresso.

As the 80s turned into the 90s, people were still drinking vodka, but this was the decade of the 'V-shaped' Martini glass.

Dick renamed the drink the espresso Martini as the 'Martini' suffix was being applied to all sorts of drinks being served in that glassware, and so the now well-known 'Espresso Martini' was born.

Finally in 1998 Dick renamed the drink the 'Pharmaceutical Stimulant' and served it on the rocks whilst he was working at 'The Pharmacy' in Notting Hill.

Mr. Bradsell is one of many famous, modern bartenders who aided the way for the cocktail renaissance. He added a score of drinks that we use in our repertoire, and enjoyed the world over. This is something that should not soon be forgotten, and so, this page is for you.

EAST 8 HOLD-UP

50ml Vodka
15ml Aperol
25ml Pineapple Juice
15ml Lime Juice
2.5ml Passionfruit Syrup

METHOD
- Shaken and strained into a rocks glass over ice
- Garnished with a lime wedge

Another drink that synonymous with London. Created by Kevin Armstrong, now co-owner of Satan's Whiskers in East London, it has one of the most unique stories behind its creation.

This is from an interview given to *'australianbartender.com.au'* in 2010:

"The first aim was to put some cocktails on a new Milk and Honey (probably the most influential classic cocktail bar to exist) menu that stylistically were served in a more traditional way but actually had real consumer appeal. All the previous menu writers had written old school menus just for the sake of it and lots of the drinks just never sold. The world needs more good vodka cocktails and clearly it was a good because they sell loads of them.

Secondly, and the best bit, is how it got its name. I've lived in E8 (a postcode in London) for ages and when I moved there it was rough as nuts so hold ups were pretty frequent, however Sam Jevons and I went out one night and I was heading home in a different direction so dropped him off in a taxi. He was walking through toward Hackney and stopped off to take a leak. He dropped his trousers and whilst pissing this guy came up behind him, stepped on his trousers and told him to hand over his wallet. It was also the beginnings of something we know now as the Hackney reach-around!

Essentially though, Sam ended up chasing this guy down the street, trousers around his ankles and his belt wrapped round his fist. Premium funny and also a vintage East 8 hold up. Hence the name."

I think this tells the tale better than anything else ever could, bravo.

EL CAMINO

25ml Rye
25ml Mezcal
10ml Benedictine
7.5ml Simple Syrup
Four dashes Peychaud's bitters

METHOD
- Stirred and strained into a rocks glass over block ice.
- Garnished with an orange peel.

A spin on the 'Vieux Carré' created at The Chestnut Club, Santa Monica, CA. The increased popularity of agave spirits sparked this creation and the result was a herbaceous, spiced, spirt-forward cocktail.

FREIGHT TRAIN SWIZZLE

40ml Aged Rum
20ml Green Chartreuse
20ml Falernum
20ml Lime Juice
Four dashes Angostura Bitters (floated)

METHOD
- Build in highball and swizzle over crushed ice
- Garnished with mint sprig, grated nutmeg and bitters

This drink is the brainchild of the legendary Sam Ross, an Australian bartender who went on to dominate New York.

Sam Ross is an alum of Sasha Petraske of Milk and Honey who went on to open Attaboy, New York and Diamond Reef, New York.

The forerunner to this style of drink was called a 'Switchel', an alcohol-free drink from the Caribbean made-up of vinegar, water, Caribbean spices and sweetened with molasses.

FRENCH MARTINI

45ml Vodka
20ml Chambord
45ml Pineapple Juice
5ml Lime Juice
One Raspberry

METHOD
* Shaken and strained into a coupe

This drink has been made by bartenders the world over, many making several hundred in their first cocktail bartending role, and beyond. This drink paved the way to many a drink with the 'Martini' prefix attached to them.

The simple cocktail compromising of only a spirit base, modifier and a juice is the creation of a restaurant owned by British-born Keith McNally. Mr. McNally went on to open several bars, restaurants and clubs in both London and New York.

The cocktail appears on the drink's menu from Balthazar, NY in 1996, and can still be found here to this day, listed as:

"Grey Goose, Lejay Crème de Cassis, pineapple, lemon."

McNally would go on to open such places as Pastis, Cherche Midi and Augustine. The cocktail which found creation at one of McNally's venues, which found its way over to the famous Met Bar in London.

During Prohibition there were many people making and shifting bootleg spirits, many of them being unpalatable and so these needed to be masked. During this time, liqueurs began the dealer's choice as a modifier to do so.

Post-Prohibition when spirits had become legal again, liqueurs had become so popular and versatile they never dropped out of popular favour. Toward the end of the 1900s when this drink was created, vodka was still the spirit of choice and so the use of juices and modifiers to create new, flavoursome drinks was at its peak.

NOTES
- Pineapple juice is key here as it offers a creamy, velvety texture without the heavy mouthfeel.
- The 'French' part comes from the use of the French liqueur Chambord, which has been produced in France since 17th Century.

GIN AND BASIL SMASH

50ml Gin
20ml Lemon Juice
20ml Simple Syrup
Six Basil Leaves

METHOD
- Shaken and fine strained into a rocks glass over ice.
- Garnished with lemon wedge and Basil Leaf.

Created by Jorg Meyer, owner of Bar Le Lion and Boilerman, Hamburg, Germany in 2008. In an interview given by Meyer he goes into how the drink came about:

> *"I was in New York drinking Whisky Smashes by the gallon. When I got back I wanted to make a Gin Smash. The I got a call from John Gakuru. John wanted to do a workshop at Le Lion, which was just six months old at the time."*

Meyer came across a recipe book that had a smash listed with basil as the garnish, and believed it wasn't a far stretch to use it in the drink and muddle both lemon and basil together. Gin was still highly popular at the time, and due to its botanical make-up, he believed it would make for a better cocktail.

Another story from Germany nonetheless, in which Hariolf Sproll is also busy opening a new bar. Funnily enough he was also working on a unique drink for his venue and was taking light from the classic 'Whisky Smash'. He says:

> *"Y'know, it wasn't such a huge leap just replacing the mint with basil, and gin also seemed like a good candidate as the right spirit."*

Sproll served his first Basil Smash in May of 2008 and Meyer published his recipe two month later. Meyer took significant advantage of social media and marketing platforms in order to make his drink an international success.

The two gentlemen had never met and yet were conceiving a drink that was virtually identical in nature and yet had obvious differences. Jörg Meyer explains:

> *"We pack a whole handful in the shaker, including the stems, which are important for the colour. And the muddling shouldn't be too heavy. Otherwise the colour turns too grassy-green and the drink goes mossy."*

Also the Basil Smash comes with slightly more lemon and sugar than it's Gin Basil Smash counterpart.

Jörg Meyer recounts a time that Hotel Nobis, Stockholm, sent two bottles of champagne to his as the hotel bar had made their own version of the drink but replaced and basil with vodka and strawberries. The drink was so popular they sold 30,000 at 22 euros a piece, quite the money-maker.

This demonstrates another dimension to the cocktail: it has become such a staple that bartenders are making their own riffs on it regardless of where you go. Even Jörg Meyer himself created a white rye version called *the* 'Green Rhino Smash'.

GREEN PARK

45ml Tanqueray 10
30ml Lemon Juice
15ml Simple Syrup
10ml Egg White
Three dashes Celery Bitters
Four Fresh Basil Leaves

METHOD
* Wet and dry shaken, then strained into a coupe

Showcasing that the American Bar at the Savoy has been designing classic cocktails since the days of Harry Craddock and Ada Coleman,

Eric Lorincz created this cocktail during his tenure as head bartender in 2011, as a riff on the 'White Lady' cocktail, stemming from the same venue in the 1900s. What a tribute from one legend to another.

GOLD RUSH

60ml Bourbon
20ml Honey Syrup
20ml Lemon Juice

METHOD
- Shaken and strained into a rocks glass over ice
- Garnished with a lemon wedge

During my time bartending, I can't tell you the number of times I have had a guest request a Whiskey Sour with no egg white, as they don't seem to trust that ingredient. The Gold Rush is my go-to in this instance, and here's the story.

Sometime, the best cocktails are the simplest, as the 'Gold Rush' – a riff on a Penicillin – proves.

The year is 2000 and Sasha Petraske opened Milk and Honey in New York. His friend and co-investor, T.J. Siegal was bartending one evening requested a Whiskey Sour with the rich honey syrup that was presently available. You wouldn't believe such a small change would make such a drastic difference.

According to Robert Simonson, a drinks author says "*The syrup dressed it up and gave it a more luxurious mouthfeel.*"

From then on, the 'Gold Rush' began an industry standard once it travelled from New York. The reason this cocktail became a modern classic is due to nature of swapping out one component for another that plays well with the rest of drink. It's just Bourbon, honey and lemon – a perfect balance.

NOTES
- A heavy corn-favoured whiskey is preferable here.
- Trading bourbon for Cognac in this drink gives you a Louisiana Purchase.

- Swapping out bourbon for apple brandy yields a Golden Delicious cocktail.

GARIBALDI

40ml Campari
120ml Freshly Pressed Orange Juice

METHOD
- Put two large, skinless oranges through a high-speed juicer
- Add Campari to small highball and top with fluffy orange juice
- Garnished with an orange wedge

The Garibaldi was revitalised by Naren Young for the menu relaunch of Cafe Dante in New York, and it has taken the world by storm.

The key difference here is the 'fluffy' orange juice providing an extra dimension to the cocktail. Naren says they use a *"high-speed juicer which aerates the juice."* Using an elbow press here would make the juice carry bitter zest from the skin, and so that would need balanced out with sugar syrup.

The flagship drink at Dante is named after an Italian revolutionary Giuseppe Garibaldi, who is credited for unification of Northern and Southern Italy in 1871. Its two ingredients – Campari from the north and as recognition to the red shirts worn by the of Garibaldi's army, and bright orange representing the Sicilian oranges – these are symbolically associated with the region.

Ideally, the cocktail should be made with Valencia oranges, however if possible and in season blood oranges are also delicious here along with aesthetically pleasant. As a note, the winter months tend to bring sweeter yielding citrus with them.

Another recipe for a drink called a Garibaldi also exists, this being:
- Amaro Averna
- Aged rum
- Velvet falernum
- Lime juice
- Orange bitters
- Sparkling water

GREENPOINT

50ml Rye Whiskey
12.5ml Yellow Chartreuse
12.5ml Sweet Vermouth
Two dashes Angostura Bitters
One dash Orange Bitters

METHOD
* Stirred and strained into a coupe
* Garnished with a lemon peel

Created in 2006 by Michael McIlroy at NYC's Milk and Honey, and named after the neighbourhood of Brooklyn sharing its name, and a relative of the classic 'Brooklyn' cocktail.

To remove confusion, it contains yellow Chartreuse, not its green counterpart like the name would elude too.

HARVEST SOUR

30ml Rye
30ml Applejack
20ml Lemon Juice
20ml Simple Syrup
20ml Egg White

METHOD
* Wet and dry shaken then strained into a rocks glass over ice

Created by the legendary Sam Ross, this split base cocktail uses the term 'Harvest' as it is a common description for drinks that have both American whiskey and American apple brandy.

I enjoy the flexibility and variety this drink has to offer. Whiskey Sours (or sours in general) are perfect vehicles for flavour, here you can easily withdraw the simple syrup in place of maple or cinnamon and you have the ideal autumnal beverage.

NOTES

- There are several variations and iterations of this cocktail, some with a form of spiced syrup, some with rum, and others containing sweet vermouth. All have been built from this drink.

HOLE IN THE CUP

45ml Blanco Tequila
5ml Absinthe
30ml Pineapple Juice
20ml Simple Syrup
15ml Lime Juice
Two Cucumber Slices (muddled)

METHOD

- Add all ingredients to tin and bruise the cucumber slices
- Shake and strain into a coupe

This cocktail was the brainchild of Lauren McLaughlin, head bartender at Fresh Kills, and formerly of Milk and Honey during this drink's inception.

According to Lauren, this drink was a riff on one of Sasha Petraske's own, his 'Gordon's Cup'. She remembers passing the service bar one evening when Sasha was correcting a member of staff, asking him to ensure there was less 'detritus' on the surface of the cocktail. No wonder it sticks out so vividly in memory.

"After a few attempts, my co-workers and I agreed that the cocktail was at its best with blanco tequila and shaken... it just became more than the sum of its parts."

INFANTE

50ml Blanco Tequila
20ml Lime Juice
15ml Orgeat

METHOD

- Shaken and strained into a rocks glass with ice
- Garnished with grated nutmeg

This Tequila-based cocktail was created by the one and only Giuseppe Gonzalez at Dutch Kills, 2009. Giuseppe is also credited with the creation of the 'Jungle Bird' and would also outrun most people on the planet.

The name stems from the late Pedro Infante, who died in 1957. He was a Mexican musician and actor held in high regards at the time.

NOTES
- This drink was riffed by Rich Andreoli, bar manager at Pammy's in Cambridge, and came up with a drink called 'The Casper'. This drink contains reposado tequila, hazelnut orgeat, lime juice and rosewater.

JASMINE

40ml Gin
15ml Cointreau
10ml Campari
20ml Lemon Juice

METHOD
- Shaken and strained into a coupe
- Garnished with a lemon peel

Paul Harrington, a bartender at the Townhouse bar in California, needed to know the science and the history behind every ingredient in front of him, likely due to his background studying architecture. Unsatisfied with the current restaurant drinks menu, Harrington looked up old cocktail books and taught himself forgotten drinks and learned the backstories of classic cocktails, to better serve his guests.

Harrington named this drink after Matt Jasmin, a friend with whom he went to architectural school with. In 1992, on a slow-service night his friend pulled up to the bar and said:

"Make me something you've never made before."

He used to push the 'Pegu Club' cocktail (gin, lime, curacao, angostura and orange bitters) so he decided to use Campari instead of angostura, and lemon juice instead of lime. Matt Jasmin tasted the cocktail and stated:

"Wow, you're good, you just invented grapefruit juice"

Harrington himself said *"It has a taste anyone could relate to. When made properly it tastes like fresh-squeezed grapefruit."*

The 'Jasmine' gained wider fame when Harrington included it in his 1998 book *Cocktails*. Years later, Harrington realised he's been spelling his friend's name wrong all along: there was no 'e', but it was too late as the cocktail was already so widespread.

NOTES
- In 1998 when the Bellagio Casino, Las Vegas opened their Chinese restaurant of the same name, the bartenders took the drink and made it their signature serve.
- As a fun poke at myself, my parents were initially going to name me Jasmine if I was to be born female.

JUNGLE BIRD

45ml Dark Jamaican Rum
10ml Campari
45ml Pineapple Juice
15ml Lime Juice
15ml Simple Syrup

METHOD
- Shaken and strained into a rocks glass over ice
- Garnished with a pineapple wedge or leaf

The first traceable recipe was written in *The New American Bartender's Guide* (1989) by John J. Poister. The original recipe had generic dark rum, Campari, pineapple juice, lime and simple syrup, as listed by Jeff 'Beachbum' Berry's book *Intoxica* (2002) recorded the recipe – with Jamaican rum to be more specific.

Then again in 2010, Cruzan Blackstrap rum was used by Giuseppe Gonzalez bringing international attention to the cocktail.

The origin of the drink is steeped in mystery, however one of the long serving members of the Hilton Hotel in Kuala Lumpur was good enough to provide some insightful information. When the hotel opened on July 6th 1973 the Jungle Bird, created by beverage manager Jeffrey Ong Swee Teik, was originally served to guests as a welcome drink. It would initially be served in a small bird-shaped ceramic vessel with a pineapple garnish, talk about a luxury hotel. The cocktail would later be listed as a permanent fixture on the menu in 1978 with the original garnish being a maraschino cherry, lemon and orange wheels along with an orchid.

The name of the drink comes from the tropical birds the guests could view from the bar, through a glass panel in a large netted area.

NOTES
• There was another famous rum cocktail to come out of the hotel, aside from the Jungle Bird, that being the Planter's Punch.

JAPANESE SLIPPER

30ml Midori
30ml Triple Sec
30ml Lemon Juice

METHOD
• Shaken and strained into a coupe
• Garnished with a bright red maraschino cherry

An unapologetically 80s cocktail, tart-sweet, electric green and fun this cocktail sprang into existence in Melbourne, Australia, at a restaurant called Mietta's – created by famed bartender Jean-Paul Bourguignon in 1984.

The name though, where does that come from?

Well in an interview given by Jean-Paul himself he says that he was learning English at the time and he was reading a book about a Japanese woman and her slippers:

"This word slipper was new for me."

And the rest, as they say, is history.

The following year Jean-Paul would leave the restaurant and take the drink with him. He would go on to consult for various business and industries all over Australia, and on very list, you guessed it, he would add the Japanese Slipper.

Interestingly enough Midori had only been on the market for around six years at this time, after it made its huge entrance at the Studio 54 club in New York. It was certainly a successful liqueur produced by the Suntory company.

NOTES
- *Midori* is the Japanese word for Green.

KENTUCKY MAID

60ml Bourbon
25ml Lime Juice
15ml Simple Syrup
Eight Mint Leaves
Two Cucumber Slices

METHOD
- Shaken and fine strained into a rocks glass over ice
- Garnished with a large mint bouquet

This is a more modern style of cocktail, yet finds a branch on the cocktail family tree, being created and solidified by the legendary Sam Ross during his time at Milk and Honey, NY.

This is a build of cocktail that contains lime juice, mint, cucumber and your choice of spirit shaken and served over ice. The first style of drink contained gin and was named 'Ol' Biddy', but Sasha Petraske wasn't found of the name and so it was renamed the 'London Maid'.

Many variations of this cocktail exist, and the name changes depending on the spirit used:
- Vodka – Polish Maid
- Tequila – Mexican Maid
- Gin – Old Maid

There have even been riffs on these drinks such as the Irish Maid from the Dead Rabbit and the French Maid from PDT's Jim Meehan. The combination of spirit, citrus, cucumber and mint seems to be a popular one even to this day.

Although the 'Maid' family was conceived at Milk and Honey, the Kentucky Maid was first served at East Side Company, another of Sasha's ventures.

LONDON CALLING

50ml London Dry Gin
15ml Fino Sherry
15ml Lemon Juice
15ml Simple Syrup
Two dashes Orange Bitters

METHOD
- Shaken and strained into a coupe
- Garnished with a grapefruit peel

What can I say about this cocktail? Ask many who know me and they'll probably roll their eyes when I bring this into conversation.

Sherry has emerged from an obscurity in recent years, still not quite to the extent as many other beverages, yet it has found its place on many cocktail menus the world over.

Adapted from a cocktail submission by Chris Jepson, formerly of Milk and Honey London, in 2002 for the *International Drinks* magazine cocktail competition, the cocktail truly comes alive even as a simple sour with the addition of sherry.

Here, more than anywhere, sherry can be seen to make the world of difference to offer something truly delicious. The drink goes through layers of flavour from dry and fruity, to nutty and citric, it really does have it all.

Tim Phillips, of Bulletin Place states "*The London Calling is the only drink to appear on every Milk and Honey menu.*" If that doesn't scream classic cocktail, I'm not sure what else will.

NOTES
- There actually exists another drink of the same name that was being served at London's Oxo Tower Bar and Brasserie, 2003: Gin and Sloe Gin, sweet vermouth and orange bitters.

LINCHPIN

25ml Aged Rum
25ml Jamaican Rum
15ml Pedro Ximénez Sherry
Two dashes Orange Bitters

METHOD
- Stirred and strained into a rocks glass over block ice
- Garnished with a grapefruit peel

A riff on a classic 'Old Fashioned' made richer in body with the base made up of two styles of rum in place of whiskey.

Created by David Molyneux from The Everleigh, Melbourne in 2017 this has become the staple rum old fashion for bartenders in recent years.

LOS ALTOS

40ml Blanco Tequila
15ml Mezcal
40ml Pineapple Juice
15ml Lime Juice
15ml Simple Syrup
Top with Soda

METHOD
- Shaken and strained into a highball over ice

I'll group these two cocktails together as they were spearheaded by the same person, David Molyneux of The Eveleigh, Melbourne.

MITCH MARTINI

50ml Zubrowka
10ml Crème de Peche
20ml Apple Juice
10ml Lime Juice
5ml Passionfruit Syrup

METHOD

• Shaken and strained into a coupe

Zubrowka bison grass vodka with cloudy apple juice, peach liqueur, and passionfruit syrup, like music to your ears. This drink was created by Giovanni Burdi at Match EC1, London, in 1998. The drink is named either after a customer called Mitch, who did voiceovers for British television, or of a powerful hurricane of the same name.

I'm firmly in the camp that this vodka cocktail should be in every bartender's arsenal of drinks.

NAKED AND FAMOUS

20ml Mezcal
20ml Aperol
20ml Yellow Chartreuse
20ml Lime Juice

METHOD

• Shaken and strained into a coupe

New cocktails are sometimes born from riffs on old classics, however this cocktail doesn't read like it should work. Joaquín Simó brought the drink into existence at Death and Co. in 2011 in which he said it is "*the bastard love child of a classic Last Word and Paper Plane, conceived in the mountains of Oaxaca.*"

Simo continues saying :

> *"There is just enough sugar to balance out the tart*
> *lime and funky, smoky mezcal, but not so much*
> *that it gets cloying ... It's a great balancing act that*

*gives the cocktail structure to let all its complex
ingredients speak in turn, rather than all at once."*

Another great example of old cocktails getting new love.

NEWARK

50ml Laird's Bonded Apple Brandy
25ml Sweet Vermouth
5ml Fernet Branca
5ml Maraschino

METHOD
* Stirred and strained into a coupe
* Garnished with an orange twist

Created by Jim Meehan and John Deragon of PDT in 2007 as they took inspiration from the classic 'Brooklyn' cocktail. According to Meehan, the popularity of rye whiskey cocktails had forced bartenders to look for other avenues to supply this insatiable demand, and as people from Manhattan do, they looked across the river to New Jersey.

There were already plenty of cocktails named after Brooklyn neighbourhoods, so they decided to go with the home of Laird's, and called it the 'Newark'.

NUCLEAR DAIQUIRI

25ml Wray and Nephew Rum
20ml Green Chartreuse
15ml Velvet Falernum
20ml Lime Juice

METHOD
* Shaken and strained into a coupe
* Garnished with a lime wedge

This cocktail was created by Gregor de Gruyther at LAB bar, London, 2005. The founder of this bar, the late Douglas Ankrah, created the Pornstar Martini and the site is now SoHo's beloved Bar Swift.

OLD CUBAN

45ml Bacardi 8 year
30ml Lime Juice
25ml Simple Syrup
Two dashes Angostura Bitters
One Prime Mint Sprig
Champagne top

METHOD

* Shaken and fine strained into a coupe
* Garnished with a mint leaf

One of the few truly 'Modern Cocktails' of our time, it has earned its stripes in the books as a delicious concoction.

Created by the one and only Audrey Saunders in 2001, she would later go on to open the famed Pegu Club in New York. Saunders and the Pegu Club were always names at the forefront of bartending, particularly at the time of this drink's creation when the cocktail culture was still being revived. Saunders honed in on technique regarding the Old Cuban, that being, to fine strain the drink. This was to prevent any ice shards, or broken mint ruining your perfect smile.

Saunders had a reputation for revitalising classic drink, and the Old Cuban is no different as it lays somewhere in the middle of the Mojito and the French 75.

She started work on the drink during her time at Beacon, New York, but the cocktail would not come to completion until she moved to Tonic, New York. Finally, the cocktail would later become the signature serve at Pegu Club, and has been enjoyed the world over.

NOTES

* The key to this cocktail is the use of aged rum – hence the use of the prefix 'Old'.
* The working title for the cocktail was 'El Cubano'.

PAPER PLANE

20ml Bourbon
20ml Amaro Nonino
20ml Aperol
20ml Lemon Juice

METHOD
- Shaken and strained into a coupe

The brainchild of Sam Ross, but first appearing on The Violet Hour bar's menu in Chicago in 2008. On this menu, under the whiskey cocktails, was a drink called 'The Paper Airplane' containing bourbon, Amaro Nonino, Campari and lemon juice.

Even though it is similar to the cocktail we are talking about, there is a reason for this. Toby Maloney helped open The Violet Hour used to work with Sam at Milk and Honey, and asked him to help him create an original cocktail for the bar. Ross based the name of drink off the song by M.I.A (actually called 'Paper Planes'). Ross was based in New York and one night after an evening of drinking, sent a voicemail to Maloney who misheard the name as "*The Paper Airplane.*"

Ross remade the cocktail the following week and realised it wasn't as balanced as he would like, "*it was slightly too bitter and the sweetness wasn't there. I subbed Aperol and was immediately satisfied with the result.*"

PALOMA

50ml Blanco Tequila
20ml Pink Grapefruit juice
10ml Lime Juice
10ml Simple Syrup
Top with San Pellegrino Pompelmo

METHOD
- Short Shake and strained into a highball with cubed ice
- Garnished with grapefruit wedge and salt rim

Described as an *"anytime drink and manageable on a hangover,"* I would say this takes the cake as the best tequila highball cocktail available. This cocktail can also be made with soda water, but traditionally it is lengthened with grapefruit soda like 'Ting' or 'San Pellegrino', or Mexican brands such as Jarritos.

As for the history of this cocktail, we're not quite sure who the first person to make one was, it could have very possibly been a person walking down the street mixing grapefruit soda and tequila together. What we do know is that there was a period of several years in which the Paloma's Wikipedia page had been completely falsified with listing of ridiculous blogs and articles.

What has been discovered are several timelines linking to the rise and popularity of the cocktail?

Firstly, the release of the grapefruit soda from 'Squirt' brand, which originated in the United States in the 1930s and then entered the Mexican market in 1955. This seems to be a critical link in the story, but it is not until the 1970s when Squirt did marketing to promote this mixture.

Later, in the 1990s, references appear of a mixture of tequila, Squirt, lime, and salt that come together as an established cocktail. A recognised area for the mixture of these ingredients seems to be a town called Tlaquepaque, just outside of Guadalajara.

Two books reference the recipe for a Paloma as something else, *A Cook's Tour of Mexico* (1997) dubs it a 'Lazy Man's Margarita', and *Cowboy Cocktails* (2000) called it 'La Paloma' (meaning 'The Dove').

The Paloma is a relatively 'new' cocktail and it has entered the market at pretty much the perfect time. With the cocktail revival, and now cycle of rediscovery, plus the rise in appreciation for agave spirits, this essentially two ingredient cocktail has won the hearts of many, and it is just the beginning.

NOTES
- The salt rim on the cocktail is, in my eyes, optional. You can simply add salt directly into the drink if you wish, it's much less invasive that way.

- There was a mid-1800s folk song named 'La Paloma', whether there is a connection here or not is unknown.

PENICILLIN

50ml Blend Scotch
20ml Lemon Juice
12.5ml Honey Syrup
12.5ml Ginger Syrup
7.5ml Ardbeg 10 Float

METHOD
- Shaken and strained into a rocks glass over ice
- Garnished with lemon wedge, candied ginger and peat whiskey float

Created in 2005 at Milk and Honey by the one and only Sam Ross, the architect of many classic drinks and cocktail culture in New York.

Ross himself states that one day there was a delivery with a newly released line of Compass Box whiskey and was playing around on a riff of a 'Gold Rush' (bourbon, honey and lemon juice), which was created by T. J. Siegal, another involved with Milk and Honey.

Scotch was a replacement for bourbon and Ross added in ginger for a spice aspect to the cocktail. The final addition was a float of Peat Monster scotch, a heavily smoked whiskey that he thought would contribute a complimentary aroma. Ross wasn't convinced, but it was a huge success:

"I was happy with it but I didn't think too much of it."

Sam Ross travelled to Los Angeles in 2007 as a consultant and introduced several bartenders to the cocktail, and many others.

"They went on to do their own programs at different places ... That's how the Penicillin spread hard throughout the West Coast."

The drink is aptly named as Nobel Laureate Alexander Fleming, who discovered the Penicillin and its therapeutic benefits, was Scottish.

When you think of it, how it took until 2005 to combine, lemon, honey, ginger and whiskey into a cocktail is truly mind-blowing. Seems like such an obvious combination to us nowadays.

NOTES
- Swap the Scotch whiskey for gin and the Islay whiskey for a spritz of rosewater and you get a 'Son of a Bee Sting' cocktail.

REDHOOK

50ml Rye
12.5ml Punt E Mes
12.5m Maraschino

METHOD
- Stirred and strained into a coupe
- Garnished with a cherry

This cross between the 'Brooklyn' and 'Manhattan' is the work of former Milk and Honey bartender Enzo Errico, in 2003. This drink builds on the classic whiskey base and doses it with the subtly bitter Italian vermouth, Punt e Mes, and sweetens it with the addition of Maraschino.

While there are a number of modern drinks that have played off the classic composition of both the Manhattan and the Brooklyn, Errico's is one of the more enduring riffs.

When I lived in Melbourne a few years back a bar I used to frequently, Spleen, was headed by a gentleman named Joel Bainbridge and this was his drink of choice when he would visit me at Bar 1806. So this cocktail is most certainly dedicated to you.

REVOLVER

50ml Bourbon
15ml Mr. Black Coffee Liqueur
5ml Simple Syrup
Two dashes Orange Bitters

METHOD
* Stirred and strained into a coupe
* Garnished with a flamed orange peel

Created by Jon Santer in 2004 at Bruno's, San Francisco, but then popularised at Bourbon and Branch. This cocktail was likely aided by the coffee movement that swept the West Coast of the United States several years ago.

The cocktail's name is a play on the spirit used, being Bulleit bourbon. Rather than reaching for a bottle of sweet vermouth, Santer used coffee liqueur to compliment the spiced flavours from the heavy rye whiskey and add additional sweetness joined by naturally bitter coffee flavours. The flamed orange peel not only adds a theatrical essence, but also contributes to highlight the desirable flavours in the cocktail.

Jeffery Morgenthaler's *The Bar Book* (2014) recalls the time he first uncovered the cocktail whilst in New York from a well-travelled patron. Couple this with the cocktail's inclusion in *Three Ingredient Cocktails* (2017) by Robert Simonson, you can see why this cocktail has been pushed to modern-classic status.

RIGHT HAND

40ml Aged Rum
20ml Campari
20ml Sweet Vermouth
Two dashes Xocolatl Mole Bitters

In essence, a rum-laced Negroni created by Michael McIlroy in 2007 at Milk and Honey, New York.

Sam Ross stated there was actually a series of 'Hand' cocktails created over the years:

'Tres Hands' was a mezcal and tequila variation, 'Smoking Hand' was an Islay and Highlands variation, and before the Boulevardier became popularised, the 'Left Hand' was a bourbon riff on this cocktail. They were inspired by the "newly released chocolate bitters from the Bittermans."

RITZ COCKTAIL

25ml Cognac
10ml Cointreau
5ml Maraschino
10ml Lemon Juice
5ml Simple Syrup
Champagne top

METHOD
- Shaken and strained into a coupe
- Garnished with a flamed orange peel

A large portion of the cocktail renaissance in New York was led by the return classic cocktails, and this was spearheaded by Dale DeGroff.

Whilst working for restaurateur Joe Baum at Aurora, Dale really came into his own. Dale and Joe envisioned making famous pre-Prohibition cocktails and as such Dale was instructed to find a copy of the *How to Mix Drinks* (1862) by Jerry Thomas, a book long out of print. The main takeaway was sticking to traditional methods when cocktails were great, and using all fresh ingredients, notably fresh citrus juice in place of sour-mix.

Dale also reviewed Ted Saucier's 1951 publication *Bottom's Up!* and noticed that there were 'Ritz' cocktails for both the London and Paris Ritz, and thus the New York Ritz required its own serve.

Dale was a showman, and was well-travelled. He had seen many luxurious venues serve their signature cocktails and had drawn inspiration from them. Champagne from the Ritz Hotels in London and New York, flamed orange peel over the espresso at Mama Leone's and the glassware at Chasen's in LA, these individual parts came together to form the Ritz Cocktail.

Dale took the Ritz of Paris cocktail and twisted it slightly with the inclusion of Maraschino liqueur. Maraschino was fairy obscure in the 1980s, however Dale was enticed by its flavour profile and brought it to the table to be included in this cocktail.

RUSSIAN SPRING PUNCH

40ml Vodka
10ml Crème de Cassis
20ml Lemon Juice
10ml Simple Syrup
Top with champagne

METHOD

* Shaken and strained into a large highball over ice then capped with crushed ice
* Garnished with mint spring, lemon wedge and a raspberry

A modern-day classic using vodka as the champion spirit. Vodka is so easily overlooked in modern-day bar-tendering, however this was not the case in the 80s or 90s. Being a punch, the accepted formula of parts that make the cocktail are four weak (generally soda water or a juice), three strong (spirit), two sour (citrus juice) and one sweet (sugar or flavoured sweetener).

Being such a well-known cocktail, there is a surprisingly finite amount of information regarding its origin. The best, and only, source of information comes the legendary Difford's Guide in which Dick Bradsell gave an interview many years ago.

This cocktail was created by Dick Bradsell in London sometime in the 1980s.

Printed in the December/ January 1998 edition of CLASS magazine (a popular drink's industry publication), Dick laid out the thought process of this drink, *"Many springs ago, I conceived the Russian Spring Punch which is basically a spiked Kir Royale over ice."* Personally, I enjoy when people are truly honest about their cocktails.

In August of 2015, Dick's full story was revealed to Difford's Guide.

"I created this drink for a friend of ours, Rebecca Pont De Bie and Peter Kent in the 80s.

Peter was a gay guy, who designed shops and married Hamish Bowles, who is editor-at-large for Vogue. They shared an extremely nice flat in the Knightsbridge end of Kensington, and they wanted to have a cocktail party but they didn't have enough money.

So I suggested that, as they didn't have quite enough cash for prestigious amounts of alcohol, they requested that everyone brough a bottle of bubbly. So if you brought rubbish, you got the drinks rubbish, and if you brought quality, you drank quality.

I stocked the bar with glasses, and in each glass was a shot of vodka, half a shot of lemon juice, two barspoons of sugar, one barspoon of cassis and ice.

It was lethal, that thing. We had people falling down the stairs and dancing around. I called it the Russian spring punch because It has vodka in it, which is Russian, and it's a Collins, or a Fizz, which is a spring drink."

And thus the highly appealing and champagne-laced cocktail was born, a raging success through the 80ss and well-deserving of a place among classic cocktails.

SPITFIRE

40ml Cognac
15ml Sauvignon Blanc
10ml Crème de Peche
20ml Lemon Juice
12.5ml Simple Syrup
15ml Egg White

METHOD
* Shaken and strained into a coupe
* Pour wine through the finished the drink

Created in 2006 by Tony Conigliaro at Shochu Lounge, London. It's a rarity that non-fortified wines are included in cocktails. Tony has nailed it here as an ingredient in this riff on a 'Delicious Sour'.

SILK STOCKINGS

25ml Blanco Tequila
20ml Crème de Cacao Blanc
25ml Half and Half
10ml Grenadine
Two Chocolate Bitters

METHOD
* Shaken and strained into a coupe
* Garnished with a grated chocolate

A modern classic, and one that does not look like it should come together. Tequila, cream and chocolate blend together to create a delicious symphony of flavour. Even if you claim not to enjoy tequila, I believe this would change your mind.

Created by Ryan Chetiyawardana in 2009, who presented this cocktail at The Cabinet Room, London during the UK finals for Diageo's World Class competition.

SUNFLOWER

30ml Gin
20ml St. Germain
20ml Triple sec
20ml Lemon juice
Two dashes Absinthe

METHOD
- Shaken and strained into a coupe
- Garnished with a lemon peel

A take on the 'Corpse Reviver No.2' cocktail created in 2008 by Sam Ross at Milk and Honey, New York. Elderflower liqueur simply replaces the Lillet Blanc within the cocktail, yet it flips it on its head to yield a floral yet herbaceous result.

TRIDENT

25ml Aquavit
25ml Manzanilla Sherry
25ml Cynar
One dash Peach Bitters
One dash Orange Bitters

METHOD
- Stirred and strained into a rocks glass over block ice
- Garnished with an orange peel

The Trident is a seafaring-inspired riff of the classic Negroni, created by Robert Hess in 2000, a cocktail historian from Seattle. Hess was working in tandem with Fee Brothers bitters company, and focusing on their peach bitters flavour in particular.

In an attempt to recreate the cocktail, Hess aligned the trio of components – strong, sweet, bitter – with those of similar flavour profile, each originating from a nautical driven country.

The gin is replaced with aquavit, Campari for Cynar, and the sweet vermouth for sherry, dashing the peach bitters on top of the cocktail.

NOTES
- Hess calls this *"one of my most successful cocktails."* However he has since revised the recipe and replaced one dash of peach bitters with a dash of orange bitters.
- This cocktail's name is also the weapon of choice of the superhero 'Aquaman'.

TRINIDAD SOUR

30ml Angostura Bitters
20ml Rye
30ml Orgeat
20ml Lemon Juice

METHOD
- Shaken and strained into a coupe
- Garnished with an orange peel

Created by Giuseppe Gonzalez in 2009 at Clover Club in Brooklyn, and was inspired by the competition winning 'Trinidad Especial' by Valentino Bolognese.

The Trinidad Especial cocktail used lime instead of lemon, and pisco in place of rye whiskey. It took a while for the Trinidad sour to catch on, even though the cocktail was balanced and had and oily texture coming from the angostura bitters.

Gonzalez himself said that it was John Gertsen who helped popularise the cocktail. Gertsen co-founded Drink in Boston before going to work at ABV, San Francisco. Drink was a menu-less bar and so he would hold it back until a guest wanted to try something truly adventurous.

Gonzalez later moved to Las Vegas to work at Herbs and Rye, when a guest order the cocktail from him, to which his reply was *"Go fuck yourself."* The guest stormed over to the owner and told her what he had said. After the debacle Gonzalez told the guest to Google the cocktail and he then put it together. The guest had tried the cocktail in London earlier that year:

"That's when I realised how big it really was."

TOMMY'S MARGARITA

60ml Arette Reposado
30ml Fresh lime Juice
15ml Agave Syrup

METHOD
* Shaken and strained into a rocks glass over ice

Created by Julio Bermejo in the late 1980s and named after his family restaurant (Tommy's Mexican Restaurant) in San Francisco, the self-proclaimed premier tequila bar in the world.

Julio became a legend in the industry due to his knowledge of agave and being a spokesperson for the tequila market, particularly 100% agave tequila. During this time the drinks industry was using 'mixto' tequila and sour mix to make tequila cocktails, Bermejo refused to follow suit and stocked his bar exclusively with 100% agave.

Bermejo travelled with the President of Mexico, back in 2001, to the UK and France in order to sign agreements recognising tequila's denomination of origin status. In doing so, he was about to liaise with influential bartenders and teach them about agave spirits, particularly how they shine in the Tommy's Margarita and spread the cocktail all over the world.

NOTES
* Bermejo preferred the use of Persian limes in his Tommy's Margarita.

TREACLE

50ml Myer's Dark Rum
20ml Clear Apple Juice
5ml Simple Syrup
Two dashes Angostura Bitters

METHOD
* Stirred and strained into a rocks glass over ice
* Garnished with a lemon peel

Another creation by Dick Bradsell, certainly one of his lesser-known cocktails in his library.

Treacle generally refers to products used in baking: golden syrup which his sticky and sweet, and then black treacle which is tarry with a bitter edge and is slightly spiced. These are British equivalents to corn syrup and molasses.

The Treacle I am referring to is course the cocktail, a combination of dark rum, angostura bitters, sugar and apple juice. Originally Bradsell used cheap bottled apple juice and said that the cocktail calls for its use specifically in order to achieve the black treacle taste.

NOTES
* Originally the apple juice is floated on top after the other ingredients have been stirred.

THE AFFILIATE

40ml Aged Cuban Rum
20ml Fino Sherry
20ml Cherry Herring
Two dashes Angostura Bitters
Two dashes Orange Bitters

METHOD
* Stirred and strained into a rocks glass over block ice
* Garnished with an orange peel

This rum based Old Fashioned style cocktail comes from Charles Joly from the Aviary, Chicago in 2013.

The story behind this cocktail is limited however how I stumbled across it is a different story. I was sat at a bar in London and my friend Ryan asked me if I could name any classic rum cocktails with sherry, I couldn't think of any at that moment. So I tasked myself with finding several, and this is the one I liked the most. It adds a dry, fruit-centric spin on normally a rather sweet take on this style of cocktail.

UNICORN TEARS

25ml Gin
25ml Fino Sherry
25ml Pineapple Juice
15ml Lemon Juice
15ml Simple Syrup
One dash Absinthe
Soda top

METHOD

- Shaken and strained into a highball over ice
- Garnished with a cucumber peel and mint sprig

Sam Ross consulted for Electra Cocktail Club, Las Vegas where we led and created the cocktail program for the venue. Located in the Palazzo Resort, Electra Cocktail Club is a venue that focuses on tropical delights and chooses to celebrate rum, pisco and mezcal as champion spirits. There is even a proclaimed pisco expert in the form of Lew Caputa on site to guide guests through a South American adventure.

One of the cocktails that caught my eye was a highball in the form of 'Unicorn Tears', an eclectic mix of gin, sherry, pineapple and absinthe. Under my restrictions, I would group this as a classic cocktail as it can be replicated the world over.

WHITE NEGRONI

30ml Gin
25ml Lillet Blanc
20ml Suze
One dash Orange Bitters

METHOD

- Stirred and strained into a rocks glass over block ice
- Garnished with a grapefruit peel

A take on a classic Negroni, spinning the cocktail to give it a more floral and fragrant aesthetic rather than a bitter one.

According to Robert Simonson this was created by Wayne Collins in 2001 at Vinexpo in Bordeaux, France. Collins was participating in a Plymouth gin competition and the brand's global ambassador was on-site, drinking a Negroni prior to judging. He decided to take a new spin on this classic and reached for two bottles of French ingredients, Lillet Blanc and Suze.

The cocktail won the competition and began its own adventure in 2003 with Simon Ford. Plymouth Gin hadn't been circulating in the United States for quite some time, so Ford brought it to New York and introduced it to Audrey Saunders of Pegu Club, the cocktail was a new addition to her menu, heightening its recognition and popularity.

NOTES
- Collins' original recipe was 1.5oz Plymouth Gin, 1oz Lillet Blanc and 3/4 oz Suze. Suze is rather heavy hitting so it may be best to dial it back within the cocktail.

WILLIAM WALLACE

50ml Blended Scotch
10ml Pedro Ximénez Sherry
10ml Sweet Vermouth
Three dashes Orange Bitters

METHOD
- Stirred and strained into a coupe
- Garnished with an orange peel

This cocktail is likely the most recent modern classic to come out of the woodwork in recent year. Created in 2019 by none other than UK bartender and bar owner, Joe Schofield who himself says:

> *"The William Wallace is inspired and takes elements*
> *from the Rob Roy and Bobby Burns and is named after*
> *another Scottish hero with an alliterate name."*

Reimaging or reinventing a stirred whiskey-based cocktail seems like a difficult thing to accomplish because so many combinations already exist, however Joe Schofield has accomplished is so seamlessly and this is a certified classic in my eyes.

WIBBLE

30ml Gin
30ml Sloe Gin
7.5ml Crème de Mure
25ml Pink Grapefruit juice
10ml Lemon Juice
5ml Simple Syrup

METHOD
* Short shake and strained into a coupe
* Garnished with a lemon peel

Created in 1999 by Dick Bradsell at The Player, London for Nick Blacknell – a prime advocate of gin. Blacknell approached the bar and asked Bradsell to make him a cocktail incorporating Plymouth gin, which he was representing at the time. Bradsell would later talk about this cocktail in an interview whilst working at Match, London in 2000:

> *"I too have recently invented a gin-based cocktail,*
> *heavily inspired by one of the reps from Plymouth*
> *coming into my bar ad asking me to invent him a drink*
> *utilising his product. I surprised myself with how nice*
> *the end result was. We called it the Wibble (It may*
> *make you wobble, but it won't make you fall down).*

Dick named this cocktail after the 1970s 'Weebles' children's roly-poly toys which were advertised with the catchphrase, *"Weebles wobble, but they don't fall down."*

BOOKS,
REFERENCES

- Ricket, Edward. *The Gentleman's Table Guide. Being Practical Recipes for Wine Cups, American Drinks, Punches, Cordials, Summer & Winter Beverages.* London, Frederick Warne & Co., **1872**.

- Thomas, Jerry. *The Bar-tender's Guide; How to mix all kinds of Plain and Fancy Drinks.* New York, Dick and Fitzgerald, **1876**.

- Barnes, Albert. The complete bartender. Art of Mixing Plain and Fancy drinks. Philadelphia, Royal Publishing Co, **1884**.

- Byron, O. H. *The Modern Bartender's Guide Or Fancy Drinks and how to make them.* New York, Excelsior Publishing House, **1884**. (First known written spec for Martinez and Manhattan).

- Fleischman, Joseph. *The Art of Blending and Compounding Liquors and Wines.* New York, Dick & Fitzgerald Publishers, **1885**.

- Johnson, Harry. *New and Improved Bartender's Manual.* New York L. Goldmann, **1888**.

- Proulx, Theodore. *Bartender's Manual.* Chicago, Chapin & Gore, **1888**.

- Boothby, W, M. *American Bartender.* San Francisco, H. S. Crocker Company, **1891**.

- Wehman, Henry. J. *Wehman's Bartenders' Guide. The Art of Preparing All Kinds of Plain and Fancy Drinks Both Native and Foreign.* New York, Henry J. Wehman, **1891**.

- Schmidt, William. *The Flowing Bowl – What and When to Drink.* New York, Charles L. Webster & Co., **1892**.

- Lawlor, Chris. F. *The Mixicologist.* Cincinnati, Lawlor & Co, **1895**.

- Spencer, Edward. *The Flowing Bowl.* London, Grant Richards, **1899**.

- Boothby, William T: *Cocktail Boothby's American Bartender: A twentieth century encyclopedia for all students of mixology (2nd ed., rev. & enl.).* San Francisco: The San Francisco News Co, **1900**.

- Johnson, Harry. *Bartender's Manual.* New York, L. Goldmann, **1900**.

- Pagem Louis. C. *The Cocktail Book: A Sideboard Manual for Gentlemen.* Boton, L.C. Page & Company. **1900**.

- Daly, Tim. *Daly's Bartender Encyclopedia.* Massachusetts, Tim Daly, **1903**.

- Spencer, Edward. *The Flowing Bowl.* London, Grant Richards, **1903**.

- Applegreen, John. *Applegreen's Bar Book.* Chicago, The Hotel Monthly, **1904**.
  (Has the equal parts martini listed as "Crisp Cocktail").

- Muckensturm, Louis: *Louis' Mixed Drinks With Hints for the Care & Serving of Wines.* Boston & New York, H. M. Caldwell Co., **1906**.

- Lowe, Paul E. *Drinks As They Are Mixed.* Chicago, Frederick J. Drake and Company, **1904**.

- Stuart, Thomas. *Stuart's Fancy Drinks – and how to mix them.* New York, Excelsior Publishing House, **1904**.

- Kappeler, George, J. *Modern American Drinks – How to Mix and serve all kinds of Cups and Drinks.* Ohio, Saalfield Publishing Co., **1906**.

- Mahoney, Charles. S,. *The Hoffman House Bartender's Guide.* New York, Richard K. Fox, **1908**.

- Paul, Charlie. *Recipes of American and other Iced Drinks.* London, Farrow & Jackson Limited, **1909**.

- Grohusko, Jacob, Abraham. *Jack's manual.* New York, McLunn & Co, **1910**.

- Raymond. E. Sullivan. *The Barkeeper's Manual.* Baltimore, Baltimore Country Club, **1910**.

- Montague, Harry: *The Up-To-Date Bartenders' Guide. A valuable ready reference guide to the art of mixing drinks.* Baltimore, I. & M. Ottenheimer, **1913**.

- Straub, Jacques. *Straub's Manual of mixed Drinks.* Chicago, R. Francis Welsh Publishing Company, **1913**.

- Ensslin, Hugo. *Recipes for mixed drinks.* New York, Fox Printing House, **1916**. (aviation and alexander recipe)

- Stockbridge, Bertha E. I,. *What to Drink. The Blue Book of Beverages.* New York & London, D. Appleton and Company, **1920**.

- MacElhone, Harry. *Harry's ABC of Mixing Cocktails.* London, Dean & Son LTD., **1922/23**.

- Vermeire Robert. *Cocktails: How to Mix them.* Connecticut, Martino Fine Books, 2015. (Originally published in 1922).

- McElhone, Harry and Wynn. *Barflies and Cocktails.* Paris, Lecram Press, **1927**.

- Requien, Marcel and Farnoux-Reynaud, Lucien. *L'Heure du Cocktail.* Paris, Corps Reviver. **1927**.

- Lowe, Paul E. Drinks. *How to Mix and How to Serve.* Toronto, The Musson Book Company, **1927**.

- Warnock, Charles. *Giggle water. Including Eleven most Famous Cocktails.* New York, Charles. S. Warnock, **1928**.

- Thomas, Jerry. *Bon Vivant's Companion or How to Mix Drinks.* New York, Alfred A. Knopf, **1929**.

- Alimbau, Jm and Milhorat, E. *L'Heure du Cocktail.* Toulouse, Imprimerie Regionale. **1929**.

- Craddock, Harry. *The Savoy Cocktail Book.* London, Constable & Company Ltd. **1930**.

- Doran, Roxana B. *Prohibition Punches; A book of beverages.* Philadelphia, Dorrance & Company Inc. **1930**.

- McElhone, Harry. *Harry's ABC of Mixing Cocktails.* London, Dean & Son Ltd. **1930**.

- Jr. Judge. *Noble Experiments. The Third Volume of the Famous Here's How Series.* New York, John Day Company, **1930**.

- Elliot, Virginia & Stong, Philip. *Shake 'Em Up.* Ohio, Brewer and Warren Inc. **1930**.

- Boothby, William T. *Boothby's World Drinks and How to Prepare Them.* San Francisco, Boothby's World Drinks Co. **1930**.

- Crockett, Albert Stevens: *Old Waldorf Bar Days.* New York, Albertine Press, **1931**.

- Ade, George: *The Old-Time Saloon. Not Wet – Not Dry. Just History.* New York, Ray Long & Richard R. Smith Inc., **1931**.

- Whitaker, Alma: *Bacchus Behave! The Lost Art of Polite Drinking.* New York, Frederick A. Stokes Company, **1933**.

- Grohusko, Jacob, Abraham. *Jack's Manual.* New York, Alfred A. Knopf, **1933**.

- Boothby, William. *World Drinks and How to mix Them.* San Francisco, The Record Printing & Publishing Co., **1934**.

- Cobb, Irvin S. *Irvin S. Cobb's Own Recipe Book.* Louisville & Baltimore, Frankfort Distilleries Incorporated, **1934**.

- Reinhardt, Charles. *Punches and Cocktails. New edition, revised and enlarged.* New York, Arden Book Company, **1934**.

- Crockett, Albert Stevens. *The Old Waldorf-Astoria Bar Book.* New York, New York Lithographing Corporation, **1935**.

- Eduardo, Jorge. *Peychaud's New Orleans Cocktails.* New Orleans, **1935**.

- Meier, Frank. *The Artistry of Mixing drinks (1st ed).* France, Fryam Press. **1936**.

- Duffy, Patrick Gavin. *The Official Mixer's Manual.* New York, Blue Ribbon Book, **1940**.

- Whitfield, W.C. *Here's How: Mixed Drinks.* Asheville, Three Mountaineers Inc. **1941**.

- Clisby, Stanley Arthur. *Famous New Orleans Drinks & How to Mix 'Em.* New Orleans, Rogers Printing Company, **1943**.

- Baker, H. Jr, Charles. *The Gentleman's Companion Being an Exotic Drink Book or, Around the World With a Jigger, Beaker and Flask.* New York, Crown Publishers, **1946**.

- Vic, Trader. *Trader Vic's Book of Food and Drink.* New York, Doubleday and Company, Inc, **1946**.

- Embury, David, Augustus. *The Fine Art of mixing Drinks.* New York, Doubleday & McLure Company, **1948**.

- *Esquire's Handbook for Hosts.* New York, Grosset and Dunalp, **1949**.

- Saucier Ted. *Ted Saucier's Bottoms Up.* New York, Greystone Press, **1951**.

- *The U.K.B.G guide to Drinks.* London, United Kingdom Bartenders' Guild, **1955**.

- MacElhone, Harry. *The ABC of Cocktails.* New York, Peter Pauper Press, **1962**.

- **1967** *Cocktails and mixed drinks* by Charles. A. Tuck

- Hogg, Anthony. *Cocktails and Mixed Drinks.* London, Hamlyn, **1979**.

- Poister, John, J. *The New American Bartender's Guide.* New York, Signet, **1989**.

- Reekie, Jennie. *The London Ritz Book of Drinks*. London, Harper Collins, **1990**.

- Regan, Gary. *The Bartender's Bible*. New York, Harper Collins, **1991**.

- Waggoner, Susan and Markel, Robert. *Vintage Cocktails*. New York, Stewart Tabori and Chang, **1999**.

- Costantino, Maria. *The Cocktail Handbook*. Devon Silverdale Books, D & S Books Limited, **2001**.

- Kiernan, Anna. *The Algonquin Bar and Cocktail Book*. New York, Barnes and Noble, **2002**.

- Berry, Jeffery. *Intoxica*. California, Slave Labor Books. **2002**.

- Broom, Dave. *Rum*. London, Mitchell Beazley Octopus Publishing Group, **2003**.

- Nicole, Beland. *The Cocktail Jungle*. Philadelphia, Running Press Book Publishers, **2003**.

- Regan, Gary. *The Joy of Mixology*. New York, Clarkson, Potter, Crown Publishing Group, **2003**.

- Argamasilla, Pepin and Dawson, Marl Aixala. *Bacardi: A Tale of Merchants, Family and Company*. Facundo and Amailia Bacardi Foundation, Inc, Bacardi and Company limited, **2006**.

- DeGroff, Dale. *The Essential Cocktail*. New York, Clarkson Potter, Crown Publishing Group, **2008**.

- Hess, Robert. *The Essential Bartender's Guide*. New York, Mud Puddle Books, **2008**.

- Hess, Robert and Miller, Anistatia. *The Museum of the American Cocktail Pocket Recipe Guide, Museum Edition*. New Orleans, The Musuem of the American Cocktail, **2008**.

- Difford, Simon, Ed. *Difford's Guide to Cocktails*. London, **2016**.

- Simonson, Robert. *A Proper Drink: The Untold Story of How a Band of Bartenders Saved the Civilised Drinking World.* New York, TEN SPEED PRESS, **2016**.

- Moger-Petraske, Georgette. *Sasha Petraske Regarding Cocktails.* New York, Phaidon Press limited, **2016**.